AF321651

LOVE, WAR, AND DIPLOMACY

Love, War, and Diplomacy

THE DISCOVERY OF THE AMARNA LETTERS AND THE BRONZE AGE WORLD THEY REVEALED

ERIC H. CLINE

PRINCETON UNIVERSITY PRESS

PRINCETON & OXFORD

Published by Princeton University Press
41 William Street, Princeton, New Jersey 08540
99 Banbury Road, Oxford OX2 6JX

press.princeton.edu

GPSR Authorized Representative: Easy Access System Europe - Mustamäe tee 50, 10621 Tallinn, Estonia, gpsr.requests@easproject.com

All Rights Reserved

ISBN 9780691274089
ISBN (e-book) 9780691274096

Library of Congress Control Number: 2025930783

British Library Cataloging-in-Publication Data is available

Editorial: Rob Tempio and Chloe Coy
Production Editorial: Mark Bellis
Jacket Design: Karl Spurzem
Production: Erin Suydam
Publicity: Maria Whelan and Carmen Jimenez
Copyeditor: Lachlan Brooks

Jacket images: Courtesy of the Metropolitan Museum of Art / Rogers Fund, 1924; University of Chicago Institute for the Study of Ancient Cultures; and © 2008 GrandPalaisRmn (Louvre Museum) / Franck Raux / Claude Valette

This book has been composed in Arno

Printed in the United States of America

10 9 8 7 6 5 4 3 2 1

Next to the historical books of the Old Testament
the Tel el-Amarna tablets have proved to be
the most valuable record which the ancient civilised
world of the East has bequeathed to us.

—A. H. SAYCE (1923, 251–52)

CONTENTS

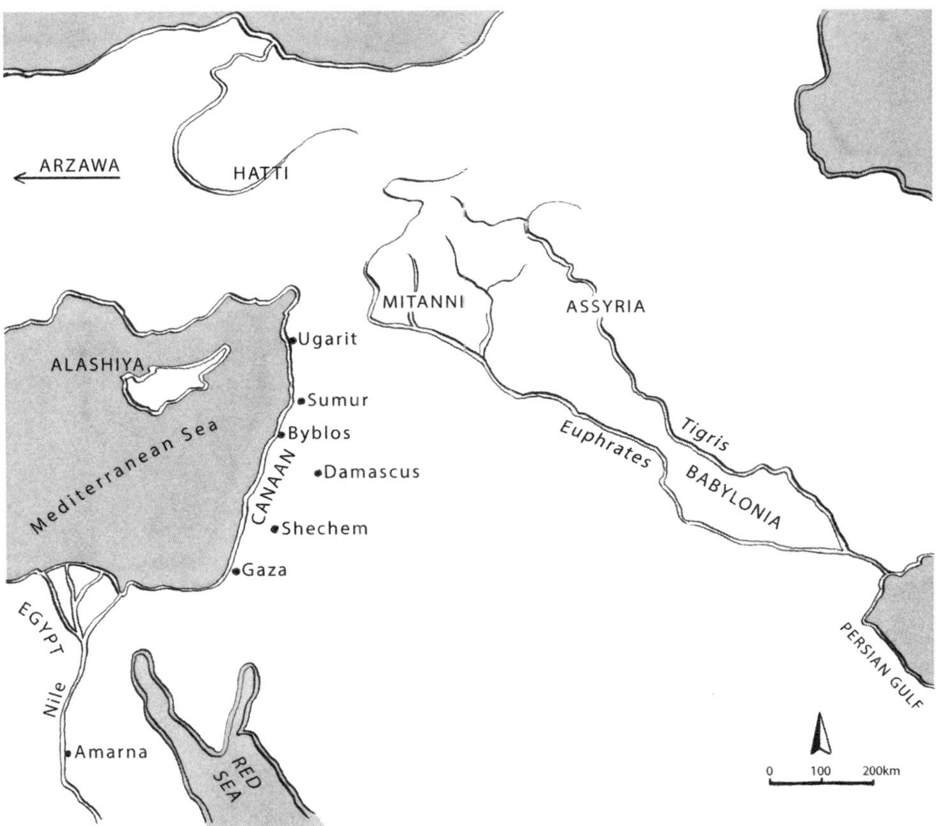

MAP 1. The Eastern Mediterranean during the Amarna Period (after Goren, Finkelstein, and Na'aman 2004, fig. 3.1). Redrawn by Glynnis Fawkes.

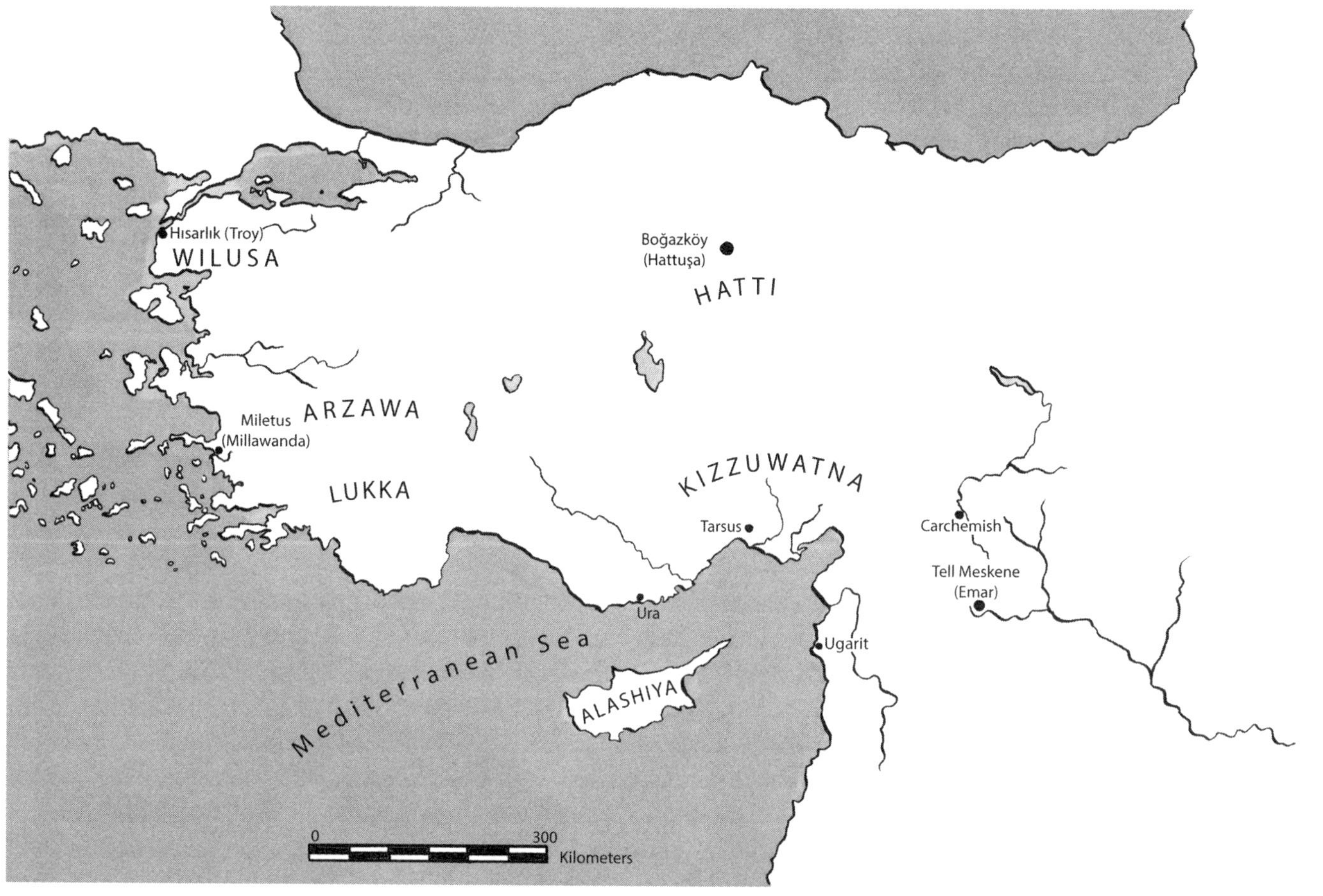

MAP 2. Anatolia during the Amarna Period (after ASOR Map Collection). Redrawn by Glynnis Fawkes.

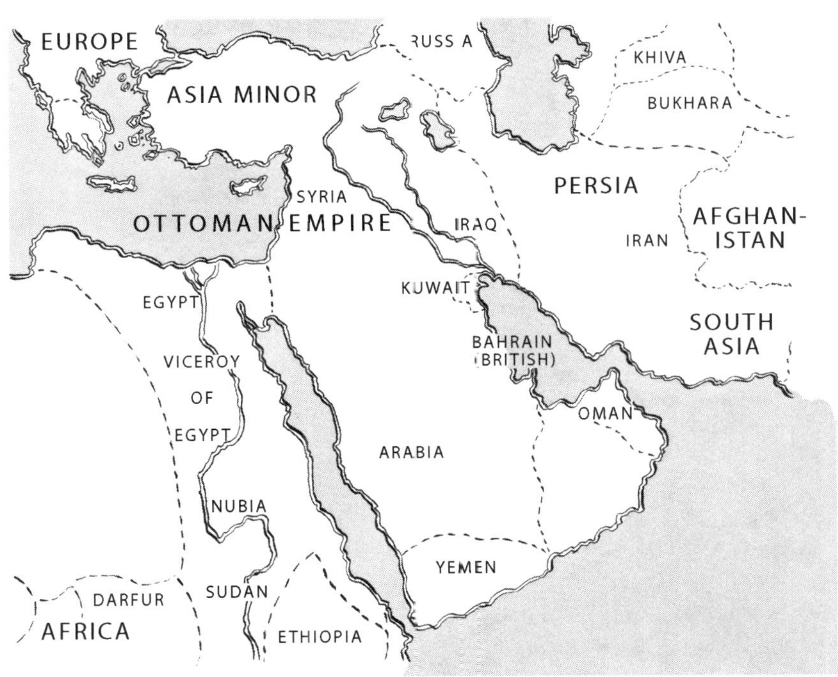

MAP 3. Middle East in 1871 (after https://timemaps.com/history/middle-east -1871ad/). Redrawn by Glynnis Fawkes.

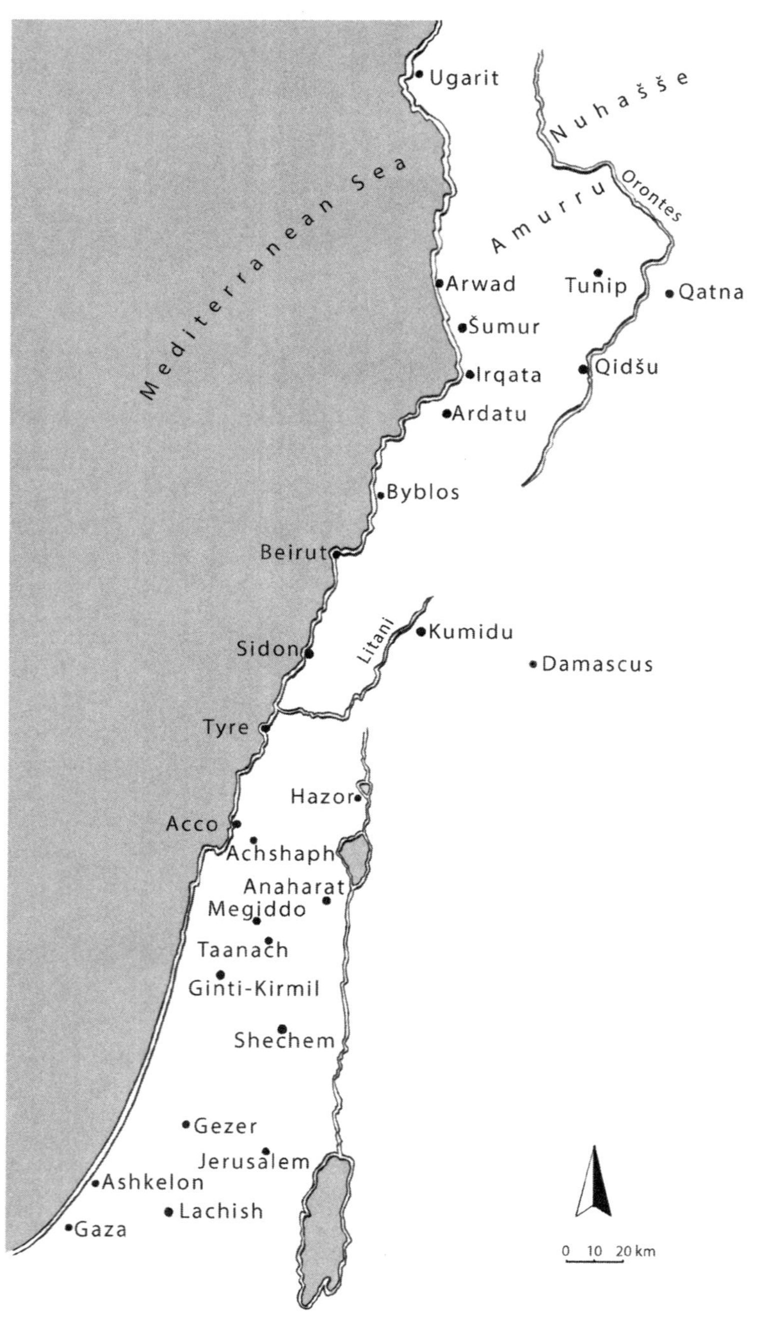

MAP 4. Main city-states in Amarna Period Canaan (after Goren, Finkelstein, and Na'aman 2004, figs. 9.1 and 12.1; Vita 2015, Map 1). Redrawn by Glynnis Fawkes.

LOVE, WAR, AND DIPLOMACY

Introduction

AN UNEXPECTED DISCOVERY

Speak to the king, my lord and my Sun god, a message from Biridiya, the
loyal servant of the king. I fall at the two feet of the king, my lord and my
Sun god, seven times and seven times. The king, my lord, should know that
after the regular troops entered Egypt, Lab'ayu waged war against me so that
we were unable to harvest. We were unable (even) to go out of the city gate
on account of Lab'ayu. Since he learned that the regular troops were not
campaigning this year, he now intends to capture Megiddo. So the king should
rescue his city. Do not let Lab'ayu seize it! . . . Lab'ayu has no other intention.
He desires to seize Megiddo.

—AMARNA LETTER EA 244[1]

THIS PLAINTIVE LETTER from Biridiya, the ruler of Canaanite Megiddo,
who was at odds with a neighboring and quarrelsome king named Lab'ayu,
was part of an archive of royal correspondence that dates to the fourteenth
century BCE, more than three thousand years ago. Written on nearly four
hundred clay tablets in all, the letters in this archive were unexpectedly discovered at the site of Tell el-Amarna in Egypt in 1887.

The usual story told about the discovery is that a peasant woman uncovered
the archive while digging for fertilizer in the ruins of an ancient city.[2] The peasant woman could never be located afterward, however. An alternate hypothesis favored by some scholars is that the tablets were actually uncovered by a
notorious Egyptian antiquities dealer named Farag Ismain (also referred to as
Farag Ismail) who would have been digging at the site, likely illicitly, perhaps
as early as the spring of 1887. While it is certainly possible that Ismain began

his excavations *because* of the initial discovery by the local woman, the thinking is that he concocted and then spread the false story to cover his own activities. Whatever the origin of their find, the first tablets were offered for sale to museums and collectors by September or October of that year at the latest (and possibly a few months earlier).[3]

In antiquity, the city in which the letters were found had been called Akhetaten (meaning "the horizon of the Aten"); it was planned and built as a new capital city by the Eighteenth Dynasty pharaoh Akhenaten. He was a figure famous in Egyptian history as the first pharaoh to worship a single deity, Aten, and was father to the most famous Egyptian of all, King Tutankhamun.

The hundreds of inscribed clay tablets unearthed at the site were part of a royal archive belonging to Akhenaten and his father Amenhotep III. They include approximately fifty letters exchanged with the other "Great Kings" (a literal translation from the Akkadian *šarru rabû*), ranging from the Hittites in ancient Anatolia to the Assyrians and Babylonians in Mesopotamia and others in Cyprus, Mittani, and elsewhere. There are also close to three hundred additional letters that were sent by both vassal and more autonomous rulers in Canaan—the region of what is now modern Syria, Lebanon, Israel, Jordan, and the Palestinian Territories, over whom Egypt ruled during the fourteenth century BCE.

The letters cover a brief period of time, just under three decades long at most (ca. 1360–1334 BCE), from about the thirtieth regnal year of Amenhotep III through the third regnal year of Tutankhamun. The vast majority were apparently found in a single building at Amarna, known today as Building 19 but originally called something like "The House of the Letters of the Pharaoh—Life, Prosperity, Health" (Fig. 1). The building served as both a records office, which explains the presence of this royal archive, and perhaps also as a scriptorium, or scribal school, for there were also school texts found here.[4]

Each of the letters was long ago (by 1915) given an "EA" number, standing for "El Amarna."[5] As Alice Mandell, a professor at Johns Hopkins University, has described it, the royal letters "are arranged counter clockwise geographically as follows: Babylon (EA 1–14), Assyria (EA 15–16), Mittani (EA 17–30), Arzawa (EA 31–32), Alashiya (EA 33–40), and the Hittite court (EA 41–44)." The additional letters, sent to and from the vassal and semiautonomous Canaanite rulers, then follow and are numbered consecutively from EA 45 onward; there are currently 349 letters amongst the 382 tablets known from Amarna (the non-letter tablets consist of scribal exercises, literary texts, and so on).[6]

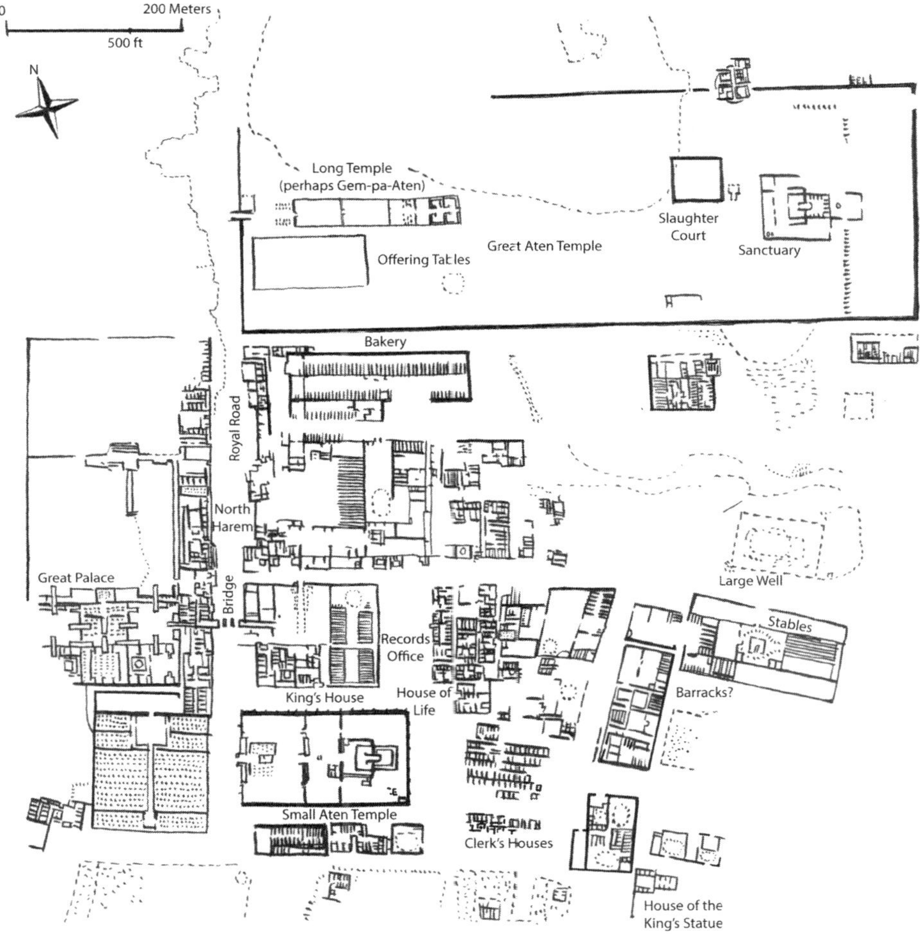

FIGURE 1. Tell el-Amarna in Egypt. Redrawn by Glynnis Fawkes.

In all of these Amarna Letters, we can hear the long-ago voices of the writers, for they were recording their problems, their concerns, their needs, and their wants, whether those of a Great King or a lowly petty ruler. But, from our point of view, they were also writing history. They are history. And we, for all intents and purposes, are forensic detectives. We are investigating their world, which has long since passed away—the ultimate cold case.

By using ancient written sources such as the Amarna Letters and piecing together the events and the people that they mention, we can begin to find out what happened in antiquity. But just like today, we cannot always take things at face value: we need to carefully read what is written, sometimes even reading between the lines. We need to weigh the evidence, judge who can be trusted and who is gaslighting, and figure out the precise order of events and the motivations in that ancient period. It is not always straightforward, and we may not always have interpreted the facts completely correctly, but overall, we are able to decipher a sense of what happened to those people in those places, way back when.

My primary aims in this book are three-fold. First, I wish to tell the basic story of the academic and scholarly competition to translate the Amarna Letters after their initial discovery in 1887. We will follow it chronologically, month by month and year by year, especially as the scholars' publications appeared during the first decade from 1887 to 1896, which is fascinating in and of itself. It is also important to accurately document the history of scholarship in this area before it is lost, especially as many of the early articles were published in venues that are not easy for everyone now to access on their own.

Second, I want to tell the story of what was happening back then, working solely from the contents of the letters themselves, for the fourteenth century BCE was a high point in the history of the ancient Near East, situated as it was almost exactly in the middle of the Late Bronze Age, which lasted from approximately the seventeenth century until the collapse at the beginning of the twelfth century BCE.[7] It was a high point especially in terms of international connections involving trade and diplomacy between all the major powers and rulers in the ancient Near East at the time, including Amenhotep III and Akhenaten from Egypt; Assur-uballit of Assyria; Kadashman-Enlil and Burna-Buriash II of Babylonia; Tushratta of Mittani; and Suppiluliuma of the Hittites. Those names may be unfamiliar to most readers at this point, but they will become known entities within the first few chapters and old friends by the end of the book. I have also included a list of the most relevant people, both modern and ancient, toward the back of the book.

I will alternate the telling of these two stories in the different sections, to keep the momentum going throughout. Then, toward the end, as my third aim, we will investigate the letters further, using some aspects of Social Network Analysis (SNA) to see if we can determine just who were the most important players among this interconnected network of rulers, both major and minor.

Overall, I hope that this volume will also demonstrate just how fascinating were the relations and history of Egypt and the Eastern Mediterranean during the fourteenth century BCE, and how in some ways things are not that different now. Even as technology and societies have changed, human nature apparently has not. In this region especially, ancient history is not always ancient nor is it always just history, for this story of people and events dating back to approximately 3,400 years ago is as intermingled with politics and fighting, diplomacy and international relations, and public posturing of one sort or another as is that same area of the world today.

PART I

The Players

1

Dealers and Destructions

BUDGE LEANED over the railing of the small steamer *Niémen*, watching the bow slice through the calm water. It was early December 1887, and a light rain was falling. Having departed London for Marseilles, he was now headed for Egypt and then Mesopotamia. His mission was to acquire antiquities on behalf of the British Museum, for he was an "assistant keeper" (curator) in the Department of Egyptian and Assyrian Antiquities. It was his second trip to the region, with stops now planned in Cairo, Luxor, and Aswan, before continuing on to Baghdad.

E.A. Wallis Budge, as he was formally known, was to become infamous as an academic anomaly during his career (Fig. 2). Officially considered an Egyptologist, he has been perhaps better described as an "omnivorous" multilingual scholar with an outsize personality and a penchant for flouting local regulations and alienating fellow scholars and colleagues.[1]

Budge was born in Bodmin, Cornwall to a mother who worked as a waitress and a father he never knew. At the time of this trip, Budge had just turned thirty years old and was at the beginning of his career. Supported and championed by William Ewart Gladstone, the future prime minister of England, as well as by Samuel Birch, a preeminent but aging Egyptologist at the British Museum, Budge had attended Cambridge and then been hired at the museum four years earlier.[2]

He had originally planned to head directly for Baghdad on this trip, but shortly before he left England, he began hearing rumors about a new find. The scuttlebutt was that hundreds of inscribed clay tablets had been discovered at the site of Tell el-Amarna in Egypt, located approximately halfway between modern Cairo in the north and modern Luxor in the south. "Whilst the official arrangements for my Mission to Baghdad were being made," Budge later wrote, "I received information from a native in Egypt that . . . a native woman

9

FIGURE 2. E. A. Wallis Budge. Illustration by Glynnis Fawkes.

had discovered at Tall al-ʿAmarnah, by accident, a large box full of pieces of clay, with what he thought was writing on both sides of each piece."[3]

His informant, whose identity remains unknown to this day but who was probably one of the numerous antiquities dealers in Cairo or elsewhere in Egypt, said that he and his friends "had secured a great many of them . . . and that the marks on back and front were *kitba mismdrf,* "nail-writing."[4] By this he meant cuneiform, a descriptive word coined from Latin by modern scholars that means "wedge-shaped." This was a writing system that had been used to inscribe various ancient Mesopotamian and Anatolian languages such as Akkadian, Hittite, and Sumerian, especially during the third through first millennia BCE, on anything and everything: examples of cuneiform range from royal inscriptions on stone to documents, diplomatic correspondence, and economic accounts written on clay tablets.

Just as there had been a race to crack the code of Egyptian hieroglyphics, most famously between the Frenchman Jean-François Champollion and the

Englishman Thomas Young, which was won by Champollion in 1823,[5] there was a similar rivalry at approximately the same time to translate the ancient texts that used cuneiform to write in Akkadian, which was the diplomatic lingua franca of the second millennium BCE in the ancient Near East. In fact, there was quite literally a competition held in 1857, at which time several scholars were given the same recently discovered cuneiform inscription and were asked to translate it. These included a British East India Company army officer named Sir Henry Rawlinson; an Irish clergyman named Edward Hincks; a German-born scholar who worked in Paris named Julius Oppert; and another British scholar named William Fox Talbot. When it became apparent that their translations were nearly identical, and that they all agreed the text could be dated to the time of the Middle Assyrian king Tiglath-Pileser I in the twelfth century BCE, the decipherment was declared a success.[6]

By the time of the accidental discovery of the Amarna Letters thirty years later, in 1887, a growing number of scholars could read Akkadian inscriptions. Known as Assyriologists, they were located primarily at universities in Germany, England, and France, with a few working in the United States and elsewhere. There were—and would continue to be, even to the present day— disputes about the transliteration of certain cuneiform signs and the specific translation and identification of items such as personal names and places, but on the whole, the code had been cracked.

———

The digging at Amarna in 1887 was unintentionally observed at the time by an Oxford professor named Archibald Henry (A. H.) Sayce (Fig. 3). However, Sayce did not realize the significance of what he had witnessed until later. In a lecture given in Manchester, UK, in early November 1889, he told the audience: "Two years and a half years ago, when coming down the Nile in a dahabiah, I stopped at . . . Tel el-Amarna. In the course of my exploration, I noticed . . . the foundations of a large building, which had just been laid bare by the natives. . . . A few months afterwards the natives, still going on with their work of disinterment, discovered among the foundations a number of clay tablets covered with characters the like of which had not previously been seen in the land of Egypt."[7]

Sayce went on to say that "the tablets soon found their way into the hands of a European who recognized that the characters were the cuneiform

FIGURE 3. A. H. Sayce. Illustration by Glynnis Fawkes.

characters of Assyria and Babylon." This, as we shall see, was none other than Budge. However, Sayce later clarified and elaborated upon the initial situation, stating in his 1923 autobiography that at the time of the actual discovery, "there was no one in Egypt who was acquainted with cuneiform" and so "the antika-dealers regarded the tablets as so many worthless bricks. Most of them were thrown into sacks and carried on donkey-back to Ekhmim." (Ekhmim is a village located about halfway between Amarna and Luxor.)[8]

According to Sayce, once the tablets arrived in Ekhmim, a few were bought by a French flour mill manager named Frénay, who occasionally acquired items on behalf of the Louvre. In an article published in 1917, Sayce further stated that an antiquities dealer named Elias had sold the tablets to Frénay, but in letters written in January and April 1888, the Egyptologist Charles Edwin Wilbour (of whom we will speak more in a moment) said that Frénay had actually bought them from a dealer based in Ekhmim named Sidrak, a Copt from whom he had bought "anteekeh" before.[9]

Frénay sent one of the tablets to Paris, where it was shown to Julius Oppert, a well-known professor of Assyriology, who had been part of the cuneiform competition back in 1857. However, as Sayce reported, "Oppert was old and blind, and pronounced it to be a forgery. The result was that no more were purchased by Frénay; the tablets were again carried on donkey-back along the banks of the Nile, and finally found their way to Luxor. By that time more than a third of them had been destroyed or mutilated, to the incalculable loss of science and history. . . . What we now have is [merely] an index of what we should have possessed had the collection been preserved uninjured and intact."[10] Sir William Matthew Flinders Petrie, the famous British Egyptologist who later excavated at Amarna himself, reported similarly that "The tablets were all grubbed out by the fellahin [the locals]; many were broken, or ground to pieces, during transit on donkey back; the authorities to whom the things were shewn, despised them; and it was very fortunate that the whole discovery was not irrevocably lost. What is saved is but a portion—perhaps not half—of what might have been preserved with proper care."[11]

We will probably never know the exact number of tablets that were destroyed during the initial discovery and subsequent transportation, although Sayce once estimated that "from one hundred and fifty to two hundred tablets were totally destroyed and fully as many broken and otherwise seriously damaged."[12] We have no idea on what basis he was able to make such a statement, but when the tablets that did remain were deciphered, they revealed that the world of the Late Bronze Age was far more impressive than anyone had previously suspected. As Sayce later wrote, "Next to the historical books of the Old Testament the Tel el-Amarna tablets have proved to be the most valuable record which the ancient civilised world of the East has bequeathed to us."[13]

———

Much later, in 1915, the Norwegian Assyriologist Jørgen Knudtzon claimed that three main antiquities dealers had been involved in selling the various tablets after their discovery. Two of them, Farag Ismain and Ali Abd el-Hajj, were both based in Giza; the third, "Tano" (whose full name was Marius Panayiotis Tano), was a dealer in Cairo. We have already briefly met Farag Ismain, the antiquities dealer who may have been responsible for the initial discovery of the entire corpus of tablets at Amarna. The other, Ali Abd el-Hajj, was probably responsible for selling 160 tablets to Theodor Graf, an Austrian antiquities dealer, who promptly resold them. They eventually made their way to a museum in Berlin along with a number of other Amarna tablets. As for Tano, he was a well-known antiquities dealer of Cypriot origin.[14]

Other sources name additional dealers. For instance, Wilbour, the American Egyptologist, noted while staying at Shepheard's Hotel on 12 November 1887 that "Tano tells me that about a hundred cuneiform cylinders have been found at Tell-el-Amarna, of which Mohammed Mohassib has fifty, the Museum twenty, and he has just sold Daninos forty." He also mentioned in a letter dated 15 January 1888 that "Frénay had some of the cuneiform tablets and that Sidrak and he both were sure they came from Haggi Kandeel [Hajji Kandil, a village located near Amarna]."[15]

We know the people and places Wilbour mentions. Mohammed Mohassib was an antiquities dealer in Luxor, who likely sold his fifty tablets to Budge, who, in turn, sent them on to the British Museum. The museum to which Wilbour referred was not the British Museum, but rather the Cairo Museum, which was located at that time in Bulaq, a district of Cairo, and known then as the Bulaq Museum. These twenty tablets may have been among the first to officially enter into the museum's possession (though see further discussion below). Albert Daninos was an Egyptian scholar who had worked with Auguste Mariette in the Antiquities Service and who was also responsible for the discovery of the famous statue pair of Princess Nofret and Prince Rahotep. The forty Amarna tablets that, according to Wilbour, Daninos had just acquired eventually also made their way to Berlin.[16] Thus, the 110 tablets that Wilbour mentioned in this one brief note were split up and sent to museums in London, Cairo, and Berlin, epitomizing the international dispersal of the tablets from this single archive.

There were a number of other, smaller dealers involved as well,[17] and by the time all was said and done, more than three hundred clay tablets had been sold in a matter of weeks or months, with most going to foreign museums. This is one of the most egregious known examples of looting and antiquity sales of an archive from the ancient world, on par with the Dead Sea Scrolls as well as with more recent examples of archives plundered and sold by looters from sites in Iraq during the past several decades.[18]

It is indeed a shame that the Amarna archive was not discovered by professional archaeologists and properly excavated, for we would then have all of the original tablets, which may have numbered as many as six hundred, if Sayce is correct in his estimation of how many were lost and broken during transport.[19]

We would also know for certain their original context at the site, which would have given us even more information about the archive.

In all, counting the additional tablets that have been found during controlled excavations, there are nearly four hundred tablets that remain to us from this archive. They are now referred to as the Amarna Letters and are scattered among fourteen museums in eight countries and ten cities on four continents. In Egypt 52 tablets remain; the rest are in Germany (202), England (119), France (7), Russia (3), the United States (3), Turkey (1), and Belgium (1).[20]

In the following pages, we will explore this story in greater detail, focusing in particular on the race between the British and German scholars to decipher the tablets. In the end, it was a hard-fought victory, for the translations of these letters, undertaken just a few decades after Akkadian itself had been deciphered, were fraught with difficulties. We will see twists and turns, follow them down blind alleys and rabbit holes, and learn of their erroneous translations before they finally figured out what was etched into the surface of the clay on each tablet. And we will discover the international diplomacy, marriages, and intrigue that were revealed when the letters were correctly translated, in which the kings of Egypt and the ancient Near East, both great and petty, participated as they competed for primacy some 3,400 years ago.

2

Budge

ʿWALLIS BUDGE'S native informant had told him to come to Egypt immediately and "take possession of all these things before the 'Mudir of Anticas' [the director of antiquities] could seize them, and cast their owners into prison." This would be a reference to Eugène Grébaut, who had taken over as director of the Department of Antiquities in Egypt following the retirement of the formidable Gaston Maspero who preceded him. With this information and after consulting with his direct supervisor as well as with the "Principal Librarian" (as the director of the British Museum was then known), Budge decided that he should go first to Cairo and then south to Luxor in Upper Egypt before continuing on to Baghdad.[1]

Upon arriving in Cairo on 19 December, Budge quickly established that the information provided by his source was correct. "Before I had been in Cairo many hours, I found that everybody was talking about the discoveries which had been made in Upper Egypt, and the most extraordinary stories were afloat. Rumours of the 'finds' had reached all the great cities of Europe, and there were representatives of several Continental Museums in Cairo, each doing his best, as was right, to secure the lion's share."[2] The phase "as was right" indicates how nineteenth-century European colonial powers treated important archaeological finds anywhere in the world—in other words, it was only right that such artifacts should be in their museums rather than kept in the country of origin.

News of the discovery had also reached Director Grébaut, because gossip was circulating that a smuggler had dropped and severely damaged one of the largest of the Amarna tablets, "about 20 inches long and broad in proportion," while bringing it to Cairo. "The man who was taking this to Cairo hid it between his inner garments, and covered himself with his great cloak. As he stepped up into the railway coach this tablet slipped from his clothes and fell on the bed of the railway, and broke in pieces. Many natives in the train and on the platform witnessed the accident and talked freely about it, and thus the news of the discovery of the tablets reached the ears of the Director of Antiquities."[3]

According to word on the street, Grébaut and his assistants were planning to seize all of the clay tablets "and to put in prison all those who were in any way mixed up in the matter."[4] Budge therefore quickly headed to Luxor, to meet with the dealers in person and see what he could acquire on behalf of the British Museum before Grébaut could make good on his threats.

As soon as he arrived in Luxor, where he enjoyed the hospitality of the antiquities dealer Mohammed Mohassib, Budge reportedly met with a man who had just arrived from Hajji Kandil, the village located near Amarna. The man, whose name we do not know, had brought with him "some half-dozen of the clay tablets which had been found accidentally by a woman," for he told Budge the version of the story that featured the local woman gathering either fuel or fertilizer at the ancient site.[5]

According to the man, she was unaware of the potential value of the tablets and regarded them as essentially worthless "bits of old clay." She therefore sold them all, the entire group of more than three hundred tablets, to a neighbor for ten piastres (a tenth of an Egyptian pound). Strictly speaking, ten piastres would have been the equivalent of about twenty-five cents, a quarter of a US dollar at today's exchange rates, but it would be more accurate to think of it as a little less than ten dollars today, once inflation and buying power since 1887 are considered. The neighbor brought the tablets to the village of Hajji Kandil and resold them for ten Egyptian pounds. That, technically, would be the equivalent of about $20 USD today, but should be considered closer to $660 when inflation and buying power since 1887 are taken into account. This means that the neighbor resold them for more than sixty times the amount that he had paid for them.

However, the man told Budge that "those who bought them [also] knew nothing about what they were buying, and when they had bought them they sent a man to Cairo with a few of them to show the dealers, both native and European. Some of the European dealers thought they were 'old,' and some thought they were 'new,' and they agreed together to declare the tablets forgeries so that they might buy them at their own price as 'specimens of modern imitations.'"[6]

The local antiquities dealers grew suspicious. Thinking that the tablets might actually be genuine, they arranged for the man from Hajji Kandil to meet up with Budge in Luxor, in order to show him some of the tablets and determine if they were forgeries or not.

Fortunately, Budge had studied cuneiform while at university:

> I could not then foresee that such knowledge of cuneiform as I possessed was to be put to a decided test in a few years' time (1887) in Egypt, and that I should be called upon to decide whether the Tall al-'Amarnah Tablets, which were written in cuneiform, were genuine or not, and whether I should acquire them for the Museum or not. No cuneiform tablets had ever been found in Egypt before 1887, and none have been found there since. If I had known no cuneiform, I should certainly have rejected them as forgeries, and the British Museum would have possessed no portion of this wonderful "find."[7]

Clearly, therefore, Budge was the unnamed European mentioned by Sayce in his 1889 Manchester lecture "who recognized that the characters were the cuneiform characters of Assyria and Babylon" as soon as he saw the tablets, as mentioned above. Budge then continued, "In shape and form, and colour and material, the tablets were unlike any I had ever seen in London or Paris, and the writing on all of them was of a most unusual character and puzzled me for hours." Eventually he decided that they were not forgeries, but also that they "were neither royal annals nor historical inscriptions in the ordinary sense of the word, nor business or commercial documents."[8] He soon understood they were letters. As he wrote in his autobiography more than thirty years later, the realization unfolded in the following manner:

While he was examining the first set of six tablets, another man arrived from Hajji Kandil, with seventy-five more tablets, some of which were quite large. Budge immediately put aside the few that he had been poring over and began to inspect this new set. "On the largest and best written of the second lot of tablets, I was able to make out the words 'A-na Ni-ib-mu-a-ri-ya,' i.e., 'To Nibmuariya,' and on another the words '[A]-na Ni-immu-ri-ya shar matu Mi-is-ri,' i.e., 'To Nimmuriya, king of the land of Egypt.'" Budge concluded that these two tablets were letters addressed to a king of Egypt called "Nib-muariya," or "Nimmuriya." On another tablet he could clearly make out "the opening words 'A-na Ni-ip-khuur-ri-ri-ya shar matu [Misri],' i.e., 'To Nipkhurririya, king of the land of [Egypt],'" and decided that "there was no doubt that this tablet was a letter addressed to another king of Egypt." From this common introductory formula, Budge decided that nearly all of the rest were letters as well. He was also certain that they "were both genuine and of very great historical importance."[9]

As it turned out, Budge was completely correct. However, a multitude of questions remain about his description of these events, especially since he was writing all of the above more than three decades later and with the benefit of twenty-twenty hindsight.

Cuneiform signs obviously could be read long before 1887. Eberhard Schrader, a German scholar considered to be one of the founders of the field of Assyriology, who held the first academic chair in Assyriology, at the University of Berlin, had already published a grammar of Assyrian and Babylonian as early as 1872.[10] However, Budge doesn't mention anywhere that he was carrying Assyriological books with him, which might have helped him to identify the cuneiform signs and thus offer a translation on the spot.

Although Budge was indeed able to provide accurate translations of the clay tablets when he was back in London surrounded by the resources in the library of the British Museum the following June, as we shall see, it is difficult to envision him doing so in Luxor six months earlier, as he claimed, by flickering candlelight in a darkened room to avoid the prying eyes of the Egyptian authorities. In short, while Budge's account is conceivable, it strains the limits of credibility. If true, it would have been a moment that he would never have forgotten, as he first held the tablets in his hands, and we can only imagine his astonishment at making out the first few words on the tablets and realizing that he was reading letters sent to Egyptian kings thousands of years earlier. It would have been as astounding as Howard Carter's first look into the tomb of Tutankhamun in 1922.

As romantic and thrilling as it might sound to be reading the cuneiform on the clay tablets by the flickering light of a candle, in reality it is far more likely that Budge simply determined—or gambled—that the tablets were legitimate and authentic, not based on what was written on them, but rather based on his observations as to their color, shape, form, and material. Whether or not he actually read what was written on them at the time, he immediately offered a reasonable price for the entire group of eighty-one tablets. His offer was accepted and records in the archives of the British Museum indicate that a payment of £512 GBP was sent to "Shipping Merchants and Agents Messrs. Bywater, Tanqueray & Co" for the collection of tablets. This would have been the equivalent of approximately £86,000 (almost $113,000 USD) in today's economy.[11]

As Budge later reported, "I then tried to make arrangements with the men from Hajji Kandil to get the remainder of the tablets from Tall al-'Amarnah into my possession, but they told me that they belonged to dealers who were in treaty with an agent of the Berlin Museum in Cairo."[12] This agent was most likely the Austrian antiquities dealer Theodor Graf, who did indeed buy 160 tablets that eventually made their way to Berlin.

There was at least one other person involved in these negotiations, for the Luxor antiquities dealer Mohammed Mohassib had facilitated Budge's meeting with the men from Hajji Kandil in the first place. Readers will remember that the American Egyptologist Charles Wilbour had noted on 12 November 1887, fully a week before Budge arrived in Cairo, that Mohammed Mohassib already had fifty tablets in his possession.[13] Toward the end of that month, on 28 November, Wilbour reported further that "Grébaut . . . says he will take the Tell-el-Amarna cuneiform tablets from Mohammed Mohassib, and pay him a thousand francs; Mohammed Mohassib has refused three thousand for them."[14] It stands to reason that Wilbour was reporting negotiations ongoing at the time between Grébaut, representing the Egyptian government, and Mohassib, in which the former offered a thousand francs for the fifty tablets and the latter protested that he had already refused an offer of three thousand francs.

In fact, Budge noted in his autobiography that, earlier in 1887, the Antiquities Service had ordered any local Egyptian who was in possession of an antiquity to bring it to Cairo to be examined and appraised. If the authorities decided to acquire any of the objects, "they would make a valuation of it, and give the possessor one half of the sum at which it was valued."[15] Thus, by offering Mohammed Mohassib one thousand francs, Grébaut was already admitting that the tablets were worth at least two thousand francs. But who would have offered Mohammed Mohassib three thousand francs? Or was that amount a negotiating tactic?

Here we may turn to Wilbour again. A few months later, in his letter dated 5 April 1888, describing raids that Grébaut had ordered to be conducted across Egypt in an effort to seize looted antiquities from specific dealers, he wrote: "I think I had told you about the seizures of antiquities [Grébaut] had made of Sidrak at Ekhmeem [Ekhmim]; of Hanna Kerass at Mensheereh; of Abd-el-Noor at Geergeh; of Mohammed Mohassib and Abd-el Megeed and Mohmood LeDeed at Luxor; and of Husseyn at Edfoo, all made by the police on one day. His main object was to get the cuneiform tablets said to be found at Amarna, but Consul Frénay tells me he got none. He himself had Sidrak's and Budge had already bought the fifty odd which M. Mohassib had at Luxor."[16]

If Wilbour is correct on two counts—that Budge bought at least fifty tablets from Mohammed Mohassib, and that the dealer already had those fifty tablets in his possession as early as 12 November 1887, several weeks before Budge even arrived in Egypt—it becomes likely that the dealer was involved as the middleman in Budge's negotiations with the men from Hajji Kandil for the eighty-one tablets that they wished to sell, since otherwise that would be a total of 131 tablets. Thus, Mohammed Mohassib's initial fifty tablets must be included within the eighty-one that Budge purchased during his visit, rather than added to them. It may well have been Budge who had initially offered three thousand francs for Mohammed Mohassib's initial fifty tablets before settling on the final amount for the entire lot of eighty-one tablets.

Regardless, three thousand francs were only worth approximately £120 GBP at the time, if one calculates the currency equivalencies. Since this is far less than the £512 that the receipt in the British Museum says Budge paid for the tablets, Mohammed Mohassib probably did turn down this initial offer, as he had told Grébaut. In fact, £512 would have been worth nearly 13,000 francs at the time. No wonder he scoffed at Grébaut's offer of a paltry one thousand francs and went with Budge's offer of more than ten times that amount. In the end, regardless of when and by whom they were brought to Luxor from the village of Hajji Kandil, by the end of December 1887, eighty-one tablets were in Budge's hands (with another one making its way to the British Museum later, for a final total of eighty-two tablets).[17]

———

Smuggling the tablets out of Egypt involved a bit of good luck as well as sheer brazen audacity. According to his own account, after traveling from Aswan first by steamer and then by train, Budge arrived at the Cairo train station one morning early in January 1888. Just outside the station, he ran into two British army officers, one of whom he knew. With their assistance, he managed to get his various bags and boxes, including the one holding the Amarna tablets, into Cairo without being searched by either the local police or customs officers.[18]

Budge decided to keep the tablets with him for the second half of his travels, to Karachi and then Baghdad. He booked passage on the *Navarino* and boarded it at Suez, with the box of Amarna tablets and his other possessions, on 12 January.[19]

After having transferred in Karachi to a ship called the *Assyria* for the remainder of the journey, he was invited to stay on the British gunboat *Comet* in Baghdad. The invitation was prompted by a suggestion from the British Consul at Basrah, Mr. Robertson, who pointed out that the boat was British territory. Storing the tablets on board would be safer than storing them in a house in Baghdad, where they might be stolen, destroyed, or confiscated by local Ottoman Empire officials. Budge was thus able to avoid showing the box of tablets to customs agents in Baghdad.[20]

Having purchased additional antiquities in Baghdad, including hundreds more inscribed clay tablets from various other periods and places, Budge packed his acquisitions into twenty-five boxes. These were then placed in the hold of the *Comet* and taken to the port city of Basrah, while Budge remained in Iraq. The boxes were transferred to the British-India Mail Steamer and thereby made their way to England. They were delivered directly into the hands of the "Principal Librarian of the British Museum" (i.e., the director) sometime in late January or early February 1888.

In the meantime, Budge traveled throughout Iraq, not returning to England until 24 April. He began work immediately on the tablets at that point, publishing his first preliminary translations by June.[21]

Though his purchase and smuggling of the Amarna tablets were contrary to Egyptian law and done in secret to avoid the authorities of at least two countries, the trustees of the museum apparently found no fault whatsoever with what Budge had done and even commended him at their subsequent meeting on 12 May for his boldness and great energy in procuring the various artifacts. Budge himself felt no guilt at what he had done, nor for his colonialist attitude. He later wrote "although the Trustees had no claim at all on the Tall al-'Amarnah Tablets . . . [h]ad I not come to a decision at once, and taken the eighty-two tablets when I had the chance of getting them, they would certainly have gone to the Berlin Museum, or into the possession of some private collector, or anywhere except to the Government Museum of Egyptian Antiquities, Cairo. When the Directors of Museums in the East make it worth the while of natives to bring their 'finds' to them, nothing of importance will find its way to Europe or America."

He added, "And if I had refrained from buying these objects on the ground[s] that I could not get them out of Egypt without devious devices, these objects would have been bought by these other men who were collecting. The objects would have been smuggled out of Egypt all the same; the only difference would have been that instead of being in the British Museum they would be in some museum or private collection on the Continent or in America."[22] Clearly Budge saw himself as a benefactor, or even a savior, of the antiquities, who was sure to write himself into historical memory as such.

3

Sayce

IN CONTRAST to Budge, the Oxford academic A. H. Sayce was late to the Amarna race because of the death of his mother. He and a friend had traveled from England to Greece and then to Cyprus "towards the end of November" in 1887, after his mother's funeral. They stayed in Cyprus for two months, after which they headed to Jaffa and Jerusalem, and only then went on to Egypt. He thus missed all the initial "Amarna tablets excitement," in Cairo, Luxor, and elsewhere.[1] Concerning that fateful period, he later wrote in his autobiography,

> I have always regarded it as a proof that I was born under an unlucky star that the only winter which I did not spend on the Nile was the one when the famous cuneiform tablets were found by the fellahin at Tel el-Amarna. I had always stopped at Tel el-Amarna, generally both when ascending and when descending the river; I was well known to the fellahin and antika-hunters—two synonymous terms there—and what they had discovered in the mounds during the previous year was always brought to me for sale. The whole collection of tablets would have passed into my possession intact.[2]

Indeed, if only the tablets had passed into his possession intact at that point, the subsequent story might have been very different. At the time, Sayce was a well-respected Assyriologist, perhaps best known for his correct declaration a decade earlier that the Hittite civilization was located in Anatolia (ancient Turkey) rather than down in Canaan as per the Hebrew Bible. He was forty-eight years old now, nearly two decades older than Budge, and had already been teaching at Oxford for more than twenty years. He was of Welsh descent, with an aptitude for languages. He had begun reading Homer and Vergil by the age of ten and was reportedly conversant with ancient Egyptian hieroglyphics, Hebrew, and Sanskrit by the time he entered Oxford at the age of eighteen. Upon his graduation in 1869, he was asked to stay on as a fellow and tutor.

The association with Oxford continued for the rest of his career, for in 1891 he was appointed to a position as the first professor of Assyriology at the university and held that post until his retirement in 1915. He was also active in several professional societies, including the Royal Asiatic Society and the Egypt Exploration Fund, and was a founding member of both the Society for the Promotion of Hellenic Studies and the Society of Biblical Archaeology, serving as President of the latter for many years.[3]

———

When he finally arrived in Cairo in early 1888, most likely sometime after 27 January, Sayce sent a long note to a British weekly periodical called *The Academy*, in which he had published frequently in previous years. His note, entitled "Letter from Egypt," was published ten days after he mailed it, on 18 February.[4] In it, Sayce said that he had just spent the past twelve days traveling overland from Jerusalem to Kantara, Egypt.

Once in Cairo, Sayce belatedly learned "that about 200 cuneiform tablets have been offered for sale here, which are said to have come from Tel el-Amarna." Of these, he said, "Some have been bought by the Bulaq Museum, but the larger number have been purchased by Danninos [*sic*] Pasha. I have not seen a specimen of them, and cannot, therefore, say to what age or class of cuneiform writing they belong. If they really have been discovered in Upper Egypt, their interest will be great."[5] "Danninos," was the Egyptian scholar Albert Daninos, mentioned previously. Though there were no longer any large groups of the tablets for sale, Sayce made the best of the situation and began arranging to see and study as many as possible of the tablets that remained in Cairo.

In his 1923 autobiography, Sayce added details about the state of the tablets at that time. He wrote "a few of them had been offered" to the museum (it is unclear if they had been purchased or not) and noted that Grébaut, the new director of the Department of Antiquities who happened to be away in Luxor at that moment, had sent word to Emil Brugsch, then the conservator at the museum, to ask Sayce, in his capacity as an Assyriology expert, for his opinion about the tablets. Unfortunately, Sayce did not record who had offered the tablets to the museum.[6]

According to this much later version, Monsieur Urbain Bouriant, the director of the French School of Archaeology in Cairo, brought Sayce the tablets that had been purchased by Frénay, the flour mill supervisor who also acted as an agent purchasing antiquities for the Louvre. Frénay had given the tablets to Bouriant, who subsequently sent one to Professor Oppert in Paris. Sayce copied these tablets and "wrote at once to Grébaut, telling him that there could be no question about their genuineness, and that he should, if possible, secure every one that had been discovered" (recall that, according to Budge, Grébaut had already begun doing this).[7] Sayce's pronouncement was, of course, in direct contradiction of the opinion offered by Oppert, who thought the tablets were forgeries.

In a summary piece published a few years before his autobiography, in an issue of *The American Journal of Semitic Languages and Literatures*, Sayce told much the same story about examining Frénay's tablets. Bouriant gave him the tablets "to examine and copy when I arrived in Cairo *toward the end of the year*."[8] The date must be slightly erroneous, for it is clear from his "Letter from Egypt" that Sayce only arrived in Egypt in late January 1888, rather than in late 1887. The error may have been because he was recollecting events that had happened thirty years earlier.

In any event, when Sayce confirmed that the tablets were genuine, Brugsch promptly telegraphed Grébaut in Luxor and suggested that he should "secure all that he could." According to Sayce, Grébaut then "seized without compensation all the tablets which were not protected by consular authority" and so "the tablets thus seized are now in the Cairo Museum" (i.e., the Bulaq Museum). Grébaut's actions turned out to be ill-advised. Either annoyed by the seizures or else excited by the prospect of finding additional tablets and the income they would bring, local residents "defaced and partially destroyed the following year" the tombs at Amarna. Sayce further noted that "a few tablets found their way into the hands of private individuals; some were bought by the Russian Egyptologist Monsieur Golénischeff, others by Monsieur Rustovich, at that time the agent of Messrs. Thomas Cook & Son, while one or two were obtained by a Greek gentleman living at Roda."[9]

Sayce's statements raise more questions than they answer. From whom were these additional tablets seized by Grébaut? How many were seized? We know that there are now fifty-two tablets in the Cairo Museum, but how many of these arrived there because of Grébaut? Furthermore, why were some "protected by consular authority"—and who was the consul in question?

Professor Jana Mynářová of Charles University in Prague, who has studied the Amarna Letters in detail, has provided some of the answers to these questions. She cites entries in the *Journal d'entrée* of the Cairo Museum dating to

February 1888, which record seventeen tablets and fourteen additional fragments that were seized in Giza. Moreover, the Norwegian Assyriologist Jørgen Knudtzon later indicated, in his volumes published in 1907 and 1915, that these particular tablets and fragments had been obtained from the antiquities dealer Farag Ismain. Knudtzon says that Grébaut purchased these items from Ismain, rather than seizing them. In return, Ismain agreed to show the authorities where at Amarna the pieces had been discovered, but when they went to that location only "some debris" was found.[10]

However, the first mention of such tablets in museum records are not twenty tablets registered in November 1887, as one might expect from Wilbour's letter cited above, but, according to Mynářová, are instead two that were purchased in January 1888 from someone named "Philip." Three more were purchased, probably in February 1888, with their provenance given as the region of Ekhmim, followed by sixteen more registered in February 1888. These come to a total of twenty-one tablets registered in January and February, which is very close to the twenty tablets mentioned by Tano and Wilbour back in November 1887. Moreover, when these are added to the seventeen whole and fourteen fragmentary tablets that were seized in Giza, we reach a total of fifty-two whole or fragmentary tablets, which is the number currently in the museum. This leaves us only with the question of why, if the museum had acquired the twenty (or twenty-one) tablets in November 1887, they weren't all registered at that time, but instead as several smaller groups in January and February 1888. This, however, is a question we may not be able to answer.[11]

From various other sources, including Budge, we also learn that the "consul" in question was possibly a man named Mustafa Agha Ayad (or Ayat), who lived in Luxor and was a "consular agent for Britain, Belgium, and Russia." As Jason Thompson has put it, he was also a known antiquities dealer and his role as a consular agent "provided international contacts as well as diplomatic protection for his large but mostly unrecorded trade in antiquities." Budge describes him as "the British Consul at Luxor," who "wanted to make the British Museum the 'best in all the world.'" Budge also notes in his autobiography the large number of antiquities that he saw while visiting Mustafa Agha Ayad in Luxor; he appreciated the connections that the "consul" was able to make for him with the locals who were actively digging up the items.[12]

It is possible that we may have the wrong man in our sights, though, for Mustafa Agha Ayad apparently died sometime before the end of 1887, which makes it unlikely that any items would still have been under his consular protection in early 1888.[13] In fact, the consular agent in question is more likely to have been Frénay, the French flour mill operator in Ekhmim, for we know from Wilbour's letter dated 5 April 1888 that he refers to Frénay as a "consul": "[Grébaut's] main object was to get the cuneiform tablets said to be found at Amarna, but Consul Frénay tells me he got none."[14]

———

In the meantime, Sayce went to work translating some of the tablets purchased by Frénay, now in Bouriant's possession. In late March and early April 1888, he published his preliminary identifications in two long articles, both of which appeared in *The Academy*, the periodical where he had published his first "Letter from Egypt" back in February. The March article was also entitled "Letter from Egypt," while the latter contained a bolder identification, with the title "Babylonian Tablets from Upper Egypt."[15]

In the articles, Sayce also complained that he had been unable to study the tablets belonging to the Bulaq Museum in Cairo. These "are locked up in the director's house; and, like several other objects of interest, are inaccessible both to the *employés* of the museum and to foreign scholars who visit Cairo during the winter, while M. Grébaut is up the river."[16]

Since Sayce does not delve into further details, we can only imagine his initial reactions while studying and translating the Frénay / Bouriant tablets. His amazement must have been similar to Budge's reaction when first studying the eighty-one tablets in Luxor, although Sayce did not have to read these tablets in secret. In hindsight, Sayce would have been wise to wait until he saw the additional tablets in the Bulaq Museum, for he misidentified what was written on the first few tablets belonging to Frénay / Bouriant as well as misdating them by nearly a thousand years.[17]

In the March 1888 "Letter from Egypt," Sayce concerned himself with a single tablet, noting that "M. Bouriant has been kind enough to let me copy one of the cuneiform tablets from Tel el-Amarna, which is in his possession." Then he got straight to the heart of the matter: "The tablet is written in a neo-Babylonian form of cuneiform script, though some of the characters are peculiar; and it belongs to the period extending from the age of Assur-bani-pal to that of Darius."[18]

Since Sayce's initial attempt to date this tablet covers a timespan of several centuries—the seventh to fifth centuries BCE—he subsequently tried to narrow down the date. In his April 1888 publication, after having seen a few more of the Frénay / Bouriant tablets, he said more specifically that the tablets were from the time of the Neo-Babylonian king Nebuchadnezzar in the late seventh century or early sixth century BCE. He stated his reasoning in no uncertain terms:

> Most of the tablets contain copies of despatches sent to the Babylonian king by his officers in Upper Egypt; and as one of them speaks of 'the conquest of Amasis,' whilst another seems to mention the name of Apries, the king in question must have been Nebuchadnezzar. The conquest of Egypt by Nebuchadnezzar, so long doubted, is now therefore become a fact of history. One of the tablets is addressed to 'the king of Egypt,' the name of Egypt being written Mitsri, as in the annals of Nebuchadnezzar, and not Mutsri, as in the inscriptions of Assyria. In others the Babylonian monarch is called 'the Sun-god,' like the native Pharaohs of Egypt.[19]

To Sayce's credit, some of these tablets, when they were eventually properly translated, did turn out to be letters from (or to) Babylonian kings. However, the kings in question ruled during the Middle Babylonian period, in the fourteenth century BCE, rather than during the Neo-Babylonian period, which began seven hundred years later.

We should perhaps not be too surprised by these misidentifications, given the haste with which Sayce translated and published these texts. Perhaps he was trying to beat Budge to the punch, for he had no way of knowing whether Budge was working on the tablets while continuing his travels to Baghdad and elsewhere before returning home to London. Perhaps he was racing to beat a number of German scholars, whom he knew had access to other tablets. Or perhaps he was simply invigorated by the challenge these new tablets presented. Over the course of his career, Sayce was involved in the decipherment and translations of a number of ancient languages, including Elamite, Urartian, Carian, Mittanian, and Hittite, in addition to his work in languages of the Assyrians and Babylonians. He was later described as having "an amazing visual memory, so that a tablet or a page of text once read was as it were photographed on his mind, and though the photograph might fade after a few days, the leading features of it would remain."[20]

Making such initial errors was also apparently not out of the ordinary for Sayce. David Gordon Lyon, the Hancock Professor of Hebrew and Other Oriental Languages at Harvard University, said just a few years later, on the occasion of the laying of the cornerstone at the Haskell Oriental Museum of the University of Chicago in 1896, "I bring gladly this just tribute to the work of Professor Sayce, although I have had, along with other Assyrian and biblical scholars, repeated occasion to regret the haste of many of his recent utterances."[21] One can hear the exasperation in his voice even now, more than 125 years later.

The Assyriologist Stephen Langdon wrote in a 1933 obituary for Sayce, published in *The Journal of the Royal Asiatic Society of Great Britain and Ireland*, that "From the point of view of an Assyriologist, Sayce must be reckoned as one of the most remarkable geniuses of the heroic age of the subject." However, in an adjacent obituary in the same journal, Egyptologist Francis Llewellyn Griffith noted ruefully that Sayce's genius came at a price and with a caveat: "Too often Sayce's conclusions were vitiated by over-hasty views. He carried with the utmost ease a vast weight of various and peculiar learning, and could concentrate all this on any particular point that came up for valuation, while his vivid imagination could draw sharply defined conclusions from the data; unfortunately, before he had tested his evidence and conclusions, his attention was too easily diverted to other matters within his vast range of interests. In short, his critical faculty was inferior to his other gifts."[22]

In another obituary for Sayce, published in the *Journal of Egyptian Archaeology*, Griffith similarly mingled admiration with condemnation:

> One cannot but feel that his marvelous gifts were out of proportion to his accomplishment. His vivid imagination and insight framed pictures of events and of interpretation in which he too often mistook the sharp lines of the picture for fact, and before he could establish or subvert his discoveries by argument, he had passed to some other field of research. His was the joyful existence of a brilliant butterfly tasting the delicious flowers of a great garden but never dwelling long enough in one spot to realize wholly its sweetness. His width of knowledge and interests was amazing, and he had little liking for the laboriousness of a specialist.[23]

However, Sayce was not at all deterred by his initial errors; nor did they appear to overly bother him, especially given the difficulties involved in identifying and interpreting the signs on these broken tablets. In fact, Sayce "was quite accustomed to making mistakes," as Griffith pointed out, for he felt that "progress in new fields is only possible by the process of trial and error." Moreover, he was also remarkably willing to acknowledge them, which is not common in academia, either then or now.[24]

Ironically, Budge, who must be seen as Sayce's main British rival in all things related to Amarna, was also accused of much of the same. In an obituary published in the *Journal of Egyptian Archaeology* when Budge died in 1934—just one year after Sayce—his fellow Egyptologist R. Campbell Thompson wrote, "The truth must be told that he suffered all his life from a desire to get things done: he was in too great a hurry to finish. Definite in all his ways, he grudged the time spent in 'rounding off the corners,' and this impatience was frequently to stand in his way."[25]

However, we should also note that, unlike Sayce, who was fairly beloved by his peers, Budge was reportedly despised by many of his colleagues. One leading Egyptologist said bluntly, in a lecture delivered at Cambridge, "Probably no Egyptologist of his stature—which none could deny him—enjoyed a worse reputation among his colleagues than did Budge at the height of his power and productivity."[26]

———

On 5 May 1888, Sayce issued an apology to Grébaut. He published a letter in *The Academy* that had been sent to him by Grébaut on 22 April, along with his own response.[27] Grébaut had written to protest Sayce's previous assertion that some of the tablets had been locked up in Grébaut's own private residence, stating instead:

My Dear Colleague,—The Assyrian tablets collected, with some difficulty, at the Boulaq Museum towards the end of last year have never left the offices of the building, where they were under the hands of the curator when you arrived in Cairo. You were misinformed when you were told that they were locked up in my house. Not being able to read Assyrian, but thinking you would come to Egypt this winter, before I departed to Upper Egypt, I had requested that the existence of the tablets should be made known to you, and that you should be asked to leave at the Museum some notes which would assist us in compiling our catalogue. I am doubly vexed at what has happened.

Above Grébaut's letter appeared Sayce's reply:

I have just received from M. Grébaut, the director of the Boulaq Museum, the following letter . . . It will be seen from it that the Babylonian tablets acquired by the Museum were after all safely deposited in an accessible part of the building, and not locked up in the private house of the director. I am exceedingly sorry that the misinformation I received should have led me to commit an act of injustice to M. Grébaut, and I hasten to repair it as soon as possible. If I am again in Cairo I hope I shall not be so unfortunate as to miss him again, or to lose the chance of copying inscriptions which throw light on Nebuchadnezzar's campaign against Egypt, and possibly also on his campaign against Judah.

While it was gracious of Sayce to admit to the larger scholarly world that he had been misinformed about the accessibility of the tablets, it is of interest to note that he still held onto his erroneous opinion regarding the date of the tablets and the Babylonian king mentioned on them, for he had not yet seen an article that two German scholars, Adolf Erman and Eberhard Schrader, had just published. It would not be much longer, however—in fact, not even a month would pass—before Sayce was compelled to change his mind publicly.

4

The Young Berliners

IN 1888, ADOLF ERMAN was a thirty-four-year-old associate professor of Egyptology at the University of Berlin. He also happened to be director of the Egyptian Department at the Royal Museum in the same city. Serving as his research assistant was Carl Friedrich Lehmann, a twenty-seven-year-old former lawyer who had just received his PhD from the University of Berlin two years earlier (Fig. 4).

The two scholars represented a new German effort to translate the Amarna tablets, meaning that Budge and Sayce now had competition. Nor were these two alone in their efforts, for they were joined, and challenged, in their efforts by several other German colleagues. As a group, we might refer to them as "The Young Berliners," for almost all were in their mid-twenties or early thirties, and most were based in Berlin. They were all either Egyptologists or Assyriologists by training and eager to work on this new discovery, alternating between cooperating and vying with each other to translate and publish the tablets, primarily those that were now in Berlin but also some in the Bulaq Museum and elsewhere.

On the Assyriological side of things was Hugo Winckler (see Fig. 4), a twenty-five-year-old archaeologist and specialist in ancient Near Eastern languages who had also just received his PhD from the University of Berlin in 1886, where he had studied with the well-known scholar Eberhard Schrader. Winckler is now more frequently cited by archaeologists and historians for his excavations at Hattusa, the capital city of the Hittites in ancient Anatolia, and for his discovery of the Hittite archives at that site, but those would not be found for another two decades. His early work on the Amarna tablets in the Bulaq Museum in addition to those in Berlin, though often overlooked by nonspecialists, is just as important as his later work on the Hittites and includes important milestones en route to the final publications of the tablets.

FIGURE 4. Adolf Erman, Carl Friedrich Lehmann, and Hugo Winckler.
Illustrations by Glynnis Fawkes.

Eventually these three scholars would be joined by Carl Bezold (Fig. 5), a young German Assyriologist who had studied at the University of Munich and then at Leipzig University for his PhD with the renowned Assyriologist Friedrich Delitzsch (who had earlier begun his own career by studying with Schrader). The fifth member of the German group of Amarna scholars was Heinrich Zimmern (see Fig. 5), a twenty-eight-year-old Assyriologist who had studied at Berlin with Schrader and then at Leipzig with Delitzsch. However, we will not meet these latter two, Bezold and Zimmern, for a while yet.

The first salvo was fired by Erman (the Egyptologist) and Schrader (the senior Assyriologist), who teamed up to coauthor a seven-page article about the Amarna tablets. It appeared on 3 May 1888, just a few weeks after Sayce's initial offerings, in a German scholarly periodical, *Sitzungsberichte der Königlich Preussischen Akademie der Wissenschaften zu Berlin*.[1]

Erman and Schrader disagreed with Sayce about the date of the tablets, stating in no uncertain terms that the tablets were from the Eighteenth Dynasty

FIGURE 5. Carl Bezold and Heinrich Zimmern.

and specifically the Amarna Period, during the reigns of Amenhotep III and Akhenaten, which they dated to the fifteenth century BCE. They did not venture to suggest any actual translations but, among other things, stated that the material included letters exchanged between those two pharaohs and Burna-Buriash II, the king of Babylonia who was known from other published documents and could now be conclusively seen as a contemporary. There were also letters exchanged between Amenhotep III and Tushratta, the king of Mittani, a kingdom located in what is now northwestern Syria and northern Iraq and that also dated to the time of the Eighteenth Dynasty, not the Neo-Babylonian period.[2]

Their work was based on the 160 Amarna tablets that had been acquired by the Austrian antiquities dealer Theodor Graf, most likely from the antiquities dealer Ali Abd el-Hajj in Giza. Graf had promptly offered the tablets to the authorities in Berlin, with the cost of the purchase covered by James Simon, a textile magnate and friend of the Kaiser. These formed the nucleus of the current collection in the Vorderasiatisches Museum, where they were eventually supplemented by other Amarna tablets, such as those originally possessed by Frénay / Bouriant as well as those purchased by Daninos.[3]

Erman and Schrader's redating of the tablets hit the scholarly world like a bombshell. Wilbour, the American Egyptologist, penned a note dated 29 May 1888:

> Schiaparelli [Ernesto Schiaparelli, an Italian Egyptologist] dined with us and was here last evening. He brought a communication from Erman to the Berlin Academy stating that they have in the Egyptian Museum one hundred and sixty cuneiform tablets from Tell-el-Amarna, bought of Theodore Graf, a Cairo merchant, who sold the great Fayoom papyrus find to the Archduke Rainer of Vienna. This will astonish people in Egypt. Professor Sayce, too, who thought to read the names of Amasis and Apries of the Twenty-sixth Dynasty on the four tablets which Frénay sent to Bouriant, will be astonished to learn that the one hundred and sixty, and probably all the rest, are of the time of Amenophis III and IV of the Eighteenth Dynasty near a thousand years before. Some are letters from kings of Babylon, big letters eighteen by ten inches, to these Pharaohs. Dooshratta writes to Amenophis III about the marriage of his daughter Ti-i-i, known well to us in hieroglyphics. The two Amenophis are called N'mmuriya and Napkhururiya near enough to Nebmara and Nefrkhepruara, their throne names. . . . There are many letters from the Governors of Syria and Phenicia [*sic*], then under Egypt. . . . The importance of this find can hardly be overestimated.[4]

Wilbour was correct on all counts, including his estimate of the importance of the find. His "Amenophis" is the Greek version of the Egyptian name "Amenhotep" and was used interchangeably until fairly recently, while Dooshratta is now more usually rendered as Tushratta, the king of Mittani. In short, the true nature of the tablets—personal correspondence between known Egyptian pharaohs and kings of contemporary empires—was now apparent. The race was on to decipher them properly.[5]

———

Within just a few weeks, in June, both Budge and Sayce published articles in the *Proceedings of the Society of Biblical Archaeology* (*PSBA*). Budge provided his initial transliterations and translations of the tablets in the British Museum. Like Erman and Schrader, Budge pointed out that Sayce had misidentified what was written on the Frénay / Bouriant tablets and had misdated them.[6]

In explaining his previous silence about Sayce's suggestions, Budge was diplomatic: "The brief examination of the tablets which I had been able to make in Egypt did not lead me to the conclusion arrived at by my good friend prof. Sayce, but as, owing to various circumstances, I was unable to verify or disprove his statements I said nothing about the matter publicly."[7]

Now, however, Budge was able to directly contradict Sayce's claims. There was no king called Amasis in the tablets and the letters were neither addressed to nor sent from Nebuchadnezzar. Instead, as Erman and Schrader had said, they were from, and to, the Eighteenth Dynasty pharaohs Amenhotep III and his son Akhenaten, "who lived at least 900 years before Nebuchadnezzar, and were kings of Egypt."[8]

Sayce clearly realized his error, for he published another note on 9 June, just ahead of his much-longer *PSBA* article, admitting his errors in assigning a date and identifications to the tablets. However, he does not credit Erman and Schrader, or mention their article, which he may not have yet seen, but rather notes the efforts of Winckler and Lehmann.

> The cuneiform tablets discovered last winter at Tel el-Amarna in Upper Egypt turn out to be even more interesting and important than I supposed. About 160 of them have been procured for the museum at Vienna [*sic*] and have been examined there by Drs. Winckler and Lehmann. The result of their examination shows that the Amasis, whose name is found on one of M. Bouriant's tablets, does not belong to the XXVIth Dynasty, as I had imagined, but to the XVIIIth, and that the tablets themselves formed part of the archives of Amenophis III and IV. They consist, for the most part, of letters and despatches sent to these monarchs by the kings and governors of Palestine, Syria, Mesopotamia, and Babylonia; and, as some of them were written by Burna-buryas, King of Babylon, their age is about 1430 B.C.[9]

Sayce went on to discuss his belief that one of the tablets contained a reference to the sun god Masu, which he believed was "letter for letter" the same as the Hebrew word for Moses. He suggested, therefore, that this was "a name already known in Egypt a hundred years before the date assigned by Egyptologists to the Exodus."[10] As we shall see, he persisted in this line of reasoning for some time, though he was later taken to task by other scholars for its incorrectness.

Today we know that Erman and Schrader in their initial article, as well as Sayce in his brief note, were off by almost a century in their dating for the Amarna tablets. After another hundred years of scholarly research, we can now clearly date them to the fourteenth century BCE, rather than to the fifteenth century. Amenhotep III is now thought to have ruled from ca. 1391 to 1353 BCE and Akhenaten from ca. 1353 to 1334 BCE. Burna-Buriash II of Babylonia overlapped with them both, ruling from ca. 1359 to 1333 BCE.[11] Still, this is far better than Sayce's original dating of the tablets, which had been off by more than seven centuries.

Budge and Sayce engaged in a back-and-forth regarding Sayce's initial dating of the tablets for more than thirty years. In his 1920 autobiography, Budge noted that "a gentleman in Cairo who had obtained four of the smaller tablets and paid £100 for them, showed them to an English [i.e., British] professor, who promptly wrote an article upon them, and published it in an English newspaper."[12] While Budge did not actually mention that it was Sayce who was the British professor in question (though there is nobody else that it could have been), he went on to say that this unnamed professor "post-dated the tablets by nearly 900 years, and entirely misunderstood the nature of their contents." Moreover, "The only effect of his article was to increase the importance of the tablets in the eyes of the dealers, and, in consequence, to raise their prices, and to make the acquisition of the rest of the 'find' more difficult for everyone."[13]

Sayce was eventually gracious enough to admit his error about the dating of the tablets and to explain how it came to be, in his own autobiography published three years after Budge's. According to him, he initially "was unable to assign a date to the tablets, as those which I had copied contained no indications of their age, and the form of the script was new and so could not be compared with anything previously known; in a letter to the *Academy*, however, I ventured to suggest the age of Nebuchadrezzar, which soon turned out to be some eight hundred years too late."[14]

———

Both Budge and Sayce were now influenced by, and indebted to, the contemporaneous work that the Young Berliners were undertaking on the tablets, not only those that had made their way to Berlin but also those that had remained in Cairo, at the Bulaq Museum. As evidence for this, we can see that in their June 1888 *PSBA* publications both Sayce and Budge cited Erman and Schrader's article that had appeared in early May. They also mention several brief notices that Lehmann had published in the popular press, intended for a general audience. Lehmann would soon thereafter publish his own scholarly article on the tablets, though it would appear later in 1888, just after those of Budge and Sayce.

Perhaps more important, though, especially in the long run, were their mentions of Winckler, the young scholar who had studied with Schrader at the University of Berlin. Although Winckler's article did not appear until later in 1888, it contained complete transliterations and translations of the cuneiform texts that he had been able to see. Sayce and Budge had both spoken to Winckler and gleaned relevant details from him while he was in Cairo working on this publication.[15]

In sum, within the first year following the initial discovery, all of the British and German scholars agreed that the tablets were dated to the Amarna Period and were from a royal archive of Amenhotep III and Akhenaten. Furthermore, all were in agreement that the letters in the archive included not only missives from minor vassal rulers of Canaanite city-states such as Byblos, Megiddo, Akko, and Ashkelon, but also letters to and from other Great Kings such as Burna-Buriash II of Babylonia and Tushratta of Mittani.[16] We shall take a look at these royal letters in the next few chapters.

PART II

The Fellowship of the Kings

5

Šarru Rabû

ONCE UPON a time, there was a king named Kadashman-Enlil I. He ruled in ancient Babylonia during the fourteenth century BCE, more than three thousand years ago. He loved his daughter very much, but he loved gold even more. Since his kingdom was on the banks of the Tigris and Euphrates Rivers, where there was no gold, he had to negotiate with the pharaoh in Egypt, who had more gold than he knew what to do with. He wrote a letter (EA 4) to Amenhotep III, the Egyptian pharaoh, saying: "As to the gold I wrote you about, send me whatever is on hand, as much as possible, before your messenger comes to me, right now, in all haste. . . . If during this summer, during the months of Tammuz or Ab, you send the gold I wrote you about, I will give you my daughter."[1]

The pharaoh was appropriately horrified and wrote back immediately (EA 1), chastising the Babylonian king: "It is a fine thing that you give your daughters in order to acquire a nugget of gold from your neighbors!"[2] Nevertheless, he did send the gold, for the sake of good trade and diplomatic relations between superpowers, and Kadashman-Enlil sent his daughter in return.

However, Kadashman-Enlil was cautious in at least one way about offering his daughter. He was well aware that his sister—unnamed in the letters—was already at the Egyptian court. Kadashman-Enlil's father, Kurigalzu, had done the same thing years earlier, sending Kadashman-Enlil's sister in a diplomatic marriage to the same pharaoh. Kadashman-Enlil therefore also inquired about his sister before agreeing to send his daughter: "Here you are asking for my daughter in marriage," he wrote to the pharaoh, "but my sister whom my father gave you is (already) there with you, and no one has seen her (so as to know) if now she is alive or if she is dead."[3]

Amenhotep III replied indignantly (EA 1), "Did you . . . ever send here a dignitary of yours who knows your sister, who could speak with her and identify her? . . . The men whom you sent here are nobodies. . . . There has been no one among them who knows her, who was an intimate of your father, and who could identify her. . . . Why don't you send me a dignitary of yours who can tell you the truth, the well-being of your sister who is here?"[4]

A simple reply of "yes, your sister named so-and-so is alive and well here; I just saw her yesterday" would have been a much more straightforward answer, but the offended Amenhotep III, with his many wives, might not have been able to recognize her himself, and perhaps wasn't even certain if she were alive or dead. We don't know how many women were in Amenhotep III's harem. We know of five or six foreign princesses and many Egyptian women chosen as royal wives for the harem, so it is possible that Amenhotep did not know either.

The matter ultimately must have been resolved to Kadashman-Enlil's satisfaction, for the marriage negotiations continued over the course of several letters (EA 2–4) and the royal nuptials eventually took place. Kadashman-Enlil returned to his concern about gifts of gold. As he wrote in one letter (EA 3) during this exchange, "You have sent me as my greeting-gift, the only thing in six years, 30 minas of gold that looked like silver. That gold was melted in the presence of Kasi, your messenger, and he was a witness."[5] Silver, a common metal in Mesopotamia and the material underlying their currency system, would not have been nearly as valued as a gift of Egyptian gold.

We don't know whether the unnamed Babylonian princess lived happily ever after in Amenhotep III's court. The fairy tale doesn't elaborate. Princess wives were rarely discussed in international correspondence between kings, and she is never mentioned again.

———

It seems appropriate to begin our discussions in this chapter as if with a fairy tale, because the correspondence exchanged between the Great Kings in the Eastern Mediterranean during the fourteenth century BCE envisioned just such a peaceful world—perhaps the first "International Society," as one scholar has suggested. Royal gifts were exchanged freely between kings of equal rank and power, and diplomatic marriages further cemented their relationships.[6]

Who were the major powers and players present in these royal letters? The early scholars often referred to them by different names and / or spellings, or sometimes got their generations mixed up, so it can be hard to discern from the translated tablets themselves.

Simply put, there were a handful of Great Powers in the fourteenth century BCE in the Aegean and Eastern Mediterranean regions. Unlike the first millennium BCE, which saw the ascendency of single empires like the Neo-Assyrians, Neo-Babylonians, or Achaemenid Persians, several powerful states balanced each other off during the second millennium BCE, much as the changing alliances in nineteenth-century Europe maintained the peace for a century until it was shattered by World War I. The kings of no fewer than five other Great Powers, not including the Egyptian pharaohs, are mentioned in these royal letters: the Hittites in Anatolia (modern Turkey); Mittani (in northern Syria); Assyria and Babylonia in Mesopotamia (modern Iraq); and the island of Cyprus. In some cases, like Egypt and Mittani, their predecessors had already been interacting in one way or another for more than a century; others were relatively new to the table. Other less powerful polities included some large city-states, like Ugarit on the Syrian coast, and the kingdom of Arzawa in western Anatolia. And, although they had been under the thumb of the Egyptian pharaoh since at least the days of Thutmose III in the early fifteenth century BCE, there were numerous small autonomous city-states scattered around the southern Levant, with familiar names like Jerusalem, Megiddo, and Gaza.

We have, at most, three generations of Egyptian kings (and one queen) who were involved in these communications, namely Amenhotep III and his wife Queen Tiyi, followed by their son Akhenaten, and grandson Tutankhamun. Together their reigns covered most of the first three-quarters of the fourteenth century BCE (ca. 1391–1323).

We also know the names and dates for their contemporaries. Assyria was ruled for almost four decades by Assur-uballit I, from ca. 1363 to 1328 BCE. In Babylonia, Kadashman-Enlil I was followed by Burna-Buriash II; all told, they were in power from ca. 1374 to 1333 BCE. Shuttarna II, followed by Tushratta, ruled Mittani from ca. 1380 BCE until sometime after 1360 BCE. The Hittite homelands were run by Suppiluliuma I, whose rule lasted from ca. 1350 until 1322 BCE. Tarkhundaradu ruled Arzawa sometime around 1360 BCE, while Ammistamru I and Niqmadu II were succeeding kings of Ugarit during this period, ruling from ca. 1360 to 1315 BCE.

As each new ruler ascended to the throne, he had to establish relations with the other powers around him to maintain his state's position in the political balance of power. We can see this, for example, in the several Babylonian

TABLE 1. Egyptian Pharaohs and their contemporaries (Thutmose IV through Tutankhamen)

King / Area	Arzawa	Assyria	Babylonia	Hittites	Mittani	Ugarit
Thutmose IV	—	Assur-nadin-ahhe II Eriba-Adad I	Kurigalzu I	Arnuwanda I	Artatama I	—
Amenhotep III	Tarkhundaradu	Eriba-Adad I Assur-uballit I	Kurigalzu I Kadashman-Enlil I Burna-Buriash II	Arnuwanda I Tudhaliya III	Shuttarna II Tushratta	Ammistamru I
Akhenaten	—	Assur-uballit I	Burna-Buriash II	Suppiluliuma I	Tushratta	Niqmadu II
Tutankhamun	—	Assur-uballit I	Kurigalzu II	Suppiluliuma I	Shattiwaza	Niqmadu II

princesses who were sent to Egypt, as well as the princesses who were sent from Mittani. As for the contemporaneity of the various rulers, including over the generations, we can see this most easily in chart form (see Table 1). I have also included them in a list of "Dramatis Personae" that can be found toward the end of the book.

———

There are few hints of war or military aggression—or even threats—in any of these royal letters. At most, there are occasional expressions of sorrow, such as when objects supposedly made of solid gold were not as they appeared or when trusted messengers were detained at a foreign court for longer than anticipated. And yet, we know from other contemporary records, including the vassal letters for instance, as well as documents and treaties signed by Suppiluliuma I in the Hittite archives found at Hattusa, that beneath the surface things were far from calm. We shall return to this later.[7]

The theme of gold being like dust in the land of Egypt, and of royal marriages, is continued in letters sent by other Great Kings. These included Kadashman-Enlil's successor Burna-Buriash II, writing to Akhenaten, as well as the Assyrian king Assur-uballit I, also writing to Akhenaten. However, they also seem to have been mistrustful of the gold shipments—and rightfully so.

For example, Burna-Buriash II brought up the topic in a letter (EA 7) to Akhenaten: "Certainly my brother [the king of Egypt] did not check the earlier (shipment of) gold that my brother sent to me. When I put the 40 minas of gold that were brought to me into a kiln, not (even) 10 minas, I swear, appeared." In another letter (EA 10), he said: "The 20 minas of gold that were brought here were not all there. When they put it into the kiln, not 5 minas of gold appeared. The (part) that did appear, on cooling off looked like ashes. Was the gold ever identified (as gold)?"[8]

Burna-Buriash gave Akhenaten the benefit of the doubt, however, saying that the gold that he had sent must have been swapped out during the journey from Egypt to Babylonia by untrustworthy deputies (EA 7): "The gold that my brother sends me, my brother should not turn over to the charge of any deputy. My brother should make a [personal] check [of the gold], then my brother should seal and send it to me. . . . It was only a deputy of my brother who sealed and sent it to me."[9]

Burna-Buriash also took issue with Akhenaten when some Babylonian merchants apparently on his payroll were attacked and killed in Canaan, which

Burna-Buriash regarded as being under Egyptian control at the time. In one very detailed and outraged letter (EA 8), he demanded that Akhenaten make sure that those responsible were brought to account and put to death, at the same time as providing compensation for the money and goods that had been stolen.[10] Unfortunately, we do not know the outcome, but presumably things were made right when Akhenaten sent a large caravan of precious gifts to Burna-Buriash, as spelled out in a later letter (EA 14).[11]

6

An Arzawan Alliance?

MARRIAGE NEGOTIATIONS were also at the forefront of discussions that Amenhotep III had with Tarkhundaradu of Arzawa, the ruler of a small kingdom that we now know was located on the western coast of Anatolia. We will meet him, and his kingdom, several times over the course of later chapters, for he was the topic of much discussion and interest on the part of the earlier Amarna scholars, though they had all mistakenly located his kingdom pretty much anywhere but western Anatolia.

Tarkhundaradu was the recipient of the only outgoing letter in the Amarna archive to have been written in Hittite, rather than in Akkadian (EA 31). One of the many things that makes this letter fascinating is that, since it was sent by Amenhotep III, it means there was at least one scribe at the Egyptian court who was bilingual in Egyptian and Hittite.[1]

The earlier scholars thought that this first letter was being sent to Amenhotep III, rather than the other way around, and also did not notice that there is a second letter related to Tarkhundaradu in the archive as well. Amarna Letter EA 32, which is in the Berlin Museum, was also written in Hittite and was in fact sent in the reverse direction, from Tarkhundaradu to Amenhotep III (thereby further indicating that there was someone at the Egyptian court who could read Hittite).[2]

William Moran of Harvard University, and other scholars, thought that the letter from Amenhotep III to Tarkhundaradu (EA 31) was the first to be sent during their correspondence. It begins with the usual type of opening found in letters between two Great Kings: ". . . with me it is well. With my houses, my wives, my children, the senior officials, my troops, my chariots, my possessions, whatever is in my lands, all is well. May everything be well with you. With your houses, your wives, your children, the senior officials, your troops, your chariots, your possessions, your lands, may all be well." The letter then picks up almost mid-stream, as it were: "Behold, I have sent to you Iršappa, my messenger. Let us see the daughter whom they will bring to My Majesty in marriage. Let him pour oil on her head. Behold, I have sent to you one *halaliya* of good-quality gold."

It is clear not only that the proposed marriage had been the subject of at least one earlier letter but that it was part of something larger as well. This, however, is only hinted at: "As for the operation about which you wrote to me: 'Send it to me,' I will send it to you afterwards. (But first) send back promptly your messenger and my messenger and let them come (to me). (When) they return to you they will bring the bride-price for the daughter."[3]

We have no idea what this "operation" involved or why Tarkhundaradu had asked Amenhotep III to "send it to him," or why Amenhotep III would only send it to him "afterwards"—in other words, presumably after the marriage had been finalized and the Arzawan princess had arrived in Egypt. However, we must consider that Tarkhundaradu's Arzawan kingdom was surrounded not only by other polities, such as the Seha River Lands and, further to the north, Assuwa and the region of Troy, but also lay in the way of the Hittites who were intent on securing all of Anatolia including the western coast at that time (see Map 2).

Thus, it was in the best interests of both Amenhotep III and Tarkhundaradu to sign a mutual defense treaty in order to stymie Hittite expansion;[4] parallel examples for such a situation can be found throughout history, up to and including the present day. It may be that such a treaty was being drawn up and would be cemented by the marriage of Tarkhundaradu's daughter to Amenhotep III (as indeed other kings had done).

The diplomatic intrigue aimed at suppressing the Hittites is shown by the subsequent lines in Amenhotep III's letter to Tarkhundaradu. These read: "Send me people of the land of Gašga. I have heard that everything is finished. And also [that] the land of Hattuša is frozen / paralyzed."[5] The Gašga, or Kaška as they are more commonly called, were a group located in Anatolia, far to the northwest of the Hittite capital of Hattusa. They were the only people to successfully sack that city, an event that is usually thought to have taken place just a few years previously, ca. 1400 BCE. It wouldn't be surprising if Amenhotep III also wished to set up an alliance with the Kaška in order to hem in the Hittites on the northwest and was using his proposed alliance with Tarkhundaradu to do so.

Moran and others thought that Amarna Letter EA 32, which is unfortunately broken, was the subsequent response from Tarkhundaradu to

Amenhotep III. This letter too picks up mid-stream: "Behold, with regard to this matter that Kalbaya said to me, 'We should establish a blood-relationship between ourselves,' I do not trust Kalbaya. He said it, but it does not figure on the tablet. If you really want my daughter, would I not give her to you? I will give (her) to you. Send Kalbaya back to me promptly together with my envoy and write back to me (about) this matter on a tablet."[6]

It is not clear from this who Kalbaya is, but some scholars had suggested that he might have been an envoy of Tarkhundaradu who was sent to the pharaoh.[7] Clearly, he was someone involved in the negotiations, both for the daughter and for whatever else was on the table. The most straightforward reading of this letter is that Kalbaya had orally delivered a message from the pharaoh, suggesting that a blood relationship should be established between the two kings, but that Tarkhundaradu did not trust the accuracy of the message since it was not also written down on a tablet that had obviously been brought to him at the same time (but which we do not now have).[8]

The letter ends with a postscript, inscribed below a line drawn across the tablet. It was not meant for the pharaoh, but rather for the Egyptian scribe whom either the Arzawan king or his scribe assumed would be replying to the letter. "[To] the scribe who reads out this tablet: may Nabu king of wisdom and the Sun-God of the Gatehouse duly protect him, and may they duly hold (their) hands around you! You, Scribe, duly write to me, also put your own name after. The tablets that are brought here always write in Hittite."[9]

Given all of the above, what was going on between Egypt and Arzawa, apart from the proposed marriage? The mystery may now have been solved, for it has been argued by several prominent scholars in recent years that we need to reverse the order of the letters. They contend that the letter from Tarkhundaradu to Amenhotep III (EA 32) is actually the earlier of the two letters, which makes a great deal of sense.[10]

If this were the case, then we should view the discussion following the revised translation and suggested order presented by the late J. David Hawkins of the University of London. He saw the situation as follows:

Amarna Letter EA 32 (sent from Tarkhundaradu): "See, this message which Kalbaya spoke to me (saying): 'Let us make ourselves a marriage-alliance,' [now] I do not trust Kalbaya. He spoke it verbally, but on a tablet it was not set down. Now if truly my daughter you are seeking, will I not indeed give (her) to you? (Of course) I will give (her) to you! Now dispatch Kalbaya back to me with my envoy in haste, and write back this matter to me by tablet."

Amarna Letter EA 31 (sent to Tarkhundaradu, in response): "Thus says Nimuwaria [Amenhotep III], Great King, King of the land of Egypt, to Tarkhundaradu, King of the land of Arzawa, speak. . . . See, I have sent you Iršappa, my envoy. Let us see the daughter whom they will bring to My Majesty for marriage. . . . Dispatch back to me your envoy and my envoy at once and let them come, and they will come and bring you the bride-price for your daughter."[11]

Hawkins's interpretation is that the opening move in this courtship dance was made by Amenhotep III, which would not be surprising. Kalbaya was clearly the emissary he had sent to Tarkhundaradu. Kalbaya apparently brought both a written letter from the pharaoh, which we do not have, as well as a message delivered orally. The oral message concerned a possible marriage alliance, but it seems that this was not also mentioned in writing on the tablet. Tarkhundaradu therefore sent his letter written in Hittite (EA 32) to the pharaoh, asking for written confirmation about the marriage proposal. The confirmation was subsequently sent by the pharaoh in EA 31, replying—very unusually and uniquely—in Hittite, as requested. All of this makes much more sense, and clarifies the role of each individual, including Kalbaya. It also shows that, even after 150 years of research and interpretation, there is still much more work that can be done on interpreting the Amarna Letters.

Unfortunately, we do not know whether the arranged marriage ever took place, or if any sort of mutual defense pact was ever signed, for these are the only two tablets left to us from what obviously had been a longer and more involved correspondence.

Additional light on tablet EA 32, among numerous others, was made by identifying the source of the clay from which the tablet was made. Yuval Goren, a specialist in sourcing clays used in archaeological materials, worked with archaeologist Israel Finkelstein and ancient historian Nadav Na'aman of Tel Aviv University, taking physical samples from many of the Amarna Letter tablets. They then compared those samples to known clay sources in areas ranging from modern Israel to Cyprus, Turkey, Mesopotamia, and Egypt, in order to determine where each of the tablets had been made. Their hypothesis was that for a common material like clay, the source used to make each tablet was probably not far from where the letter was written. They also made use of previous studies involving Neutron Activation Analysis of the clay, which examined the chemical composition of clay pots and other vessels from these same locations.[12]

Although they were unable to find a matching clay source for Amarna Letter EA 32, it turned out that the chemical composition of the clay from the earlier project involving neutron activation analysis placed its source in northern Ionia, on the western coast of Anatolia—where Arzawa was located. This leaves us confident that this tablet was sent by Tarkhundaradu from his kingdom in Arzawa in western Anatolia.[13]

7

All's Fair in Love and War (and Diplomacy)

THE ONLY other royal letter in the Amarna archive that was not written in Akkadian is one written in Hurrian, a language used primarily in Mittani (located in what is now northern Syria), which was sent from Tushratta to Amenhotep III (EA 24). It also concerns an upcoming marriage, this time between Amenhotep III and Tushratta's daughter, Tadu-Heba.

It is surprising that this letter is written in Hurrian, for in the archive there are a total of nine letters (EA 17–25) that Tushratta sent to Amenhotep III, in addition to one that he sent to Queen Tiyi (EA 26), and another three that he sent to Akhenaten (EA 27–29). All of these other letters are written in Akkadian. What makes it even more curious is that the contents indicate that this one was neither the first nor the last in the series of letters that Tushratta sent to Amenhotep III.

In the customary opening to the letter, in which Tushratta provided the traditional well-wishes toward Amenhotep III's wives, children, senior officials, horses, chariots, troops, land, and possessions, he referred to himself as Amenhotep III's father-in-law. This should mean that his daughter Tadu-Heba was already married to the Egyptian pharaoh. He wrote: "Say to Nimmureya, the king of Egypt, my brother, my son-in-law, whom I love and who loves me: Thus (speaks) Tushratta, the king of the land of Mittani, your father-in-law, your brother."[1]

However, later in the letter he indicated that the marriage had not yet happened. "And now, when the wife of my brother comes, when she will be shown to my brother, may she be attired as my flesh of my flesh, and as my flesh may she be shown. And may my brother assemble the entire land and all the other countries and the honored guests (and) all envoys should be present. And may they show his dowry to my brother, and may they spread out everything in the sight of my brother."[2]

He also mentioned, rather matter-of-factly, "Now, my father's daughter, my sister, is herself there, and the tablet of her dowry is itself available; and my grandfather's daughter, the sister of my father is herself there." Thus, this would be the third generation of Mittanian princesses who had been sent to Egypt, for at the time that Amenhotep III requested that Tadu-Heba be sent to him, Tushratta's sister and his aunt were apparently both already there. They had been given to Amenhotep III by Shuttarna and Artatama, the previous kings of Mittani.[3]

So, just as there were two generations of Babylonian princesses in Amenhotep III's harem (Kadashman-Enlil I's sister and daughter), there would now have been a total of three generations of Mittanian princesses in the harem / court of Amenhotep III:

1) Artatama's unnamed daughter: She was Shuttarna's sister and Tushratta's aunt, who had been sent to Egypt by Artatama (Tushratta's grandfather) in order to marry Thutmose IV (Amenhotep III's father) and presumably remained in the royal harem even after the death of Thutmose IV.

2) Shuttarna's daughter Kelu-Heba: She was Tushratta's sister who had been sent to marry Amenhotep III.

3) Tushratta's daughter Tadu-Heba: She was now being sent to marry Amenhotep III.[4]

What this also means is that each king of Mittani, as he ascended the throne, felt the need to renew relations with the Egyptian pharaoh who was reigning at the time. Sending a daughter to marry the pharaoh, and thus creating anew the bond(s) between the two families quite probably went hand in hand with defensive treaties and the like, even if such treaties have not survived to us today. We have already seen that the Babylonian kings did the same.

In this letter, Tushratta emphasized the fact that he would send Amenhotep III "gifts for sure," as indeed he did, according to the itemized lists contained in some of the other letters, and pronounced his wish that Amenhotep III would give much in return to Tushratta, especially in the form of gold, "for . . . gold . . . in his [your] land, is plentiful; in the eyes of my brother it is not expensive, so may my brother not hold it back." Interestingly, he also asked specifically for an image of his daughter made of molten gold, which Amenhotep III should "lovingly" send to him.[5]

The numerous other letters, all written in Akkadian, which Tushratta sent to Amenhotep III and for which we have no replies, are each primarily concerned with the upcoming marriage and / or with gift giving. Two of these (EA 22 and 25) are simply long lists of gifts sent from Tushratta to Amenhotep III, including necklaces, rings, and other items made of precious metal and stones, as well as textiles, scented oils, and other expensive objects. These show the extent of the international connections at the time, which allowed for the trade and acquisition of the raw materials to make such finished luxury items for gifting between kings.

Some of these letters, such as EA 19 and 20, are concerned with gifts that Tushratta wanted Amenhotep III to send to him, primarily quantities of gold (Fig. 6). He wrote at one point, "in the land of my brother gold is plentiful like dirt," and so "to my brother I said: 'May my brother always surpass ten times what he did for my father!' And I requested of my brother much gold."[6]

As a result of gifts sent as a bride price for Tadu-Heba, Tushratta then declared mutual support between the two rulers: ". . . so we between us . . . are we one. The Hurrian land and the Egyptian land are therefore between them as one single land and support one another. I am like the lord of the Egyptian land and my brother is like the lord of the Hurrian land."[7] We might imagine Amenhotep III's irritation at being informed that Tushratta was "like the lord of the Egyptian land," although undoubtedly he would not have minded being considered the ruler of Mittani as well as Egypt.

A few lines later Tushratta reiterated the nature of the mutual defense treaty: "But in case sometime an enemy of my brother invades his land, (and) my brother writes to me and the Hurrian land, armor, weapons and all together everything that pertains to the enemy of my brother will be at his disposition. However, on the other hand, should there be an enemy of mine—if only he did not exist!—I will write to my brother, and my brother will send the Egyptian land, armor, weapons, and all together everything that pertains to my enemy."[8]

Another letter (EA 17) sheds light on why Tushratta was asking for a mutual defense treaty, harkening back to his earliest days on the throne of Mittani. "When I sat on the throne of my father, and I was young, then Pirhi did some unseemly deeds in my land and slew his lord. And because of this he was not permitting me friendship with anyone who loved me. But I, moreover, because of these unseemly things that were done in my land, was not remiss and as for the people who murdered Artashumara, my brother, with all that belonged to them, I slew them."[9]

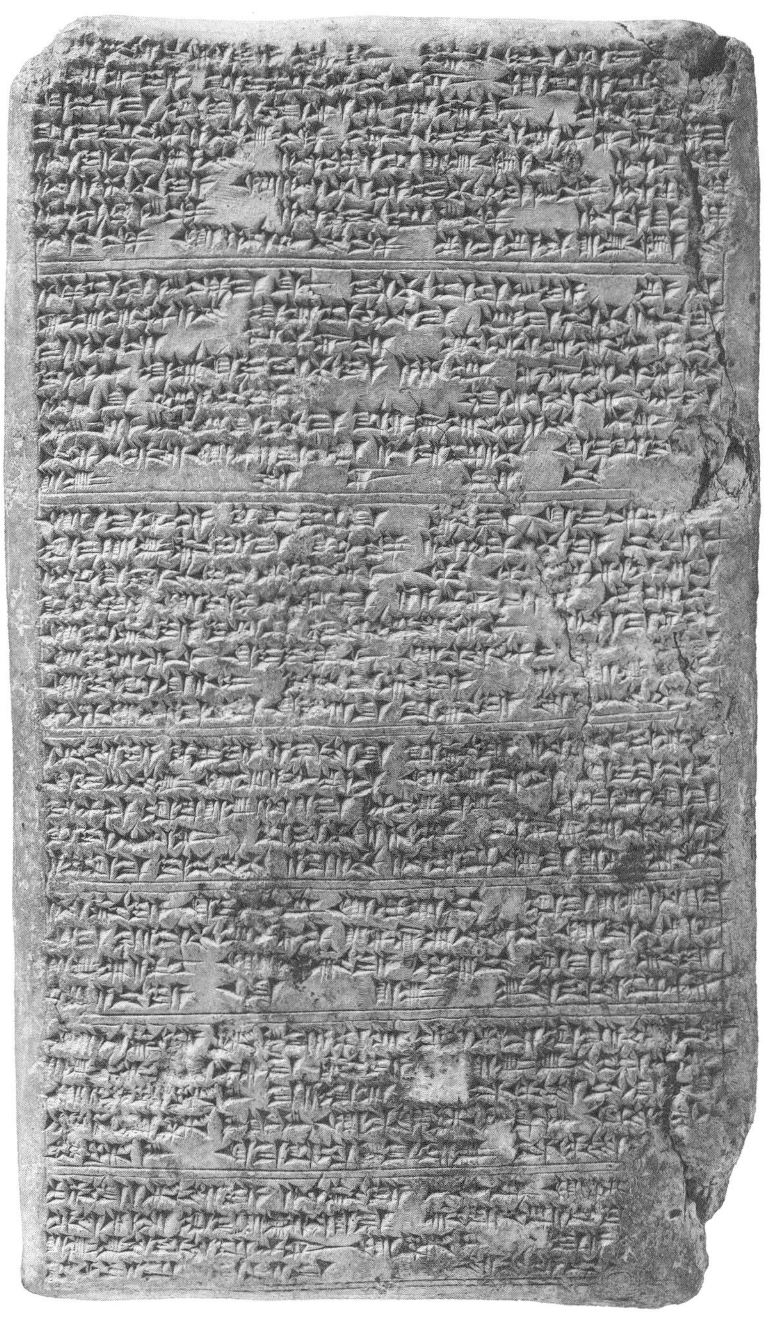

FIGURE 6. Amarna Letter EA 19 (Tushratta to Amenhotep III); BM E29791.
© Trustees of the British Museum.

It is not quite clear who Pirhi was, and whom he slew, but it is clear that Tushratta was probably not supposed to have succeeded his father on the throne and only did so because his older brother Artashumara had been murdered, perhaps in a coup attempt. He continued, "Inasmuch as you were friendly with my father, then because of that I have written and I have spoken to you so that my brother may hear of these things and so that he may rejoice."

Tushratta also mentioned that the Hittites (possibly led by Suppiluliuma I when he was still crown prince, but perhaps by his predecessor) had attacked his kingdom after he took the throne, but that he had defeated them. As proof, he said that he was including a chariot and two horses, as well as a boy and a girl, taken "from the spoil of the land of Hatti" among the greeting gifts that he was sending to Amenhotep III.[10]

We can understand Tushratta's fears, for even though he was now firmly in control in Mittani, his land was landlocked and surrounded, with trading partners who could turn against him in the blink of an eye. The Hittites lay immediately to the west and were always a source of potential problems. The Assyrians, now ruled by Assur-uballit I, lay directly to the east and south, with territory overlapping that of Mittani. Assur-uballit had already defeated Tushratta's father Shuttarna in battle ca. 1360 BCE, to begin Assyria's rise to prominence during this period. Babylonia lay further to the south, just below Assyria and allied now with Assur-uballit through an arranged marriage between his daughter and Burna-Buriash II.[11]

It is indeed a testament to Egyptian diplomacy, beginning first in the time of Hatshepsut, and reinforced by the campaigns of Thutmose III, that by the time of Amenhotep III's reign he had either established alliances, or was on speaking terms, with virtually all of the Great Powers and was able to maneuver through the realpolitik of the day.

We should not overlook or discount the power and influence of Amenhotep III's wife, Queen Tiyi, to whom Tushratta also sent at least one letter after Amenhotep III's death (EA 26). This tablet is now in two separate fragments, the larger one making its way to the British Museum and the smaller one ending up first at the Art Institute of Chicago and then the Oriental Institute at the University of Chicago (now the Institute for the Study of Ancient Cultures).

Tushratta was concerned with keeping good relations with Egypt, even as power transitioned from Amenhotep III to Akhenaten. He correctly surmised that Queen Tiyi was the essential bridge between father and son. He reminded Tiyi that they were related by marriage through his daughter Tadu-Heba, her daughter-in-law, and complained that Amenhotep III's son and successor,

Akhenaten, was sending statues of wood plated with gold, rather than the solid gold statues Tushratta had requested.[12]

Tushratta subsequently continued to write directly to Akhenaten (EA 27–29). In the first of these (EA 27), Tushratta took the liberty of reminding Akhenaten that Tadu-Heba, now Akhenaten's wife, was his daughter and thus they too were related by marriage. He spent the rest of the letter telling Akhenaten how good his father Amenhotep III had been in terms of sending gifts of gold to Tushratta and complaining directly about receiving the wooden statues plated with gold, rather than the solid gold statues that he had requested.[13]

Amarna Letter EA 28 turned out to be another long complaint from Tushratta, in which he grumbled that Akhenaten wasn't sending back the Mittanian messengers who accompanied the various gifts and messages sent to Egypt.[14] The third letter (EA 29) is also very long, but very informative, for it listed the names of several generations of Mittanian rulers (Artatama, Shuttarna, Tushratta) as well as Egyptian pharaohs (Thutmose IV, Amenhotep III, Akhenaten). It also included again the fact that there were no fewer than three Mittanian princesses who had been sent to marry the various Egyptian kings, as he had said in the letter written in Hurrian (EA 24). And, yes, Tushratta also took this opportunity to complain once again about the gold statues.[15]

But that was it; after this, the letters from Tushratta suddenly stopped. Scholars have hypothesized, based on textual evidence primarily in the Hittite archives, that Suppiluliuma I launched his First Syrian War at about that time, somewhere between five and ten years after Akhenaten had begun to rule. According to Suppiluliuma's boastful claims, this first major campaign of the Hittites against Mittani and its Syrian vassals lasted only a single year (though scholars have now suggested that it may have actually lasted as long as five years). Regardless of its length, the Hittites were able to reach and sack the Mittanian capital city of Washukanni, with Tushratta fleeing for his life (or so the Hittites claimed). Sometime soon therafter, Tushratta fell victim to a palace conspiracy and was assassinated, which led to his son Shattiwaza being installed upon the throne as a puppet king loyal to Suppiluliuma. This explains the sudden cessation of letters to Egypt from a previously prolific correspondent.[16]

As ancient historians, we are indebted to Tushratta for his prolific correspondence during his lifetime. It is through his letters that we are able to reconstruct his family history, for instance, as well as corroborate many of the facts and events associated with his reign and elsewhere in the ancient Near East before he disappeared from the scene.

8

The Hand of Nergal

ASSYRIA TOOK full advantage of the problems caused by the Hittites to get out from under the shadow of Mittani. This provides us with a context for the only letters (EA 15–16) sent to Amarna by the Assyrian king Assur-uballit I, who was eager to take his place at the table with the other Great Kings.[1]

In the first of these letters (EA 15), Assur-uballit specified that he was the first of his family to write to the Egyptian pharaoh: "Say to the king of the land of Egypt: Thus Assur-uballit, the king of the land of the god Assur. . . . I have sent my envoy to you to see you and to see your land. Up to now, my fathers have not written. Today, I have written to you." For never having written before, he certainly knew proper protocol, for along with this letter, the Assyrian king sent a greeting gift for the pharaoh, consisting of a chariot, two horses, and a piece of genuine lapis lazuli, probably imported from distant Afghanistan.[2]

The second letter (EA 16) clearly was written after Akhenaten had sent messengers in response to the first letter. It is written in a pure Assyrian dialect rather than the standard Akkadian (Fig. 7). Assur-uballit promptly launched into his own request for gold but padded his request. Speaking directly to Akhenaten by name (Naphuriya) this time, he wrote: "When I saw your ambassadors, I rejoiced greatly. May your envoys dwell in my presence in great solitude." After briefly listing a few more greeting gifts that he was sending (two more chariots and two more horses, plus a cylinder seal of lapis lazuli), he then got immediately to the point of the letter, using the common refrain: "Gold in your land is dirt. They gather it up. Why does it delay with your approval? I am engaged in building a new palace. Send as much gold as needed for its adornment and its needs."[3]

Perhaps being new to all of this negotiating business, he offered nothing in return beyond the greeting gift that he had just mentioned. Instead, he listed

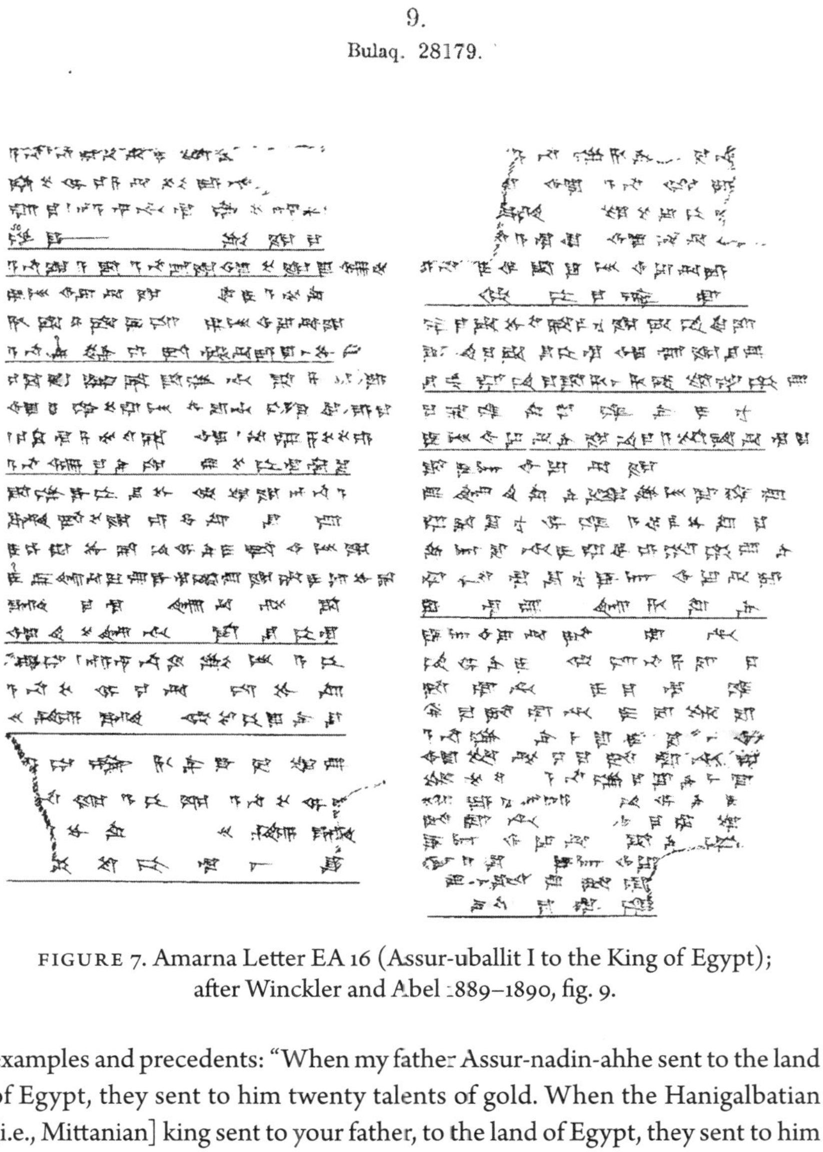

9.

Bulaq. 28179.

FIGURE 7. Amarna Letter EA 16 (Assur-uballit I to the King of Egypt); after Winckler and Abel 1889–1890, fig. 9.

examples and precedents: "When my father Assur-nadin-ahhe sent to the land of Egypt, they sent to him twenty talents of gold. When the Hanigalbatian [i.e., Mittanian] king sent to your father, to the land of Egypt, they sent to him twenty talents of gold." Coming full circle, and embracing his new-found status, he then wrote: "I am equal to a Hanigalbatian [Mittanian] king but you send to me x minas of gold. It is not sufficient for the going and returning and the wages of my envoys."

Note that the actual number of minas being sent is unclear in the letter. We also know, from other sources, that the Assyrian king Assur-nadin-ahhe II, who is mentioned in this letter as having also corresponded with Egypt, perhaps with Thutmose IV, and whom Assur-uballit here calls his "father," was not his actual father but more likely his uncle. Eriba-Adad I—who is not mentioned in this letter but who was probably the brother of Assur-nadin-ahhe and was the actual father of Assur-uballit—ruled in between the two of them on the throne of Assyria.[4]

In any event, Assur-uballit finally remembered his manners and ended this section of the letter with an offer, saying: "If your intention is truly genuine, send much gold, and as for that house of yours, send to me so that they may bring what you need." He ends the letter less diplomatically, with a complaint that his envoys had apparently been kept waiting outside in the sun when they first arrived at Amarna and asking if the pharaoh was trying to kill them on purpose.

Assur-uballit seems a little too brash, a little too eager, and a little too pushy—nouveau riche, we might say now, or literally a new kid on the block—which Akhenaten may not have appreciated. A little decorum would have gone a long way. It is possible that Assur-uballit eventually learned better manners, but we will never know because these are the only two letters exchanged between the two courts that are now left to us from the Amarna archive.

———

There are very few other letters exchanged between the Great Kings in the Amarna archive that are not related to alliances and marriages (proposed or otherwise) or to gold and trade or gifts. Even those exchanged with Alashiya / Cyprus (EA 33–40) and with the Hittites (EA 41–44) are concerned with these matters.

Of the four letters sent from the Hittites, all are written in Akkadian rather than in Hittite, perhaps surprisingly. The first one (EA 41, which is in the Cairo Museum) is known to be from Suppiluliuma I, since it specifically gives his name. It is addressed to "Huriya," whom he calls "my brother" (i.e., his political equal), and who is most likely Akhenaten. In this letter, Suppiluliuma began by touching on the same themes as the other kings, requesting friendly relations between himself and Akhenaten, as there had been in the time of Akhenaten's father (Amenhotep III).

Without much further preamble, Suppiluliuma then brought up the topics of both gift exchange and a marriage agreement, beginning by asking, "Why have you withheld the shipment that your father sent when your father was alive?" He continued: "Now, my brother, you have ascended the throne of your father, and just as your father and I desired greeting gifts between us, so now may you and I thus enjoy good relations between us, and the request that I made to your father, to my brother will I make: 'May we make a marriage agreement between us.'"

He also requested specific gifts, as seems to have been almost normal, namely two statues of gold and two statues of silver as well as "much lapis lazuli."[5] One would never know, from the tone of this letter, the havoc that Suppiluliuma had been causing in northern Canaan at this time, a region under Egyptian oversight, as we shall see below when we get to the vassal letters in the Amarna archive.

The other three related letters (EA 42–44, two of which are in Berlin and the other in the Ashmolean Museum at the University of Oxford) are more fragmentary. One of these might be also from Suppiluliuma to Akhenaten, while another appears to be from a Hittite prince named Zidan, who may have been Suppiluliuma's brother; the third is so fragmentary that it does not have the opening lines, so we are not sure about either the sender or the recipient.[6]

As we know from other texts found elsewhere, a marriage agreement between Hatti and Egypt was eventually made. It occurred a bit later and was most unusual, for instead of a Hittite princess being sent to Egypt to marry the pharaoh, it involved a Hittite prince named Zannanza being sent to Egypt to marry the widowed queen—most likely Nefertiti, widow of Akhenaten (though it might have been Ankhsenamen, widow of Tutankhamun). Unfortunately for all concerned, it ended in disaster and death, for the young Hittite prince was assassinated en route, thereby providing Suppiluliuma with an excuse to invade northern Canaan yet again and fight with the Egyptians, bringing home, by his account, thousands of prisoners of war.[7]

As for the letters from Cyprus / Alashiya, in Amarna Letter EA 33, neither king is specifically named: "To the king of Egypt, my brother: Message of the king of Alashiya, your brother." However, it is generally thought that this was sent to Akhenaten, since it also says, "Moreover, I have heard that you are seated on the throne of your father's house." It then continues with a mention of two hundred talents of copper, a key export from Cyprus, and suggests further that messengers should be sent between the two kings each year and that "gifts of peace" should also be exchanged.[8]

In a second letter (EA 34), possibly a follow-up, the Cypriot king said that he was sending his messenger with a hundred talents of copper for the pharaoh, as well as a few other gifts, ranging from an ebony bed to sweet oil to linen robes and shawls. The point, he said, was that "an alliance should be made between the two of us, and my messengers should go to you and your messengers should come to me."[9]

Another letter (EA 39), sent from the king of Cyprus to the king of Egypt with no specific names given, is concerned only with the welfare of specific Cypriot merchants who were doubling as messengers and whom the king of Cyprus wished to have sent back.[10]

Similarly, another very important letter (EA 35) concerns the sending of a Cypriot ambassador to Egypt (Fig. 8). In it, the king of Cyprus refers to a plague ("the hand of Nergal") that was ravaging the island at the time. "I herewith send to you 500 (talents) of copper. As my brother's greeting-gift I send it to you. My brother, do not be concerned that the amount of copper is small. Behold, the hand of Nergal is now in my country; he has slain all the men of my country, and there is not a (single) copper-worker. So, my brother, do not be concerned. Send your messenger with my messenger immediately, and I will send you whatever copper you, my brother, request." He added that a man from Alashiya had died while in Egypt and that the ambassador was needed in order to bring the body back to Cyprus.[11]

This is one of the few contemporary mentions of plague that we have from the time period—the other principal example is the Hittite tablet known as the "Plague Prayers of Mursili," in which Suppiluliuma's immediate successor recorded the fact that the Egyptian prisoners of war captured during the conflict that began after the murder of Zannanza had brought plague to the Hittite homelands, resulting in the death of Suppiluliuma himself and many others in the royal family, in addition to untold numbers in central Anatolia.[12] This event is not mentioned in the Amarna Letters, but it would explain the sudden cessation of correspondence between the Egyptian pharaohs and the Hittite king after the Zannanza Affair.

In another letter (EA 36), the Cypriot king said that he was sending another 120 talents of copper and that he was apparently prepared to send far more: "May the ships be many, send them here." There was also always a price to be paid, even if only in "gifts," for the Cypriot king continued, "Since they have prepared much copper, grain in ships from the province of Canaan send to me as in former days, so that I may make bread."[13]

In the previous letter (EA 35), the Cypriot king had likewise concluded: "You are my brother. May he send me silver in very great quantities. My brother, give me the very best silver, and then I will send you, my brother, whatever you, my brother, request . . . Whatever greeting gift he (my brother)

FIGURE 8. Amarna Letter EA 35 (King of Alashiya to the King of Egypt); BM E29788. © Trustees of the British Museum.

sends me, I for my part send back to you double." The message about the need for sending silver in return was not to be ignored, for in a subsequent letter (EA 37), the Cypriot king reiterated the request: "Send me pure silver. May my brother dispatch my messenger without delay."[14]

———

From the viewpoint of an ancient historian, the Amarna Letters exchanged between the Great Kings are like nuggets of gold and silver themselves. Putting ourselves especially in the shoes of the British and German scholars working on the first translations, the new information that was gleaned and the suppositions that were confirmed by these letters opened up vast new areas of understanding of the political and economic situation of the fourteenth century BCE.

As will already be clear, this was a time when the Egyptian pharaohs interacted on a daily basis with the other Great Kings across the region, stretching from what is now modern-day Turkey to modern-day Iraq. It was a glorious period—quite possibly the most spectacular era of the Late Bronze Age in this region.

However, the situation with the many petty Canaanite rulers was quite different from that of the Great Kings in their capital cities, for in those letters we can see that there was infighting and political intrigue at the local levels all up and down Canaan. Without these additional letters, we would be restricted to royal pronouncements carved on stone, which were more like propaganda and so do not offer insight into the power dynamics, negotiation strategies, and changing relations that we can see from the Amarna documents. All of this became apparent to Sayce, Budge, and the Young Berliners throughout 1888 and beyond, as they began to translate the tablets from the Canaanite rulers, at the same time as continuing to work on the correspondence of the Great Kings.

The Rules and the Race

9

No No Necho

IT WAS in the June 1888 copy of the *Proceedings of the Society of Biblical Archae-ology*, appearing just a few pages before Budge's article in the same issue, that Sayce officially published his preliminary translations of Frénay's thirteen tablets, which he had been shown by Bouriant. These new translations were very different from his earlier erroneous version sent to *The Academy* (which Sayce strategically does not mention in this new article), and he now agreed, once again, that the tablets dated to the fifteenth century BCE (rather than the fourteenth century, as is now accepted).[1]

However, there were still numerous problems with his translations, for Sayce made grievous errors in his suggestions regarding each of the thirteen tablets, most of which turned out to be letters sent by vassal kings. Some of these mistakes were his fault entirely, caused in part by his eagerness to find mentions of biblical people and places in the tablets, but others came from the general status of the field at the time.

Although the mistakes are somewhat understandable, and although we must also have sympathy for his fledgling efforts, the error-filled translations by Sayce stand in stark contrast to the more correct offerings being published virtually contemporaneously by the Young Berliners, and one can only imagine their reactions upon reading the statements and suggestions made in his article. I will highlight here only a few of the errors in Sayce's publication of these thirteen tablets in order to demonstrate the problems involved in being one of the first to attempt a translation of these letters.

Sayce thought that one of the tablets (EA 290) was a letter sent to the pharaoh from someone named "Arudi," who was concerned with someone else named "Melech the son of Marratim" and cities called Gaturri, Gimti, Kilti, and "Sadu-rurusi." This turned out to be very far afield, for we now know that it is actually a letter sent to the pharaoh by Abdi-Heba, who was the ruler of

Jerusalem and who was concerned at that moment with a military action by Milkilu of Gezer (not Melech the son of Marratim), who had used his own troops as well as those of Gath and Qilti to attack Jerusalem.[2] By 1890, Sayce and other translators belatedly realized that it was, in fact, Jerusalem that was being named (rather than "Sadu-rurusi"), but it took even longer than that for the other people and places named on the tablet to be correctly identified.

Other misidentifications involved a tablet (EA 146) that Sayce thought mentioned Pharaoh Necho of Egypt (who lived seven hundred years later). It was actually a letter sent by Abi-Milku, the ruler of Tyre, who—as it turned out—had sent a number of additional letters also found in the archive.[3]

Another tablet (EA 157), which Sayce thought also mentioned Pharaoh Necho or rather "of the country of Necho," does not do that either. Instead, it is a letter sent by Aziru, the ruler of Amurru, a kingdom in northern Syria located to the south of the city of Ugarit; it is one of many letters either sent by Aziru or that mention him. Rather than discussing Necho or his country (which would have been Egypt), Aziru was actually discussing the Hittites in Anatolia, whom Aziru worried would declare war against him.[4]

Sayce also elaborated on the tablet (EA 211) that he had included in his 9 June *Academy* note and that he thought mentioned Moses fully "a century before the date of the Exodus." Unfortunately, this identification too was erroneous. It is simply a letter sent by someone named Zitriyara, the ruler of an unnamed city, who also sent three other letters to the Egyptian pharaoh.[5]

Sayce did a better job on his translation and interpretation of the eighth tablet (EA 33).[6] He correctly identified the sender as the king of Alashiya, which is now generally accepted as the Bronze Age name for all or part of ancient Cyprus, and the recipient as an unnamed pharaoh of Egypt. He was also almost correct in thinking that there were "200 pieces of bronze" mentioned, although scholars now more usually think that copper is meant, rather than bronze (and, in fact, the word after the number two hundred is missing, so modern renditions usually supply "talents" for the ancient measurement rather than simply "pieces").

However, he was wrong in asserting that there was a mention in this letter of "the black stone of Solomon" at one point (line 14). The mistake by this linguistic expert is understandable, for the cuneiform signs preserved in one of the lines reads "[. . .]-te-mè šu-ul-ma-na." One can see how the word *šu-ul-ma-na* (which we now know means "well-being") could easily be mistaken for the name "Solomon" by someone like Sayce who was keen to find Biblical allusions, especially given how broken the text is at this point.[7]

In his translation of this same letter (EA 33), Sayce also completely mangled what turns out to have been the traditional opening in such royal correspondence. He translated the lines as: "To the king of the land of Egypt my son, I speak. The king of the land of Alashiya thy son towards me is at peace. For the family of Kausikkid . . . For he killed . . . openly the king of the country of Akkapisukka, and against two-thirds of your country exceedingly he approached . . ." (lines 1–8). The contemporary, and more accurate, translations now see this as simply reading: "To the king of Egypt, my brother: Message of the king of Alashiya, your brother. For me all goes well. For you may all go well. For your household, your wives, your sons, your horses, your chariots, and in your country, may all go very well."

The formulaic opening of such letters was soon clarified in subsequent articles by other scholars, especially those published by the Young Berliners; included in their publications were other letters sent by the king of Cyprus to the Egyptian pharaoh with a similar opening paragraph. A two-volume set published several decades later by the Norwegian Assyriologist Jørgen Knudtzon, who included all the tablets known to that point, corrected Sayce's additional errors regarding this tablet.[8]

Sayce also continued to claim that the sixth-century BCE Egyptian pharaoh Amasis was mentioned in line 9 of the ninth tablet (EA 107), as he had previously declared in several of the earlier "Letters from Egypt." Instead, that line has nothing to do with Amasis but is part of a declaration by Rib-Hadda, the ruler of Byblos, swearing that he is a loyal servant of the pharaoh and always speaks the truth.[9]

Rib-Hadda also sent the tenth and eleventh tablets, though Sayce managed to read the tenth tablet (EA 122) backward, so that what he thought was the front side is actually the back side, and vice versa. His translation, therefore, has the opening lines of the greeting from Rib-Hadda to the unnamed king of Egypt in the middle of the letter, rather than at the beginning as it should have been. This mistake was also eventually caught and rectified in Knudtzon's 1915 publication of the same tablet.[10] Sayce repeated this same mistake with the eleventh tablet (EA 103), again leaving it to be corrected by Knudtzon nearly thirty years later.[11]

Finally, Sayce mangled in grand style the thirteenth and final tablet (EA 14), which actually consisted of two large fragments. As he phrased it, "the nature of the tablet to which these fragments belonged is very evident. It was an inventory of certain property belonging to the Egyptian king, and stored by him in his new capital of Khu-Aten, 'the glory of the solar disk.'"

We now know that the two fragments come from a letter containing a very long list of goods that were being sent as a gift *from* Akhenaten *to* Burna-Buriash II, the king of Babylonia, upon the occasion of Akhenaten's marriage to the latter's daughter, either as a bride-price or simply as a gift. The opening of the letter is now seen as reading, "[These items Naphuru]re'a, great king, [king of Egypt, s]ent [to his brother, Burna]burariash [Great King, king of Karaduniash] [when he (Burnaburiash) gave his daughter to] him." In Sayce's defense in this case, the tablet is not in good shape and many of the signs have had to be restored, including part of the verb "sent."[12]

The extent of these errors may, on the surface, seem surprising, especially given Sayce's status as a highly respected philologist and Orientalist. However, as British Egyptologist Griffith said in his obituary for Sayce, his "vivid imagination and insight framed pictures of events and of interpretation in which he too often mistook the sharp lines of the picture for fact."[13] His ability to admit his errors and change his mind as necessary was therefore crucial, given this style.

———

For his part, Budge must have been working day and night in the race to produce the initial translations of the eighty-one tablets that comprised his own June 1888 publication (i.e., all of the tablets that he had purchased for the British Museum while in Egypt in December 1887).[14] His translations were much better than Sayce's. For example, among Budge's tablets was also one of the letters from the king of Alashiya to the pharaoh of Egypt (EA 35), but in contrast to Sayce, Budge nailed the formulaic opening of the letter: "[To] the king of Egypt, my brother [from] the king of Alashiya, thy brother. I, and my houses, my wives, my sons, my nobles, my horses, and my chariots have peace. May peace be multiplied in my countries! To thee, brother, to thy houses, to thy wives, to thy sons, to thy nobles, to thy horses, and to thy chariots may there be peace! May peace also be multiplied in thy countries!"

Budge also hedged his bets much more than Sayce. Instead of attempting a word-for-word translation of each, he summarized or paraphrased the contents by paragraph . . . and was for the most part correct. Thus, immediately after the opening, Budge simply wrote, "The king of Alashiya next says that he is sending his own ambassador with that of the Egyptian king into the land of Egypt. These are the contents of the first two paragraphs."[15]

Budge did the same thing with all the other letters, providing transliterations for some but almost never a literal translation for any of them. He did, though, provide commentary in more detail for some of them. A few of the details are wrong, though there are not nearly as many errors as Sayce published.

Among the more interesting British Museum tablets that Budge now published, for instance, was the fragmentary letter that Tushratta, king of Mittani, sent to Queen Tiyi, the wife of Amenhotep III, with a mention of both her son Akhenaten and her husband (EA 26); we will see this again in just a moment.[16] There were also several of the additional letters that Tushratta had sent to Amenhotep III and to Akhenaten as well, including one (EA 19) that was fully eighty-five lines long, split into thirteen different paragraphs on the tablet.[17]

There was also a letter (EA 9) that was sent to either Tutankhamun or Akhenaten from Burna-Buriash II that mentions the Babylonian king's father, Kurigalzu (Fig. 9).[18]

———

As a final event during this very busy month of June 1888, Oppert, the German-born scholar based in Paris, finally weighed in on the race for translation, which had begun when he had been sent a single Amarna tablet approximately six months earlier and declared it a forgery. In a paper presented on 22 June to the Académie des Inscriptions et Belles-lettres as a response to Erman and Schrader's article published the previous month, he expressed great regret that "the French School in Cairo did not acquire this collection for France."[19]

In defending his initial impression that the tablets were forgeries, Oppert said that the tablet that he had been sent was very small, had only sixteen lines inscribed on it, and that "the content was absolutely insignificant." Since he had seen only the single specimen, his doubts about it could not be resolved, unlike the situation with the collection that had subsequently been brought in its entirety to Berlin where authenticity was able to be confirmed.

He reiterated again that "the appearance of the tablet did not satisfy me," but he also noted specifically that "You can't judge the value of a collection that you haven't seen. But this impediment does not exist for the people who are on the spot and who alone can decide the questions relating above all to the place of provenance and the circumstances which accompany the discovery."[20]

That was as much of an apology as he was prepared to give. Ironically, the tablet that he had been sent, the first Amarna tablet ever read by a specialist, cannot now be located.[21]

FIGURE 9. Amarna Letter EA 9 (Burna-Buriash II to either Tutankhamun or Akhenaten); BM E29785. © Trustees of the British Museum.

10

Lost in Translation

A FEW MONTHS later, the second major Amarna article by a German scholar appeared, in one of the newest academic journals on the scene, the *Zeitschrift für Assyriologie*. The journal, still a leading publication today, was only three years old at the time. It was edited by Carl Bezold, the young German Assyriologist who had studied at the University of Munich and then at Leipzig University for his PhD with the renowned Assyriologist Friedrich Delitzsch. While Bezold was the principal editor, he was assisted by Oppert in Paris, Sayce in Oxford, and Schrader in Berlin.

The lengthy article addressed the Amarna tablets in Berlin. It was written by Carl Lehmann, the twenty-seven-year-old former lawyer turned Egyptologist, who was now also Erman's research assistant. Lehmann had published two short newspaper pieces on the tablets for the general public, but this was his first full-length scholarly article on the topic.[1]

Lehmann had been unable to consult or cite either Sayce's or Budge's recent articles, since they had appeared while his manuscript was still in press. However, he was able to draw from the article published by Erman and Schrader and cited it approvingly. Lehmann had also been consulting with Winckler about the various readings of the texts while the two men were working on this new material. There are, however, later hints that Winckler might not have been too happy with Lehmann having beaten him to print. There may have been as much rivalry as collaboration between the two young scholars.[2]

In his article, "Aus dem Funde von Tell el Amarna" ("On the Finds from Tell el Amarna"), Lehmann described and analyzed what he considered to be the most important letters in the Berlin collection. The first news of the find had reached Berlin "through the sending of plaster casts of several clay tablets, from which I could see, when they were presented to me for examination, that they showed an unusual type of writing and that some of them were probably letters sent to a king."[3]

It was unclear at first as to the dates when the documents were written, said Lehmann. It was only when a large number of the actual tablets arrived in Berlin, including one large tablet with "beautiful writing," which turned out to be a letter from Burna-Buriash II of Kara-Duniash (Babylon) to the king of Egypt (whose damaged name was later identified as Akhenaten), that the date and the context became clear.[4]

Lehmann next discussed some of the letters sent by Burna-Buriash, of which there were now at least five in the Berlin collection, including one in which Burna-Buriash reminded the Egyptian pharaoh that his father had sent "plenty of gold" to Kurigalzu, the previous ruler of Babylonia. Lehmann noted further that Burna-Buriash, in fact, called himself "son of Kurigalzu" in one of the letters and so he (Lehmann) proceeded to try to reconstruct the order of successive kings of Babylonia from this time period, according to the information contained in the new tablets.[5]

Lehmann then moved on to the numerous letters of Tushratta, king of Mittani, that had found their way to Berlin. Most of them were the ones concerned with the marriage of Tushratta's daughter to Amenhotep III. Among these were the "largest clay tablets which, to our knowledge, have been found up to now: one of them reaches a height of nearly ½ meter." One (EA 27) had a note in Egyptian hieratic script painted in black on the margin of the tablet that Erman had translated as "[year] 2, first month of winter, day . . . when the court was staying at the southern residence."[6]

The remainder of the article was taken up by a discussion of where Mittani might have been located, among other matters. Lehmann concluded by reproducing a hand-drawn copy of the large tablet sent by Burna-Buriash II to Akhenaten, showing all of the cuneiform signs, along with a transliteration and a few brief comments.[7]

Lehmann's article marked the official beginning of the study of the contents of the tablets, in terms of the information that they added to our understanding of the history of the period and the region. He went beyond what had been done in any of the previous articles. He and the other Young Berliners had begun to master, and tame, the nuances of what has come to be known as "Amarna Akkadian," with its own unique peculiarities.[8] In addition, it is not difficult to imagine the excitement with which they were devouring this material, so crucial to this fascinating period of history. That there would be periods of rivalry in addition to scholarly collegiality among the young scholars is perhaps only to be expected, just as there was quite obviously a rivalry between Sayce and Budge in England.

One thing that should also be noted from all the above is that Assyriology was a male-dominated field at the time. Although there were women involved in Egyptology in general during this period,[9] there are no indications of any women being involved with the Amarna Letters during the first few decades after their discovery. Fortunately, that has now changed.

———

Soon thereafter, in November / December 1888, Winckler published his own detailed article. It contained snippets of translations, as well as depictions of the actual cuneiform, from a few of the tablets on which he had been working. These were from the collection in Berlin as well as those in the Bulaq Museum in Cairo.[10]

Among the tablets in Berlin that Winckler now dealt with in his article were four of the letters sent between Akhenaten and Burna-Buriash II of Babylonia, which Lehmann had mentioned a month earlier in his own article. Winckler translated the beginning of one of them (EA 6): "[Just] as before you and my father were friends with each other, so now I and you [friendship] should share." The translation went on: "What[ever] you desire in my country, write to me and it will be brought to you; and what[ever] I desire in your land I will write to you and it shall be brought to me."[11]

Regarding another letter (EA 11) sent to Akhenaten by Burna-Buriash II, Winckler suggested that the latter was invoking the memory of much gold being sent to his ancestor, Kurigalzu, by Amenhotep III.[12] There was also a letter sent to Akhenaten by Assur-uballit, king of Assyria. This letter was also concerned with gold: "Gold in your country is like dirt; one simply gathers it up." We now know that this is one of the few letters sent from or to Assyria in the archive.[13]

Winckler included an actual drawing, or hand copy as it is called, of the cuneiform signs written on a tablet sent to the King of Egypt from the King of Alashiya, which was among those in Berlin. He noted that a similar tablet was in the Bulaq Museum; at the end of the latter was a small inscription in black ink, in Egyptian hieratic script, rather than cuneiform; we shall address this further below.[14]

Winckler's article included partial translations from a group of letters that he identified as correspondence between Tushratta, the king of Mittani, and

Pharaohs Amenhotep III and Akhenaten. Some of these had been previously referred to by Ehrman and Schrader earlier that year. All had been purchased and taken to Berlin, but they were very clearly related to letters between these kings at the British Museum on which Budge had been working; not one in this series remained in Cairo.[15]

One of the letters in Berlin (EA 22) is the extremely long list of wedding gifts sent by Tushratta to Amenhotep III on the occasion of the latter's marriage to Tushratta's daughter Tadu-Heba. Another (EA 25) is the additional inventory of gifts also sent by Tushratta as a wedding dowry, although the tablet is broken and it is not clear when or to whom they were being sent; they may have been yet more gifts sent at the time of Tadu-Heba's marriage. It is quite possible that it is one of these two that could be the very large tablet accidentally dropped by one of the antiquities dealers while boarding a train for Cairo. It has never been clear whether the dealer picked up those pieces or just left the shattered tablet where it lay; one suspects that he gathered up the pieces, or at least the larger ones . . . that is, if such an event even occurred.

In addition, among the letters in the Bulaq Museum that Winckler had been allowed to study was the letter (EA 31) from Amenhotep III to Tarkhundaradu. This was the first occasion when Winckler identified him as the king of a place called "Ar-sa-pi," though he didn't know where that kingdom was located. He also noted here for the first time that the letter was not written in Akkadian like the others, but rather was written in what he thought might be Hittite. The gist of the text, he thought, had something to do with the daughter of the king.

As we have seen, Winckler was correct about virtually all of this, although he thought that the letter had been sent to Amenhotep III rather than being sent by him. We also now identify Tarkhundaradu as the king of Arzawa, not "Ar-sa-pi" as per Winckler, and we know that it was a kingdom located in western Anatolia, as we have seen above. In his defense, since the cuneiform sign ZA can also be read as either "ṣa" or "sa$_3$," while the cuneiform sign PI can also be read as "wa," Winckler was actually correct in his reading of the signs; he simply chose the wrong sounds for some of the characters that had multiple choices—both "Ar-za-wa" and "Ar-sa-pi" are technically correct readings of the cuneiform, but we now use "Ar-za-wa" as the modern designation, based upon historical information, rather than Winckler's "Ar-sa-pi."[16]

In all these cases, Winckler's transliterations and translations of these tablets were greatly superior to those attempted by either Sayce or Budge on the tablets that they had examined. There is, in fact, very little substantial difference between the currently accepted interpretations and those offered by Winckler in 1888, more than 130 years ago. Moreover, as we shall see in a moment, his transliterations and translations had a direct and immediate impact, especially upon Sayce, after Winckler courteously sent him a copy of his article when it appeared.

———

Just as the year came to a close, Sayce published another "Letter from Egypt," in the 29 December issue of *The Academy*.[17] In it, among other items, he mentions some of the same letters in the Bulaq Museum that Winckler had just discussed in his article, including the letter sent to "Tarkhundara [Tarkhundaradu], king of the country of Arzapi." (Note that he was one step closer to our modern transliteration, spelling it Arzapi rather than Arsapi like Winckler, though, like Winckler, he thought that it was being sent to Amenhotep III rather than the other way around.) He also mentioned the letter sent from Alashiya that included a few lines written in hieratic Egyptian. Sayce thought that the hieratic inscription mentioned "the land of Alosa," rather than Alashiya, and voiced his belief that it lay in Syria. Despite the overlaps, Sayce had not seen Winckler's article yet, though he would soon enough.[18]

Sayce also discussed a third letter, which he thought was sent from Aziru of Amurru to his father Dûdu, concerning a garden that Aziru had been laying out. Indulging himself in one of his biblical flights of fancy, Sayce linked the name Dûdu to the name David in the Hebrew Bible, which had never been found outside the Bible, and noted that "it is interesting to find it [the name] borne by a high official at the court of the Pharaoh in the century before the Exodus." As will be no surprise by now, Sayce was wrong, either partially or entirely, about all three of these tablets, as he eventually learned when they were republished more accurately by other scholars.

In mid-January 1889, just two weeks later, Sayce published yet another "Letter from Egypt" in *The Academy*.[19] It was essentially a continuation of his December 1888 "Letter," for it was concerned with some of the same tablets in the Bulaq Museum, which he said that he had finally been allowed to see and had now finished copying. "I have had little difficulty," he wrote, "in copying all the tablets and fragments of tablets from Tel-el-Amarna, now preserved at Boulaq, before my departure from Cairo." He noted again the letter from a "king of Arzapi" which, like Winckler, he thought was written in Hittite (or a "Hittite dialect," as he phrased it).

Sayce also noted that there was a long letter sent to Amenhotep III "from a certain Lan-makhsi, who calls himself 'king of the country of Karandu,' about the marriage of his youngest daughter." Once again, Sayce got the crucial details wrong, although he was correct about the intended upcoming nuptials. We now know that "Karandu" is actually "Karaduniash," in other words Babylon / Babylonia. Its author-sender was the Babylonian king Kadashman-Enlil, who did indeed send his daughter to Amenhotep III (as his father, Kurigalzu, had done before him). This is now identified as Amarna Letter EA 3, which is still in Cairo.[20]

11

Flights of Fancy

JANUARY 1889 and the months afterward also saw new figures appear in the Amarna discussions, barely a year after the first published announcement of the letters by Sayce. First was Father Alphonse J. Delattre (Fig. 10), a Jesuit priest based in Belgium, who published a short piece on the discovery of the Amarna tablets, based primarily on Budge's 1888 article in *PSBA* but also referencing the 1888 article by Erman and Schrader. He followed this up with another article in late October of the same year, after the additional publications by German scholars appeared, spending much of his time in the latter article defending himself against perceived attacks on his scholarship by Winckler.[1]

The next commentator, in February 1889, was the British surveyor and military officer Claude R. Conder (Fig. 11), better remembered for having led a team of British army engineers in a ground-breaking survey of Western Galilee in the 1870s. The survey, which was conducted at some risk to the participants, resulted in a series of volumes that were published by the Palestine Exploration Fund.[2] Its contours still mark the modern boundary between northern Israel and southern Lebanon.

Educated at University College London (UCL), Conder pumped out a good number of publications regarding the ancient Near East over the years, all while maintaining a full-time career on active military duty (and in military campaigns) and then working full-time for the Home Ordnance Survey in England. Among these were a series of notes, articles, and even a book on Amarna, all of which appeared between 1889 and 1893 while Conder was directing the Engraving Department for the Ordnance Survey from Southampton.[3]

Conder began with a very brief note in *The Academy* in February 1889, in which he simply commented on Sayce's earlier discussion of the language used in the Tarkhundaradu letter and whether Akkadian could be compared to Hittite. He followed this up with a short note that appeared in the first 1889

FIGURE 10. Father Alphonse J. Delattre. Illustration by Glynnis Fawkes.

issue of the *Quarterly Statement of the Palestine Exploration Fund*. Conder summarized the discovery of the Amarna Letters and the scholarly thinking to that point, noting that they probably dated to about 1430 BCE, which "would represent the time of Joshua, but perhaps more probably preceded the Hebrew conquest of Palestine," as he put it. He also mentioned that the tablets indicated that the kings of Egypt and Mesopotamia appeared to be allies at that time, that there were royal marriages, and that there were trade and political alliances. He also noted, by the by, that probably by that time "the Semitic race had occupied Northern Syria, mingling with the Hittite population."[4]

Several months later, in June 1889, Sayce published the full details of the Bulaq Museum tablets in the *PSBA*. However, contrary to what he had published in

FIGURE 11. Claude R. Conder. Illustration by Glynnis Fawkes.

The Academy back in January, he stated that he had not, in fact, copied all the tablets in the Bulaq Museum, "owing to circumstances into which I need not enter." He had only been able to copy "most" of them. Those "circumstances" are still unclear.[5]

Sayce further acknowledged receipt of the article that Winckler had published on the Bulaq tablets in late 1888. Winckler's work had directly impacted his own thinking on the subject. Not only had Winckler included translations of some tablets that Sayce had missed in the Bulaq Museum, including a letter from the king of Assyria identified as "Assur-uballit," but Winckler's publication also indicated that some corrections were necessary to Sayce's *PSBA* article of a year earlier.[6]

It must have been difficult for Sayce to admit these points publicly, but it was likely necessary from a professional point of view, for it was now plain to all his colleagues that Sayce's previous publications on the tablets were riddled with errors. However, he did not draw attention to the fact that he also had to emend one of his identifications and translations, which he had only mentioned a few months earlier in January, although that became clear in the article.

Among the thirty-three tablets that Sayce discussed in this June article were a number of those that he had briefly mentioned in his December 1888 and January 1889 "Letters from Egypt."[7] These included the tablet from Alashiya in the Bulaq Museum, for which Winckler had already published the cuneiform but not a translation.

As we have previously noted, Winckler had observed that there was a small hand-written inscription in ink, in Egyptian hieratic script, below the cuneiform text on this tablet. Just as he had done in his shorter "Letter from Egypt," Sayce now translated this as "the correspondence of the prince of the land of Alosha" and concluded that the country should be identified with "the Syrian district of Alosha." He was, again, incorrect, since it says "Alas[hiy]a" rather than "Alosha" (or Alosa, as he had said previously), now identified as Cyprus. However, he did provide a reasonable transliteration and translation of the cuneiform of this tablet that Winckler had not previously published.[8]

Sayce also discussed in detail, once again, the letter to King Tarkhundaradu of Arzawa, though he continued to identify the country as "Arzapi" and to believe that it had been sent to Amenhotep III rather than the other way around. Within the footnotes at the bottom of each page, he now contrasted the differences between his transliterations and translation with those of Winckler's 1888 article. Sayce was able to state securely that the king was offering his daughter in marriage to Amenhotep III, but that the negotiations had not yet been completed. Apart from the first two lines, which were written in Akkadian, Sayce reiterated his belief that the remainder of the letter was written in a dialect of Hittite, in which he agreed with Winckler.[9]

Sayce also discussed a number of tablets that were either concerned with, written by, or sent to various kings or officials in Canaanite city-states. Among these was another of the letters that Sayce had mentioned in his 29 December 1888 "Letter from Egypt," which was the one that he thought was sent from Aziru of Amurru to his father Dûdu.[10] Sayce was now of the opinion that Dûdu was a high official at the court of the pharaoh and was even possibly stationed in Phoenicia (i.e., Canaan). He was still particularly excited by Dûdu's name, seeing it as "the Biblical Dodo, Dod or David, [which] has hitherto never been found outside the Old Testament," and by the fact that the father of a Canaanite minor ruler could have held such a high position at the Egyptian court.

We now know that Dûdu was indeed a very high Egyptian official, for he was a royal vizier whose name we now usually read instead as Tutu. He was not, of course, Aziru's actual father. In the Amarna Letters this was simply a term of respect used for a political superior and had nothing to do with actual kinship. Aziru's real father was named Abdi-Ashirta, as we will see time and again below. Moreover, Tutu's name has nothing to do with David, Dod, or Dodo.[11]

Sayce had also gained access to additional tablets that were in three private collections, those of "Rostovitch-Bey, M. Golénisheff, and the Rev. Ch. Murch." He included these in his new article, noting that they hadn't been copied or reported on before and that "the tablets belonging to Rostovitch-Bey and one of those belonging to M. Golénisheff are . . . of exceptional value and interest."[12]

Thus, within this category of letters relating to Canaanite petty rulers, Sayce also discussed three of the tablets that belonged to "M[onsieur] Golénisheff," including one that he said had been sent by Rib-Addu, whom we now render as Rib-Hadda, the king of Byblos. This, Sayce claimed, contained a mention of the Canaanite city Megiddo. This is presumably the tablet to which Sayce was referring when he said that there was a tablet of exceptional interest in Golénisheff's collection. By process of elimination, this must be Amarna Letter EA 70, which is indeed a letter sent by Rib-Hadda to the Egyptian pharaoh.[13]

And yet, although the tablet is badly broken, with many restorations necessary, no subsequent translators have ever restored Megiddo as Sayce did. Instead, it is probably to be restored as Magdali or Magdalu, a city whose location is unknown. We now know that there are a number of other Amarna tablets that either mention Megiddo or Biridiya (the ruler of Megiddo), scattered among the Cairo, British, and Berlin Museums, but this letter cited by Sayce cannot be included within the small subset of Megiddo letters.[14]

Sayce then returned to one of the tablets that he had mentioned in his January 1889 "Letter from Egypt." He had identified this as a letter "from a certain Lan-makhsi . . . king of the country of Karandu" and thought it concerned the marriage of his youngest daughter. Now Sayce inched closer to a proper identification of the country, rendering it as "Kar-Duniyas," which is quite close to our present transliteration of "Karaduniash"—Babylon / Babylonia. However, he did still mangle the king's name, reproducing it as "Ris-takullimma-Sin" rather than our current understanding of it as Kadashman-Enlil. Regardless, he was correct that it was concerned with the marriage of the king's daughter to Amenhotep III, as we have discussed (although we still don't know her name).[15]

Sayce also briefly discussed a small fragment belonging to the Rev. Chauncey Murch, who had purchased it in Luxor. Murch was an American missionary who had a personal penchant for collecting Egyptian artifacts but often also served as an intermediary for purchases made on behalf of the British Museum. The fragment, which Sayce recognized as containing a number of royal names in the text, including both Amenhotep III and Akhenaten, later disappeared for a number of years, only to be rediscovered again and published in 1916. It was found among items from Murch's collection at the Art Institute of Chicago, where it had been since 1894.[16]

We now know, courtesy of Professor John Brinkman of what was then the Oriental Institute of the University of Chicago, that Murch's fragment joins with the much larger piece known as Amarna Letter EA 26. This was the tablet that Budge had just published in his article as the one sent by Tushratta, king of Mittani, directly to Queen Tiyi, the wife of Amenhotep III, and that was concerned with continuing the good relations between the two countries now that Akhenaten was on the throne of Egypt. Brinkman made the connection when the British Museum portion was brought to Chicago as part of an Amarna exhibit.[17]

Four additional tablets that Sayce studied belonged to Alexandros Rostovitch, a Greek expatriate living in Cairo, who later gave all of them to the British Museum in addition to donating many other items to the National Archaeological Museum in Athens.[18] One of these (now known as Amarna Letter EA 28) was sent by Tushratta, king of Mittani, to Akhenaten. It mentions Queen Tiyi, and plainly states that Tushratta's daughter was married to Akhenaten—"Tushratta, king of Mittani, your father-in-law who loves you, speaks thus"—thereby making it a very important tablet for those involved in reconstructing the history of this period.[19]

Unfortunately, Sayce was unable to make out the daughter's name at the time, rendering it with a question mark as "Šaka-kansak (?)." From Amarna Letters EA 20–21 and 23–24, it is now clear that her name was, in fact, Tadu-Heba, and that she had actually been given in marriage to Amenhotep III and had only been transferred to the harem of Akhenaten after Amenhotep III's death. Moreover, as mentioned, we now also know (from Amarna Letter EA 17) that Amenhotep III had earlier married another Mittanian princess, Kelu-Heba (or Gilu-Heba), who was Tushratta's sister (having been sent to Amenhotep III by Shuttarna II, Tushratta's father), thereby making the two men brothers-in-law as well as father-in-law and son-in-law.

Sayce was by now cautious enough to note that all of his translations were preliminary. He concluded this long publication of the thirty-three tablets with: "Let it be borne in mind that the translations I have given above are but first attempts, with all the imperfections that are inevitable in first attempts. But the first attempt is better than none at all, and the primary duty of the Assyriologist is to assist others in understanding the texts which he edits."[20]

Later the same year, Sayce republished six of these translations in a series that had been started the previous year, in 1888, and for which he himself was editor. It was called *Records of the Past* and was meant for the general public, featuring translations of ancient inscriptions and texts by eminent scholars, such as Sayce, the French Egyptologist Gaston Maspero, and others.[21]

One thing that becomes clear is that Sayce's translations in this June 1889 article were better than any that he had done previously. It is fairly obvious that he took full advantage of having Winckler's 1888 article in hand and followed most of the same transliterations and translations of the various cuneiform signs, and entire words, to good effect, as he consistently cites Winckler throughout this new article. However, there was still an embarrassment of errors in Sayce's translations—so much so that one wonders what the German scholars were now thinking of him.

Sayce did also note further in this article that seeing the tablets in the Bulaq Museum had allowed him to make several additional corrections on the readings and translations that he had previously published of the Frénay / Bouriant tablets. However, he also specifically complained about not being allowed to see the tablets that Budge had sent to the British Museum. This, he said, had directly resulted in some of the improper readings or translations that Sayce had earlier proposed—"Had I had access to the collections of the British Museum," he lamented, "these corrections would not have been required."[22] The bitterness was obviously aimed at Budge, and it seems to confirm that, by now, there was either a rivalry or an intense dislike between the two.

As for tablets in the British Museum, we learn from archival sleuthing conducted by Jana Mynářová that the publication of their tablets was recommended by Peter le Page Renouf, the Keeper of Oriental Antiquities at the museum. The motion was discussed and approved by the Trustees on 9 March 1889.[23] Since Renouf had been in charge before the tablets had arrived at the museum just about a year previously, it seems a bit surprising that nothing had been done with them in the interim, until one realizes that the museum was virtually flooded with tablets coming in and being added to their collection at the time, from other museum projects at sites like Kuyundjik (ancient Nineveh) and elsewhere. Despite approval by the Trustees, nothing would be done with the Amarna tablets in the British Museum for quite a while to come.

———

Some of the translations and interpretations proposed by the various scholars during these early years seem ludicrous from our viewpoint now. However, we must remember just how much was still unknown about Bronze Age Egypt and the Near East, and even Mycenaean Greece and Minoan Crete, in the 1880s. Just to put it into perspective, Schliemann had recently finished his work at Troy (1884) when the Amarna tablets were discovered. Even the important fact that the Hittites were located in Anatolia rather than in Canaan had only been correctly suggested by Sayce, much maligned in this tale, a decade earlier. The discovery of these Amarna Letters in 1887 took place a decade before Petrie found the Merneptah Stele that mentions "Israel" (1896); twelve years before Arthur Evans began excavating at Knossos on Crete (1899); almost twenty years before Winckler began excavating at Hattusa and found the Hittite archives there (1906); and thirty-five years before Howard Carter found King Tutankhamun's tomb (1922).

12

Winckler and Abel

MEANWHILE, THE Young Berliners also continued to work on the Amarna Letters during this time. Winckler was especially productive in 1889, first with a long article appearing in a periodical devoted primarily to the ancient Egyptian language, the *Zeitschrift für Ägyptische Sprache*, and then a shorter notice in the *Zeitschrift für Assyriologie*.[1]

The latter piece consisted merely of a few comments about the appearance of Rib-Hadda, king of Byblos, in the Amarna tablets. In the same volume, Carl Lehmann published a brief article with minor notes and corrections to his article of the previous year, emending it based on Winckler's article that had appeared a month after Lehmann's.[2]

The longer article by Winckler was a tour de force. It was innocuously titled "Verzeichniss der aus dem Funde von el-Amarna herrührenden Thontafeln" ("Index of the Clay Tablets Originating from the Find of el-Amarna"), but it was much more than that, for he provided a preliminary catalogue and a summary of the contents of the various tablets, so that scholars could get an idea of what was contained in each.[3]

He began by noting that the tablets were now spread among museums in Berlin, London, and Cairo, and that some had already been published by Sayce, Budge, and others. He then proceeded to list the tablets, splitting them into two large groups. Into the first group he placed all the letters sent between the Great Kings, arranged in subsets according to the geographical area and the king who was responsible for sending or receiving each letter. Thus, the first subset included tablets to and from Babylonia, among them those to and from Burna-Buriash II discussed above, with some attempts at translation.[4] The second consisted of a single letter sent by Assur-uballit I of Assyria to Akhenaten, with translation offered by Winckler.[5] The third included only the Tarkhundaradu "of Arsapi" letter written "in an unknown language"; Winckler

37

ruminated on many of the words in this letter but didn't attempt a translation.[6] The fourth subset consisted of fragmentary letters to and from the kings of Alashiya (Cyprus), with a few lines of translation attempted.[7] The fifth section had two incomplete and untranslatable letters in it,[8] while the sixth consisted of letters to and from the kings of Mittani.[9]

The second large group in Winckler's article consisted of letters sent to and from the minor rulers in Canaan, again split into subgroups according to region and ruler. Thus, for example, Winckler grouped together letters concerning Aziru of Amurru. He also pulled together letters to and from Rib-Hadda of Byblos; as well as "Pitia" [probably Yidya] of Ashkelon; Biridiya of Megiddo; and a variety of others.[10]

This was the first attempt of its kind, and it set the stage for all subsequent research. By and large this is the format that is still standard today, in terms of grouping and presenting the tablets. Rather amazingly, it was published just two years after the discovery of the archive and little more than a year after the first attempts at translation.

Winckler was even more ambitious, however, and had more in mind than this single article. It is now clear, long after the fact, that the article was intended to accompany a multivolume set that he was working on with Ludwig Abel, for the formats of both the article and the books were identical.

The first volume of this set appeared later that same year. It was entitled *Der Thontafelfund von Tell-Amarna* (The clay tablets found at Tell-Amarna). In a note included at the beginning of the first volume, with the date of May 1889, Winckler included a full citation of his just-published article, along with the earlier publication by Erman and Schrader and the publication by Lehmann. He also noted that this first volume contained the letters from "Asiatic kings" to Amenhotep III and IV, while the second volume, which he said had already been started, would contain the letters from the petty Canaanite rulers, thus mirroring the division of the letters into two large groups as presented in his lengthy article. A third volume would contain additional materials as needed.[11]

The order and arrangement of the letters within the various sections in this first volume mirrored the scheme followed in Winckler's 1889 article as well. Just as in the article, the first section in the book featured eight letters to or from Babylonia, of which six were in Berlin and two in the Bulaq Museum. The second section had just one letter, that of Assur-uballit I from Assyria, while the third contained only the letter sent by Amenhotep III to Tarkhundaradu—with his kingdom once again identified as Arsapi—which

Winckler still thought had been sent the other way, from Amenhotep III rather than to him. The fourth section contained seven letters to and from Alashiya (i.e., Cyprus). The fifth had three letters from unidentified kings, while the sixth section had seven letters specifically to and from Tushratta of Mittani. In all, there were a total of twenty-seven letters in this first volume.[12]

No transliterations or translations were attempted here; that would have to wait for a later publication. Instead, for each of the tablets that were featured in the first volume, primarily from the collections in Berlin and Cairo, Winckler's colleague Abel provided hand-drawn copies with the cuneiform signs precisely reproduced. Some tablets were even photographed, thereby making them fully accessible for study and interpretation by all scholars. Winckler later complained that he really should be credited as the sole author of the volumes, and that Abel only did the "autographs" (i.e., the hand-drawn copies of the tablets), but most scholars refer to this edition as by Winckler and Abel, rather than simply by Winckler alone.[13]

———

The second volume appeared in two halves in 1890, the very next year; there was no need for a third volume. In a note that appeared at the beginning of the first half of this volume, dated February 1890, Winckler said as much: "For external reasons, contrary to the original intention, it seemed expedient to have the second part of the publication of the el-Amarna texts appear in two editions [i.e., halves], the first of which is hereby released to the public. . . . The second delivery of the second part will probably also be ready for publication in a short time."[14]

This first half of the second volume contained another sixty or so letters sent to and from the petty Canaanite rulers, most of them now in Berlin but some in the Bulaq Museum in Cairo. Again, each tablet was hand drawn by Abel, replicated precisely on the page, and with photographs of some of the tablets included. No transliteration or translation was given for any of them either. Those would also appear years later, authored by Winckler alone.[15]

When the second half of the second volume appeared later that same year, it was much like the first half, but with around 150 more letters to and from the petty Canaanite rulers. In all, this multivolume set was meant to be a first effort at a definitive publication of the tablets to which the German scholars had access, for nearly 240 letters were now available for anyone with sufficient training to study and attempt to translate.

Charles Wilbour, the American Egyptologist, commented about all this early in 1890, in a letter dated 26 January, which he wrote after the first volume appeared: "The Tell el Amarna cuneiform tablets at Berlin have begun to be printed, [but] not translated. Sayce read me a letter from Dooshratta, King of Babylon, to the Heretic King, in which it appears that Aten Makt his daughter, whose torso I have, had a Babylonian mother, Dooshratta's daughter; the Heretic King's mother was Dooshratta's sister and the mother of his father Amenophis III or Memnon, was Dooshratta's aunt. So my girl was seven-eighths Babylonian in blood. No wonder that the Egyptians thought it time to change the dynasty."[16]

Wilbour had things somewhat mixed up, since Tushratta was incorrectly identified here as a king of Babylonia, rather than a king of Mittani, and Akhenaten's mother was not Tushratta's sister. It is clear by this point, though, that Sayce had already procured a copy of this first Winckler-Abel volume, since he was reading the contents to Wilbour, according to this letter. It is therefore possible that the errors can be attributed to Sayce rather than to Wilbour.

Meanwhile, in London on 9 July 1890, Renouf reported that the publication of the British Museum tablets would be further delayed, and this time specifi-cally said it was because Budge hadn't had time to revise his manuscript "due to the 'pressure of the general work in the Department of Egyptian and Assyr-ian Antiquities.'" He also noted that the matter of publication had become urgent, saying that the British Museum's tablets should be published before or at the same time as the publication of the Berlin tablets. However, that horse had already left the barn. It would be two more years before the volume of British Museum tablets finally appeared in 1892.[17]

———

Just a few months after the full publication of the 1889–1890 volumes, and with Winckler's express permission, Heinrich Zimmern, the twenty-eight-year-old Assyriologist who had studied at Berlin and also at Leipzig with Delitzsch, utilized the new volumes to put together his own article about the tablets.[18] Soon thereafter Zimmern would become the first official professor of Assyriology at the University of Leipzig, but at the time of this publication he had just received his Habilitation (the highest degree possible) from the University of Königsberg.

Entitling his article "Briefe aus dem Funde in El Amarna in Transcription und Uebersetzung" ("Letters from the Finds in El Amarna in Transcription and

Translation"), Zimmern began by stating that he was presenting complete transcriptions and translations of some of the cuneiform letters found at Amarna, because "only on the basis of such publications is it possible for the non-Assyriologist to make his own judgment about the character and the value of these documents." For that reason, he said, he had chosen for presentation only those letters that were preserved the most completely, "since these are best suited to provide an insight into the nature of this correspondence."[19] He then first presented a full transcription and translation of the same letter that Lehmann had featured in his article of late 1888—the letter from Burna-Buriash II to Akhenaten (EA 7).[20]

Zimmern's translation was well done. He pointed out that Burna-Buriash began by complaining that he had been ill and that Akhenaten had not even bothered to ask how he was doing, only to subsequently be told by the messengers that Egypt was much further away from Babylonia than he had thought. As the most recent translation in English by the late Tel Aviv University Professor Anson Rainey (slightly more complete than Zimmern's) puts it, Burna-Buriash said: "When my body was unwell and my brother [i.e., Akhenaten] did not express concern for me, I was filled with anger, saying 'That I am sick, has my brother not heard? Why has he not shown concern for me? His envoy, why did he not send and did not look into my situation?' The envoy of my brother said this to me, saying: 'It is not a territory close by that your brother should hear and that he should send greeting to you. The land is far away.'"[21]

Upon hearing this, Burna-Buriash was no longer angry at the Egyptian king. He then promptly moved on to his reason for writing, which was to remind Akhenaten of the previous good relations between their two countries and to request that Akhenaten "send me much high quality gold" for he had undertaken a new project (though he did not give the specifics). He also mentioned that there had been a problem with a previous shipment of gold, which had not been as much as had been promised ("as for the forty minas of gold that they brought, when I cast it into the kiln . . . only x minas came forth"), and furthermore that two of his trade caravans had been robbed in Canaan.[22]

Along with this letter, Zimmern also included a transcription and translation of two more letters that had been sent from Burna-Buriash to Akhenaten (now identified as Amarna Letters EA 8 and 9). One was in Berlin, and continued with the topic of plundered caravans and murdered merchants. The other was at the British Museum, and continued with the request for gold; Zimmern was able to include this letter because Budge had published a faithful rendition of the cuneiform, and a less-faithful attempt at transliteration, in his 1888 *PSBA* article.[23]

The last letter that Zimmern included in this article was chronologically earlier, having been sent from Tushratta of Mittani to Amenhotep III (EA 19). This was the long letter that we have mentioned several times, in which Tushratta reminded the Egyptian king of previous relations between the two countries, and between the two kings themselves, including the fact that Tushratta had sent his daughter to marry Amenhotep III. However, this letter too was primarily written to ask for gold, just as Burna-Buriash would later request the same from Akhenaten, although Tushratta phrased his request more elegantly—not only as a request for use in building a mausoleum for his grandfather but also as part of the bride price for his daughter.[24]

From all of this, it is clear that the German scholars were already getting a sense of the problems and aggravations afflicting the Great Kings at the time. The distances that were involved in their ongoing trade and interactions, including problems with gold shipments and brigands attacking the caravans, were also becoming more obvious. However, they were also getting a sense of what was troubling the petty kings in Canaan at the same time and so it is to some of these that we will now turn our attention. In so doing, we will get an idea of the ailments, alignments, successions, and conflicts that roiled day-to-day life in the region, creating a world quite different from that experienced by the elite Great Kings ensconced in their capital cities during the same period.

PART IV

Lab'ayu and Sons, Inc.

13

The Lab'ayu Affair

IN ALL, there were less than fifty letters written and sent by the Great Kings that were found in the Amarna archive. By way of comparison, there were six times as many letters (more than three hundred in all) which were sent and / or received by the petty rulers in Canaan. These letters shed light on the intense rivalries and almost constant infighting that were the hallmark of this region during the period. In stark contrast to the world painted by the letters exchanged between the Great Kings, the letters sent to the pharaoh by the Canaanite kings portray a much darker realm, one of rival petty rulers, alliances made and broken, caravans robbed, and even assassinations and rulers sent into exile.[1]

The letters read like the protracted bickering of a large dysfunctional family or a bunch of squabbling children with deadly toys. As one political scientist, Professor Steven David of Johns Hopkins University, has said, they include primarily "a litany of aggression, conquests, and urgent pleas for assistance."[2]

Most of the letters revolve around several major disputes that involve many of the vassal rulers, some during the reign of Amenhotep III and others during the reign of his son Akhenaten. When one looks closely at the letters from these petty Canaanite rulers, it is clear that the same geographical areas that are in conflict today, from Syria in the north to Gaza in the south, were also conflicted back then, even during the golden age for the Great Kings. Steven David was not exaggerating when he continued, "Chariots, infantry, and archers may have been replaced by modern armies and nuclear weapons, but the threat they posed to neighboring states was as intense as exists today."[3]

———

The Amarna vassal letters all follow the same basic formatting conventions. The local ruler who was sending the letter began by stating the identification of the addressee, sometimes mentioning the pharaoh specifically by name (i.e., Amenhotep III or Akhenaten) but more often just called the king of Egypt. He then identifies himself as the sender, stating his name and location, and expresses his inferior status to the king of Egypt, usually by saying that he was falling at the king's feet ("seven times and seven times over"). The opening lines that gave the name of the recipient were sometimes quite effusive, as studies by Jana Mynářová of Charles University in Prague and Ellen Morris of Barnard have shown.[4] They range from a simple "Say to the king of Egypt" to a much more complex and convoluted "Say to the king, my lord, my Sun, my god, the Sun from the sky."

They continue to the heart of the matter, usually either 1) responding to the pharaoh about a matter they had previously been discussing; 2) requesting something from the pharaoh; 3) reporting on events in their locale; or 4) discussing something of mutual interest. It is this section in each of the letters that provides us with much historical data concerning the individual vassal rulers and the details of what was going on at the time. The letters usually conclude with additional greetings to the pharaoh and sometimes mention gifts that were being sent to accompany the letter.

There were only a limited number of major players among the Canaanite vassal kings—two dozen at most. Among these, about half a dozen monopolized the discussions. Some were ruling in cities that still dominate the news headlines today, such as Jerusalem, Byblos, Beirut, Tyre, Damascus, and Gaza. Others were ruling in cities and areas that are more familiar only to the archaeologists and ancient historians of the region or known from the Bible, including Megiddo, Hazor, Acco, Shechem, and the region of Amurru (in northern Syria).

Just as we have two or even three generations of Egyptian rulers to whom the letters were addressed (Amenhotep III followed by Akhenaten and then possibly Tutankhamun), along with two to three generations of other Great Kings elsewhere, these vassal letters provide us information about several generations of rulers in some of the Canaanite cities. For example, Surata and then Satatna ruled Acco, while Lab'ayu and his sons were at Shechem. There were also Yapah-Hadda and Ammunira of Beirut, Rib-Hadda followed by his brother Ilu-rapi in Byblos, and Abdi-Ashirta and his sons, especially Aziru, of Amurru.

These rulers were constantly fighting among themselves, and frequently appealed to the pharaoh to intervene, much as bickering children would plead for assistance from a parent or authority figure. Ultimately, these boil down to several primary but ongoing sets of conflicts. For example, more than seventy letters are related to problems caused by Abdi-Ashirta and his son Aziru in the region of Amurru in northern Canaan. These came close to causing a war between the Egyptians and the Hittites, which did eventually happen, albeit a bit later.

Another two dozen letters are related to the events and problems swirling around Abdi-Heba in Jerusalem, as well as Milkilu of Gezer and Shuwardata of Qilti. (Qilti is usually identified with biblical Keilah and, by some scholars, with modern Hebron.)[5] Some fourteen other letters are related in some way to the so-called "Lab'ayu Affair" in and around Shechem and Megiddo, which also involved some of the same rulers, such as Gezer's Milkilu and Qilti's Shuwardata.

Of the remaining letters, a number involve other rulers, such as Biryawaza of Damascus, who are sometimes also tied into the main conflicts. There are also approximately seventy more letters responding to Akhenaten's order to get ready for an Egyptian campaign in the region. The rest concern a variety of minor matters unique to each of the individual petty rulers.

In the following discussions, and in the subsequent chapters, I will summarize as well as quote directly from these letters, so as to give voice to the ancient vassal kings and the Egyptians with whom they were corresponding.[6] Hopefully, my reconstruction of the history of this region and its conflicts during the Amarna Period will be less fanciful and a bit more grounded in reality than some of the initial translations that were suggested.

———

A good place to begin is by discussing what Amarna scholars commonly call the "Lab'ayu Affair." This was a dispute between several of the petty Canaanite rulers that escalated until it involved at least eight different leaders over two generations in what seems to have been an ancient Hatfield-and-McCoy feud combined with a Bronze Age mafia don running wild and knocking off his competitors.

The tangle of related conflicts was initiated by Lab'ayu, the ruler of Shechem, near the modern Palestinian city of Nablus in the northern part of the central hill country of ancient Israel, and then continued by his two sons after he was ambushed and killed. They ultimately involved Biridiya of Megiddo; Yashdata of Taanach; Ba'lu-meher of Yoqneam; Shuwardata of Qilti / Keilah; Surata and then his son Satatna of Acco; Milkilu of Gezer; and Abdi-Heba of Jerusalem, at the very least.

The story began with Lab'ayu's initial actions during the time of Amenhotep III, but then continued into the reign of Akhenaten. However, since we are not certain of the chronological order of the letters, which is not helped by the fact that most of them do not actually give the specific name of the Egyptian pharaoh to whom they were sent, we cannot be sure that we have the events themselves in proper order.[7] Nevertheless, what is presented below is a plausible scenario and timeline.

We enter with the conflict already in mid-action: Biridiya, Megiddo's ruler, has written to the pharaoh and reported that he was at war with unnamed enemies. He ended his letter (EA 242): "Behold, all of the cities are at peace, but I am at war."[8] He elaborated in a second letter (EA 244), which is the one quoted on the opening page of the introduction to this book, by describing the specific threat to Megiddo posed by Lab'ayu of Shechem, apparently after a unit of the Egyptian army that was posted in the vicinity of Megiddo had been called home. He began this letter, "Speak to the king, my lord and my sun god, a message from Biridiya, the loyal servant of the king." He then informed the king that Lab'ayu had been waging war on him ever since the Egyptian troops had left. The situation had become so bad that the citizens of Megiddo were unable to leave the city to harvest their grain or tend to their flocks. And now, said Biridiya, he thought that Lab'ayu intended to try to capture Megiddo and begged the pharaoh to "provide a garrison of 100 men in order to guard his city."[9]

In an additional letter (EA 243), he gave more details. A group known collectively as the *'apiru*, who were on the fringes of society and frequently caused problems through their raiding of Canaanite cities and roadways, were also causing problems for him. He told the pharaoh that by now he was literally guarding Megiddo both day and night: "By day I am guarding from the fields in chariots and by night I am guarding the walls of the city of the king, my lord. But now, the hostility of the *'apiru* is severe in the land, so may the king, my lord, care for his land."[10]

However, Lab'ayu was no stranger either to warfare or diplomacy, for he also sent several letters to the pharaoh, protesting his innocence. In one letter (EA 252), Lab'ayu attempted to gaslight the pharaoh and represented himself as being the injured party, with two of his towns seized by an unnamed enemy. It seems quite likely, though, that he was actually the aggressor in this conflict. Certainly, he was aggressive in the letter that he sent to the pharaoh, dismissing the claims made about him and stating boldly, "Slander was spoken about me before the king, my lord."[11]

Even while continuing to protest and to proclaim his innocence, Lab'ayu seems to have been attacking other cities as well. In a second letter to the pharaoh (EA 253), he defended himself against an unspecified accusation that apparently centered around the fact that he had "entered" (perhaps even captured?) the city of Gezer. He wrote:

> I have obeyed the commands that the king, my lord, sent to me on a tablet. Look, I am a servant of the king like my father. The father of my father was a servant of the king from long ago. Neither am I a criminal nor am I derelict. See, my crime and, see, my offense is that I entered Gezer, (and) I said: "The king punishes us!" Here now, I have no other intention apart from serving the king. Whatever the king commands, I will obey. The king should assign me to the authority of my commissioner in order to guard the king's city.[12]

Lab'ayu continued this line of argumentation in the next letter (EA 254), again about Gezer and specifically its ruler Milkilu, repeating almost verbatim much of the above and then complaining of being slandered by the Egyptian commissioner. (There were nearly a dozen of these commissioners, each of whom was assigned to oversee one or more administrative districts in Canaan on behalf of the pharaoh; we shall meet several of them in the following chapters.) According to Lab'ayu, he had done nothing wrong, and he repeated his claim that his only crime was entering the city of Gezer and complaining in public about how he was being treated: "The king takes my possessions, but where are the possessions of Milki-'ili [Milkilu]? I know Milki-'ili's action against me."[13]

Lab'ayu also took the opportunity to address another issue, accusations of consorting with the 'apiru—which Biridiya had mentioned in his letter—and even threw one of his own sons under the bus in the process, all while protesting his undying loyalty (Fig. 12). "I did not know that my son was associating with the 'apiru," he told the pharaoh, "but behold, have I not turned him over to Haddaya?"

The first phase of the Lab'ayu Affair came to an end when Lab'ayu suffered an early demise, as we find out in one of the later letters sent by Biridiya from Megiddo (EA 245). In it, Biridiya informed the pharaoh of the events that had culminated in the capture and then the killing of Lab'ayu. Although we once again begin in medias res, since this is obviously the second tablet of what was once a two-tablet letter, Biridiya reported that Lab'ayu had been captured and then turned over to Surata, the ruler of Acco, so that he could be sent to Egypt for further action (perhaps disciplining or even a trial) by the pharaoh. However, Lab'ayu apparently bribed Surata, who allowed him to escape, along with

FIGURE 12. Amarna Letter EA 245 (Biridiya of Megiddo to either Amenhotep III or Akhenaten); BM E29855. © Trustees of the British Museum.

another man named Ba'lu-meher (who was probably the ruler of Yoqneam and who had also been causing problems). Immediately thereafter, however, there was an ambush and a fight during which Lab'ayu was killed.[14]

We do have letters from Surata (EA 232 and 233), but unfortunately, we cannot tell if they were sent before or after this incident, because in them Surata simply assured the pharaoh that he would do whatever was requested of him.[15] Moreover, Biridiya's testimony was not that of a firsthand witness, for he had not personally been present at the ambush or witnessed the death of Lab'ayu, reportedly because of a delay caused when his horse had earlier been shot out from under him. Instead of being at the ambush, he had to ride with Yashdata, the king of Ta'anach, who had been driven from his own city and was now staying at Megiddo with Biridiya.[16]

We have no way of knowing whether Biridiya's claim about his horse was actually true or not, but his actual words, in which he washed his hands of the killing, were as follows: "[And so] I entreated my brothers: 'If the god of the king, our lord, acts and we reach Lab'aya, then it is alive that we must bring him [i.e., we must bring him alive] to the king, our lord.' But my mare was taken away [i.e., it was shot], so I stayed behind and rode with Yashdata, but by the time of my arrival, they had killed him [i.e., Lab'ayu]."

14

The Sons of Lab'ayu

UNFORTUNATELY FOR Biridiya of Megiddo, and probably for the rulers and inhabitants of other cities as well, even the death of Lab'ayu did not bring any peace, for Lab'ayu had two sons, although we are never told their names. Upon the death of their father, these two sons simply picked up where Lab'ayu had left off and took up arms against Biridiya. Moreover, they enlisted the 'apiru men as well as men from the "land of the Sutu" (the Suteans), a nomadic or seminomadic group who are also mentioned in several other Amarna Letters. We know all of this because, in one of his letters to the pharaoh (EA 246), Biridiya wrote: "Now, the two sons of Lab'aya are giving their silver to 'apiru and to Suteans in order for (them) to wage war against me. The king should care for his land."[1]

We find out more from letters sent to the pharaoh by other rulers at this time. There is, for instance, a letter (EA 250) written by a man named Ba'lu-[UR.SAG], possibly the ruler of a town called Rahabu or Rehob (perhaps Tel Rehov, a town in the Jezreel Valley). He wrote to the pharaoh (most likely Akhenaten) to report on the further activities of Lab'ayu's two sons. "The king, my lord, should know," he said, "that the two sons of the evildoer against the king, my lord—the two sons of Lab'ayu—intend to make the land of the king, my lord, go out of the king's control after their father made it go out of (his) control."

Furthermore, he said, Lab'ayu's sons had personally threatened him, saying: "Wage war against the men of the land of Qina because they killed our father! But if you do not wage war, we are your enemy." Ba'lu-[UR.SAG] therefore requested that the pharaoh tell him what steps he should take against these two sons of Lab'ayu. He also asked the pharaoh to send one of his senior officials to Damascus and order Biryawaza, the ruler of the city, to join the fight against the sons of Lab'ayu.[2]

102

Unfortunately, we do not know how this continuing saga ended, for there are no other letters from the archive that mention Lab'ayu's sons. However, we do meet some of the other rulers again, in different situations. For example, Biryawaza of Damascus is named in at least a dozen other Amarna Letters and was clearly involved in many machinations during this time period.[3]

To give just one illustration, in another one of the royal letters sent by Burna-Buriash to Akhenaten (EA 7), which we discussed above, Burna-Buriash complained specifically that Biryawaza had robbed a caravan sent from Babylon, as had Pamahu, another local Canaanite ruler. "Furthermore," Burna-Buriash wrote, "twice has a caravan of Salmu, my messenger whom I sent to you, been robbed. The first one Biryawaza robbed, and his second caravan Pamahu, a governor of yours in a vassalage, robbed. When is my brother going to adjudicate this case?"[4]

These were not the only such incidents that took place, and Biryawaza and Pamahu were not alone in their actions, for in another letter (EA 8), again sent to Akhenaten, Burna-Buriash again complained that his merchants had been attacked and killed in Canaan and this time specifically identified one of the culprits as Satatna of Acco, the son of Surata (the same man who had been bribed by Lab'ayu). The sequence of events was straightforward: "Now, my merchants . . . were detained in the land of Canaan on business matters. . . . Shum-Hadda son of Ba'lumme (and) Satatna son of Saratu of the town of Akka [Acco] sent their men and they attacked (slew) my merchants and they carried off their silver." He then demanded that the Egyptian pharaoh do something about it. "Investigate them; pay the money that they took away and as for the men who slew my servants, kill them; requite their blood. But if you do not execute these men, they will do it again; they will attack either my caravan or your envoys."[5]

It is not clear in which order the incidents took place. Those for which Biryawaza and Pamahu were reportedly responsible may have taken place either slightly earlier or slightly later than the one for which Satatna was responsible, but they were likely fairly close in time. This may have been part of a general phase of brigandry and unrest, for we have another letter that was sent by Satatna to the pharaoh (EA 234), and that mentions Biryawaza specifically, so we know that they were contemporaries.[6]

Anson Rainey suggested that the pharaoh then sent the Egyptian army in retaliation for this attack by Satatna (though we might want to include those of Biridiya and Pamahu as well). He based his hypothesis on a letter (EA 367) sent by Akhenaten to a man named Intaruta, who ruled Akshapa (a town near Acco). Rainey interpreted this letter as an order "to prepare supplies for the arrival of the Egyptian army, which probably took place after the robbing of [the] Babylonian caravan by Satatna of Acco." In it, the pharaoh wrote: "Herewith the king is dispatching to you Hanya, the son of Ma'iriya, the king's stable master in the land of Canaan. That which he commands to you, obey it very carefully lest the king find guilt in you. Very carefully obey and perform every command that he speaks to you. And be on guard, be on guard! Do not be negligent! And you should prepare much food and much wine (and) everything else for the arrival of the king's regular troops. Now, he will reach you very quickly and cut off the head of the king's enemies."[7] However, other scholars, such as Itamar Singer of Tel Aviv University, have suggested that the mobilization of the Egyptian army was not in retaliation for what Satatna had done, but rather for events having to do with the Hittites and Amurru, as we shall see below.

———

Other Amarna Letters confirm that Biryawaza was quite the troublemaker in central Canaan during this period, for he is also mentioned by other rulers, primarily in complaints registered against him and sent to the pharaoh. In one letter (EA 151), for example, Abi-Milku, the ruler of Tyre, told the pharaoh that Biryawaza was at war with Aitukama, the prince of Qadesh, as well as with Aziru, the ruler of Amurru. He didn't provide any further details about that conflict, but the letter has generated much scholarly interest, for Abi-Milku also reported that the king of the land of Danuna (in southeastern Anatolia) had died and the king's brother was now reigning in his place; that fire had destroyed half of the royal palace in Ugarit; and that there were no troops of Hatti there (i.e., at Ugarit, perhaps meaning that the Hittites didn't have anything to do with the events).[8] We will revisit this letter in a future chapter.

Aitukama of Qadesh himself wrote to the pharaoh (EA 189), also complaining about Biryawaza, most likely in connection with this same conflict: "My lord, I am your servant, but the evil Biryawaza was defaming me before you, my lord—and while he was defaming me before you, he captured from me the entirety of my paternal estate outside of the land of Qidšu [Qadesh], and he sent my cities up in flames." He then specified that Biryawaza was working with the 'apiru men:

Wherever (there is) hostility towards the king, my lord, I myself go together with my troops, together with my chariots, and together with all of my brothers. But, look, Biryawaza permitted all the cities of the king, my lord, (to go) to the 'apiru in the land of Tahšu and in the land of Apu. But I arrived—your gods and your Sun god were going before me—and I restored the cities to the king, my lord . . . and I made the 'apiru go away. So the king, my lord, should rejoice concerning Aitukama, his servant. I serve the king, my lord, together with all of my brothers. . . . I serve the king, my lord, but Biryawaza caused all your lands to go out of (your) control. His intention is to do violence, but I am your servant in perpetuity.[9]

By way of defense, Biryawaza wrote to the pharaoh several times to give his side of the story. In one letter (EA 195) he doesn't deny working with 'apiru men, but instead says that he deliberately hired them, along with others, as mercenaries to supplement his troops. He also reiterated his allegiance to the pharaoh, in the typical fashion of such letters from a vassal to the Egyptian king: "Speak to the king, my lord, a message from Biryawaza, your servant, the dust of your feet and the ground upon which you tread, a chair upon which you sit, and a footstool for your feet. I fall at the feet of the king, my lord, the Sun god of the morning, seven times plus seven times." He continued: "Now, I, together with my troops and my chariots, and together with my brothers, and together with my 'apiru, and together with my Suteans, am (ready) for the front of the regular troops, wherever the king, my lord, commands (them to go)."[10] None of this would seem out of the ordinary, given the circumstances of the time, were it not for the complaints of the other local rulers about Biryawaza's aggressions, probably with these same troops.

In another letter (EA 196), Biryawaza reported to the pharaoh that the locals had gone over to the side of the Hittites. He claimed to be the only ruler who had remained loyal to the pharaoh. In return, he requested that Egyptian troops be sent to help protect him: "The king, my lord, should dispatch 200 men to me in order to guard your servant and in order to guard the cities of the king, my lord, until I see the regular army of the king, my lord."[11]

In a final letter (EA 197), Biryawaza appears to specifically address the story that Abi-Milku, the ruler of Tyre, told the pharaoh about Biryawaza being at war with Aitukama, the prince of Qadesh. Not only does he not deny it, but he put it into a larger context, claiming that it was actually Aitukama and several other leaders, including Aziru, the ruler of Amurru, who had instigated the conflict. He then proceeded to describe what subsequently happened, including mentioning both Aitukama and troops from Aziru, but also laying the ultimate blame at the feet of the Hittites.[12] From our vantage point, it is hard to know whom to believe and who might be presenting alternative facts to the pharaoh.

———

If we consider at face value all of the details in the letters discussed in this chapter, even if we do not take sides as to who may have started the various conflicts, it is clear that some of the local conflicts were just that—local conflicts, such as those fought between Lab'ayu and Biridiya, as well as between Lab'ayu's two sons and other rulers. However, additional conflicts, such as perhaps between Biryawaza, Aitukama, and Aziru, were actually mini-wars fought by proxies on behalf of the Great Powers, as the Hittites attempted to woo vassals away from their Egyptian overlords.

We shall see this in more detail below, when we look at the conflicts involving the region of Amurru, for in these earlier Amarna Letters, sent by local rulers blaming each other as they participated in conflicts fought in the shadow of the Egyptian and Hittite empires, it is now quite clear that we are seeing the beginnings of what would eventually break into all-out war between the two superpowers. Less than a century after Amenhotep III, Akhenaten, Suppiluliuma, Biryawaza, Lab'ayu, and Biridiya had exited the stage, these local conflicts eventually culminated in the Battle of Qadesh, fought in 1274 BC, when the two great(est) powers of the day—the Egyptians and the Hittites—fought to a stalemate and then subsequently signed a peace treaty, cemented once again by a foreign princess sent to marry an Egyptian pharaoh.

PART V

The Game: Winners and Losers

15

Jerusalem, O Jerusalem

IMMEDIATELY AFTER Winckler and Abel published their volumes, a steady stream of publications about the Amarna Letters began to appear. These were written by a variety of scholars and other interested parties, both distinguished and otherwise. For instance, there was immediate interest in trying to decipher and translate the language of the single Tushratta letter that was not written in Akkadian (EA 24).

In 1890, a trio of articles appeared in the *Zeitschrift für Assyriologie und verwandte Gebiete* on "the language of Mittani," which eventually turned out to be Hurrian. One of these was written by Sayce, not unexpectedly, but the other two were composed by scholars who we have not met before. One was a German Assyriologist named Peter Jensen who had studied with Delitzsch at Leipzig and Schrader at Berlin (where he received his PhD in 1884) and who held the first professorial chair in Assyriology at the University of Marburg. The other was a German American Orientalist named Rudolph Brünnow who was eventually appointed to a chair of Semitic Languages at Princeton University.[1]

Sayce himself made immediate use of the volumes published by Winckler and Abel to produce his own English translations of some of the tablets in Berlin and Cairo that he deemed most important. He did this in the same series, *Records of the Past*, for which he served as editor.

He began: "In the following pages I have given translations of the most important letters, from a historical point of view, which have yet been published. They are mostly to be found in the magnificent publication of Messrs. Winckler and Abel . . . of which two parts have appeared containing the texts of a considerable number of the Tel el-Amarna tablets at Berlin and Cairo." Sayce then proceeded to sling another arrow at Budge: "The promptitude and carefulness with which they have been edited contrasts favourably with the tardiness of the authorities of the British Museum in putting the collection of Tel el-Amarna tablets that exists there at the service of scholars. Of the eighty-one tablets now in the British Museum four only have been published (by Mr. Budge . . .)."[2]

Sayce then presented his translations of eleven Amarna Letters. For most of them, these were the first English translations that had appeared. The letters included one from "Assur-Yuballidh" [Assur-uballit] of Assyria to Akhenaten; two from "Burna-Buryas" [Burna-Buriash] of Babylonia to Akhenaten; one sent by Aziru of Amurru to his "brother" Khu and another sent by Aziru to his "father" "Dûdu." There was also one from "Rib-Addu" [Rib-Hadda] of Byblos to the king of Egypt; and four from "Dusratta" [Tushratta] of Mittani, two of which were sent to Amenhotep III and two of which went to Akhenaten.[3]

Since Sayce was now not only able to use the expert drawings of the tablets and the cuneiform signs upon them that had been created by Abel but also to take advantage of the various publications by Winckler, Zimmern, and others, his translations of these eleven tablets were much better than his previous efforts. For instance, he got a number of the important details correct, including the genealogy for Tushratta of Mittani. Although Sayce still referred to Tushratta himself as Dusratta, he was correct that Tushratta's father was named Shuttarna and his grandfather was Artatama. However, he also repeated some of the errors that he had made previously, including thinking that Aziru was the son of the Egyptian vizier Dûdu and that Dûdu's name was related to that of David, when, in fact, Dûdu was actually named Tutu and was not Aziru's father, as we have seen.[4]

We meet Conder again at this point, for he published a lengthy article in the *Quarterly Statement of the Palestine Exploration Fund* entitled "A Hittite Prince's Letter." In it, he again took up the topic of Tarkhundaradu of the "Arzapi" letter, agreeing with Sayce and Winckler that it was written in Hittite, but continuing to locate the origin of the letter, and the king, in northern Syria rather than in western Anatolia. He also claimed to have now identified and translated about 150 Hittite words, based on this letter. He incorrectly brought up comparisons to Turkic, Mongol, and related languages for these words, mistakenly thinking that Hittite was most likely part of the so-called Altaic language family, which it is not.[5]

The breakthrough in translating Hittite would not take place until ca. 1916, which still lay some twenty-five years or so in the future, when the Czech linguist Bedřich Hrozný was able to decipher the Hittite tablets that Winckler found in the archives at the Hittite capital Hattusa beginning in 1906. Winckler did not live to see the breakthrough by Hrozný, for he died in 1913 after a "long illness," just a few months shy of his fiftieth birthday, likely from malaria he had contracted while excavating at Sidon a few years earlier.[5] At this point in time, though, in the early 1890s, his untimely passing still lay several decades in the future.

———

A new French scholar enters the scene at this point, Joseph Halévy (Fig. 13). He was an Orientalist and biblical scholar originally born in Turkey but now based in Paris. In the first of his publications, which appeared in French in 1890, within the *Revue des études juives* as part 20 of the ongoing "Revue Biblique" series, Halévy attempted to assess the content of various Akhenaten letters in the Amarna archive within the context of Near Eastern history as described in the Hebrew Bible.

He castigated Sayce for announcing that he had identified Moses in the Amarna Letters, beginning by saying that "to be truly useful to the progress of history and exegesis, it is necessary to begin by barring the way to any hasty or exaggerated hypothesis, to any conclusion which is not based on an exact interpretation of the texts." Without explicitly mentioning Sayce by name, he added that nothing had been more prejudicial to the study of these new texts than the haste by which "the discovery of the names of Moses and of the Hebrews in the tablets preserved at Boulak" had been announced. "Usually such claims," he said, "have their source in the misinterpretation of a word, sometimes even of a single letter. We regret to say that the starting point of the astonishing pre-Hebraic discovery which I have just mentioned is no more solid."[7]

Halévy's next 1890 publications appeared in two sections in the *Journal asiatique* and were actually the first installments in a series that continued through 1891. He produced the first transliterations and translations in French for the various texts whose hand-drawn copies had been published in the first of Winckler and Abel's volumes on the Berlin tablets.[8] Their goal had been to make these publications available to all scholars, not just those who could travel to see them in person. The work by Halévy and the other new scholars who were not part of the initial Amarna group was evidence that they achieved that aim.

———

One additional biblical topic set the scholarly world abuzz in 1890 concerning the tablets. First in April and then twice in October 1890, brief notices

FIGURE 13. Joseph Halévy. Illustration by Glynnis Fawkes.

appeared in *The Academy* that asserted that Jerusalem had been identified in the Amarna tablets.

The first mention was by Sayce in his by now familiar "Letter from Egypt" column. This one was published in the 19 April 1890 issue of *The Academy* and contained in the very last paragraph a brief mention that he had identified Jerusalem in a single Amarna tablet. "I have examined afresh one of the letters from Southern Palestine contained in the Tel el-Amarna collection," he said, "in which mention is made of the cities of Keilah, Kirjath, and what I read doubtfully as Ururusi. . . . My copy, however, subsequently made me think that it really was . . . the name reading *Uruśalim*, or Jerusalem. Another inspection of the tablet has shown me that my conjecture was right, and that the city of Jerusalem already existed under its familiar name in the fifteenth century B.C. It was at that time a garrison of the Egyptian king."[9]

We should note that less than six months earlier, during his lecture in Manchester in early November 1889, Sayce had not yet realized that "Ururusi" was in fact Jerusalem: "We seek in vain in later history for the name of Ururusi, which appears as a city of equal importance with Gath and Gaza."[10]

Sayce was absolutely correct that Ururusi was actually Jerusalem, but one has to ask, of course, why he had decided to examine "afresh" this one tablet (EA 290). A compelling reason is readily found, for the second mention in *The Academy* that year was an anonymous note that appeared six months later. This note stated that there were now five Amarna tablets in Berlin that had been identified as mentioning Jerusalem: "Among the tablets from Tel el-Amarna, now in the museum at Berlin, five have lately been found which were sent from Urusalim or Jerusalem to the Egyptian kings. Their writer was a certain Additaba or Hadad-tob [now identified as Abdi-Heba], who claims to have been a tributary and protected prince, and not merely an Egyptian governor." The anonymous writer went on to acknowledge that Sayce had also discovered the name of Jerusalem in one of the tablets that was now in the Cairo Museum.[11]

We do not know the author of this note, but the process was clear. Winckler and Abel's second half of the publication of the Berlin tablets had appeared during the early part of 1890. In this second volume, the name Jerusalem appeared on six tablets in Berlin, rather than five, which Winckler and Abel published as numbers 102–6 and number 174 in their volume. Rumors must have been flying soon afterward, probably compelling Sayce to hastily reexamine his own tablets and publish his note in April 1890.

These specific tablets were mentioned by Zimmern in a brief article that he published in the *Kölnische Zeitung* on 1 October 1890, just three weeks before the notice appeared in *The Academy*. It seems extremely likely that Zimmern was in fact the anonymous author of the note in *The Academy*, for he discussed the tablets twice more the next year (1891), as we shall see.[12]

The anonymous note in the 18 October 1890 issue of *The Academy* was followed by a fuller, and more specific, discussion by Sayce, as a response published in the 25 October issue. Here he expanded on his notice from the previous April, though curiously he does not mention that earlier note in this longer response. "The discovery of despatches from Jerusalem to the kings of Egypt in the fifteenth century B.C., announced in the *Academy* of last week, throws light on one of the tablets from Tel el-Amarna, belonging to M. Bouriant, which I copied three years ago. The imperfect condition of the tablet prevented me at the time from realizing its importance, though I was able to identify in it the names of the cities of Gedor, Gath, Keilah, and Rabbah. But I see now that it also contains a reference to Jerusalem, which is of considerable interest. The passage is as follows . . ."

Sayce then took the opportunity to provide a suggested transliteration and translation, which he rendered as "the city of the mountain of Jerusalem, the city of the temple of the god Uras: (his) name (there is) Marruv; the city of the king, adjoining (?) the locality of the men of the city of Keilah." He then continued: "Here Jerusalem is distinctly marked out as situated on a mountain, and as being the seat of a famous temple. . . . At all events, we must see in the deity whose temple stood on 'the mountain of Jerusalem,' the *êl elyôn*, 'the most high God,' of Gen. xiv.18."[13]

A similar discussion, following Sayce's lead on this translation, was undertaken the following year, in May 1891, by William St. Chad Boscawen. He was a young Assyriologist who had been Budge's immediate predecessor at the British Museum but who had been let go by the museum after just a few years for unstated reasons.[14] Unfortunately for both men, while the letter to which Sayce refers does mention Jerusalem, it does not say that Jerusalem was the seat of a famous temple or anything about a deity named Uras.

Sayce's misinterpretation regarding a deity named Uras was based on an erroneous translation of some of the words in this passage, as Zimmern subsequently pointed out in his longer 1891 article in *Zeitschrift des Deutschen Paläistina-Vereins* (*ZDPV*). Instead, these lines simply say: ". . . a town belonging to Jerusalem, Bit-dNIN.IB by name, a city of the king, has gone over to the side of the men of Qilti (Keilah)."[15] In short, the letter is concerned with political and military matters, not religious. It is yet another cautionary tale about Sayce's translations and his desire to connect the material in the Amarna archive to the Hebrew Bible whenever and wherever he could.

Near Eastern scholars looking for biblical connections at this time was not unusual, particularly since many of them were also practicing ministers with degrees in theology. Sayce, who was an ordained minister, was similarly intent on linking these texts to the biblical accounts. He had begun his 1889 Manchester lecture by saying:

A marvelous discovery has recently been made in Egypt, so marvelous, indeed, that had a prophet arisen to predict it to our fathers or our grandfathers they would have listened to him with scornful incredulity. We have been suddenly brought face to face with the civilised world as it existed in the days when the Israelites were groaning under the burdens of their Egyptian taskmasters; we can handle the very letters that were written by the princes and governors of Canaan when as yet Joshua was unborn, and we can trace the course of events that led to the mission of Moses and the exodus of Israel out of Egypt.[16]

[...]

Consider for one moment what an important bearing such a discovery must have upon the criticism of the Old Testament. We have hitherto taken it for granted that the world of Moses was narrow and circumscribed, that a knowledge of letters was confined to a few in the cultivated kingdoms of Egypt and Babylonia, and that the populations of Canaan were as illiterate as the populations of Europe in the Middle Ages. Suddenly the veil has been drawn aside which has for centuries hidden that ancient world from our eyes, and we find it a world much like our own, educated and literary, constantly informed of all that was passing in the countries around it, and enjoying an advantage which we no longer possess—that of a common medium of literary intercourse.[17]

A much more recent discovery contains many parallels. In the 1970s, when Italian excavators discovered the archives at the site of Ebla in Syria, initial claims were made by one of the epigraphers that he could see the city names of Sodom and Gomorrah and the biblical figures of Abraham, Isaac, and Jacob on the tablets. All of those identifications turned out to be completely erroneous, for though the tablets had been inscribed in cuneiform, which the epigrapher thought had been used to record texts in Akkadian, it soon turned out that the cuneiform signs actually were being used to write a previous unknown language, now known as "Eblaite" or "Eblaitic." As soon as this was realized, and proper translations were done, Sodom, Gomorrah, Abraham, Isaac, and Jacob disappeared from the texts, leaving only a memory of that initial attempt to find connections to the Bible, just as with Sayce's attempts to connect the Amarna Letters eighty years earlier.[18]

16

Publish or Perish

IN 1891, Winckler published another note in the *Zeitschrift für Assyriologie und verwandte Gebiete*. Its genesis was rooted in Winckler's pique at one or more unnamed scholars, for he wrote near the beginning, "After my edition of the el-Amarna texts was complete, I was able to tackle the processing of the material in context . . . it is natural that other researchers, whose time is not taken up by the tedious and exhausting reading of the originals, and who can therefore devote themselves entirely to the study of what is made accessible to them, would be faster in completing investigations than the one who first has to finish publishing the texts."[1]

He stated in particular that unless one had seen the original tablet(s), one should not make "public judgments about the reading of such cases, and that in particular, one who is ignorant of a particular newly published original is hardly entitled and able to estimate the value or merit of the publication of the same."[2] It is not clear at all whom Winckler had in mind when he wrote this, or even if it was directed at anyone in particular, though it certainly seems aimed at someone. To make such a public comment also seems quite strange, since Winckler (along with Abel) was the one responsible for publishing the hand-drawn copies of the tablets in the Berlin and Cairo museums, which was what allowed other scholars who were unable to see the tablets in person to suggest their translations, however far-fetched or erroneous.

It may well have been one of the reviewers of his volumes who was the subject of Winckler's wrath, or his colleagues Zimmern or Lehmann. However, it seems much more likely to have been aimed at Sayce, Conder, Boscawen, or one of the other scholars (whether established, marginal, or "wannabe") who were now attempting transliterations and translations. Delattre in particular comes to mind, for he had already been the target of Winckler's fury, but it may well have been either Sayce, appointed that same year to a position as professor of Assyriology at Oxford, or Conder, since both of them had published articles in the previous year based on Winckler's work.

Winckler also pointed out, quite correctly, that with "an unexplored class of documents" such as the Amarna Letters, one needed to decide whether to understand a text fully before publishing it or to "paint what one sees" even before that point is reached. Therefore: "It will . . . seem understandable to everyone if I have the wish, after I have had the unpleasant part of the work behind me, to present some of the fruits of my reading myself."[3]

Winckler proceeded to discuss a few points pertaining to some minor Amarna Letters in the rest of the article, leaving the reader with the impression that his point in publishing this note was to defend his other publications as well as to condemn (or even warn off) some of his colleagues or rivals. One can hardly blame him, especially if he were trying to keep the field clear for his forthcoming translations, although those were still a few years away.

Zimmern also continued to publish on the Amarna Letters, with several articles appearing during this year. One was a short technical article on the actual language of the tablets, entitled "Kanaanäische Glossen." The second was specifically devoted to the Amarna tablets that mention Jerusalem, which he published in the *Zeitschrift für Assyriologie und verwandte Gebiete*. The third was a more general article, published in the *Zeitschrift des Deutschen Paläistina-Vereins* (*ZDPV*), in which he attempted to reconstruct and describe the history of the southern Levant around the year 1400 BCE based on the Berlin tablets. In this longer article, Zimmern specifically gave credit to Sayce for having been the first to publish about the occurrence of Jerusalem in the tablets, citing Sayce's note in the April 1890 issue of *The Academy*.[4]

These were not the only scholars writing on the Amarna Letters in 1891. Halévy published four more installments of his series in the *Journal asiatique*, totalling nearly two hundred printed pages of his transliterations and translations into French on the Berlin and Cairo tablets. Conder published two more of his takes on the Amarna Letters, including one in the *Quarterly Statement of the Palestine Exploration Fund* and another in *The Scottish Review* (which was, perhaps surprisingly, apparently published in London). Sayce also published another article containing additional translations in his *Records of the Past* series.[5]

Delattre, the Jesuit priest in Belgium, also published four fairly short articles at this same time, in the *Proceedings of the Society of Biblical Archaeology*, appearing in December 1890 and March, April, and June 1891.[6] They all involved various Amarna tablets that had caught his interest. Most notably, in discussing some of the letters written by Aziru of Amurru, he pointed out that Aziru's real father was named Arad-Asirtou or Arad-Asratou [now rendered as Abdi-Ashirta] and was able to state fairly conclusively that the Egyptian "Doudou" (Sayce's "Dûdu") was only his father in a figurative sense, contrary to Sayce's claims. Delattre had already pointed to this use of false kinship terms in some of the Amarna Letters sent between the Great Kings in an article he had published in 1889. Here he established that there were false kinship relationships used as part of the opening greetings and rhetoric in the Aziru letters. Whether we can give credit to him for being the first to note this seems very likely, for we don't see it mentioned by anyone else at this time.[7]

Sayce's next installment in his *Records of the Past* series in 1891 began with an effusive endorsement of the Royal Museum of Berlin, and Winckler and Abel in particular, for rapid publication of the tablets in their possession. "The authorities of the Royal Museum of Berlin have laid scholars under an obligation by their speedy publication of all the cuneiform tablets found in the ruins of Tel el-Amarna which are now at Berlin. . . . Drs. Winckler and Abel, to whom the copying and editing of the texts have been entrusted, have performed their task with marvellous accuracy and skill, which can be fully appreciated only by those who have themselves attempted to copy the extremely difficult inscriptions of Tel el-Amarna."[8]

He compared and contrasted this prompt action with the snail-like pace of Budge and the British Museum, "which has for three years withheld the tablets in its possession even from the sight of students." He then added "until they are published our knowledge of the collection will not only be incomplete, but doubtless at times misleading."[9]

Sayce's article attempted translations from the hand copies published by Winckler and Abel on the letters from the petty Canaanite rulers in the southern Levant, which had appeared in the third part of Winckler and Abel's volumes (the second half of volume 2). He cautioned once again that his translations "must be received with the indulgence due to the first translations of ancient texts. The language of the letters is full of forms and expressions which are new to the Assyriologist; the large number of tablets, however, which we can compare with one another, has thrown light upon many of these, and explained words and idioms which would otherwise have been obscure." He also acknowledged that Delattre had attempted his own translations of some of the same texts.[10]

Sayce persisted in presenting the name of the ruler of Jerusalem as Ebedtob instead of Abdi-Heba and continued to talk about Jerusalem as "the seat of the worship and oracle of the god 'Salim, whose temple stood on 'the mountain' of Moriah." He explained this to his readers by stating that the word *uru* meant city, which it does, and that therefore *Uru-'salim* meant "the city of the god 'Salim." Though this is not out of the question, the meaning of the name has been much debated over the years, and this is by no means the only possible interpretation, though Sayce's biblical focus kept him on this track.[11]

In one of the letters, Sayce claimed the ruler of Jerusalem wrote to the pharaoh that "The country of the king is being destroyed, all of it. Hostilities are carried on against me as far as the mountains of Seir, and the city of Gath-Karmel." According to Sayce, the king continued, "(There is) peace to all the (other) governors, but war against myself is raised," and then quoted an "oracle of the mighty king" saying, "While (there is) a ship in the midst of the sea . . . the conquests shall continue of the country of Nakhrima and the country of Babylonia. And now the fortresses of the king the Confederates are capturing. Not a single governor remains (among them) to the king my lord; all are destroyed."[12]

While the essential meaning of Sayce's translation of this letter was correct, large parts of it were not, including the so-called oracle that Sayce quoted. These lines are now translated as: "The king should show concern for his land. The king's land is out of (his) control. Its entirety has been seized from me. (There is) hostility towards me. From the mountains of Šeru to Gintu-Kirmil, (there is) peace for all of the city rulers, but (there is) hostility towards me!"

Modern translations continue thus, "I am placed like a ship in the middle of the sea! The strong hand of the king captured the land of Mittani and the land of Cush, but now the *'apiru* are capturing the king's cities. There is not a single city ruler belonging to the king, my lord. All are out of (his) control!"[13]

———

At the same time that these exchanges were taking place, William Matthew Flinders Petrie began excavating at Amarna, having started in 1891 and continuing into 1892. During the latter season, a very young Howard Carter—the future discoverer and excavator of the tomb of Tutankhamun—was assigned to work with Petrie at the site. Petrie wrote in his private journal: "Mr. Carter is to come here to work, not exactly with me, but on parts of the ground which I may assign to him. I [have] no responsibilities about his work, except to the Gov[ernment] here."[14]

Born in May 1874, Carter was seventeen years old at the time. As others have pointed out, he failed to make much of an impression on Petrie, who noted in his journal that "Mr. Carter is a good-natured lad, whose interest is entirely in painting & natural history; he only takes this digging as being on the spot & convenient to Mr. Amherst, & it is of no use for me to work him up as an excavator."[15]

Petrie found additional Amarna tablets during his field season. In his private journal, he noted:

> At last I have got touch of the cuneiform tablets. A bit of one was found in re-clearing the house in which they were said to have been found; & there, most unexpectedly, we found in old rubbish pits under the <house> walls a lot of scraps of the peculiar clay, bits of broken tablets, a large tablet broken up before being written on, where the scribe had scrawled about & dug into the clay with his stylus & tried the point of it here & there, also a tablet idly covered with some fifty presses of a small seal of Khuenatens [Akhenaten].[16]

Petrie began hypothesizing to himself:

> So it's certain that such things never were sent from Babylonia. I read it thus: The Babylonian scribe who did the cuneiform correspondence, lived up there, outside the palace, some way to the east. Outside his house were sand pits, dug for sand when building it. His rubbish was thrown in there. Then the store rooms were built over those pits, & the tablets from Babylonia stored there close to the scribe's house. These tablets have all been cleared out now; but the scribe's rubbish, memoranda, spoilt pieces, & a charm cylinder of clay, were left in his old rubbish holes beneath. It throws an entirely new light on the correspondence.[17]

While it is certainly not out of the question that there might have been a Babylonian scribe (or two) living at Amarna and helping with translating the incoming letters from Burna-Buriash II and the other Babylonian kings, as well as helping to craft the pharaoh's replies, Petrie's scenario has not found much favor among scholars. Just as likely, or perhaps far more likely, is that the Egyptian scribes at Amarna were also conversant in Akkadian (as well as probably other languages, such as Hittite and Hurrian) and could both read the various incoming letters and compose the outgoing replies themselves. It is notable that Sayce, who was responsible for publishing these new fragments in Petrie's 1894 publication on his excavations, did not comment on such musings or pose any such hypotheses himself, nor did Petrie include anything along such lines in his final report.[18]

17

Bezold and Budge, Finally

THE BRITISH Museum volume finally appeared in 1892, some three years later than originally planned. The Young Berliner Carl Bezold—who was thirty-three years old and working at the British Museum at the time—was listed as the primary author of the volume, with Budge as second author.[1] It will be recalled that Bezold was also the principal editor of the journal *Zeitschrift für Assyriologie und verwandte Gebiete* and had been since its inception in 1886. By the time the British Museum volume saw the light of day, the journal had already published six articles on the Amarna tablets: three by Winckler, two by Lehmann, and one by Zimmern.

The long-awaited volume began with a brief fifteen-page introduction and a lengthier sixty-page summary of the eighty-two tablets included in the volume, both written jointly by Bezold and Budge. The rest of the volume, some 141 pages, was taken up with facsimiles of each of the tablets, with the cuneiform signs reproduced in type so that other scholars could study them and attempt their own translations. Though the tablets were not hand drawn to reflect or reproduce the exact shapes of the individual tablets and signs, as Winckler and Abel had attempted to carefully do for the Berlin and Cairo tablets, photographs were provided for each of the British Museum tablets, in twenty-four plates within the volume, to show the script in its original context.

The long introduction and summary in the volume marks the first occasion that Budge had discussed the Amarna Letters in print since his initial June 1888 article in *PSBA*, which had appeared just after he returned from his travels in Egypt and Mesopotamia. In that article, Budge had given an introduction to the tablets and their discovery but only attempted actual translations for very few of the tablets. Instead, he had provided an overview of what was in each, although he did include actual line-by-line transliterations for a couple of the more interesting tablets.

Now, in this volume, he and Bezold did essentially the same thing, beginning by briefly introducing the story of the discovery of the tablets, commenting on a few of them, and putting them into the context of the period during which they were written some 3,400 years ago. They itemized the tablets as follows:

> The documents were most probably written between the years B.C. 1500–1450. They consist of: A letter from Amenophis III to Kallimma-Sin [Kadashman-Enlil]; three letters from Burraburiyash [Burna-Buriash] King of Karaduniyash, to Amenophis IV; three letters from the King of Alashiya to the King of Egypt; three letters from Tushratta, King of Mittani, to Amenophis III; a letter from Tushratta, probably to Thi [Tiyi], wife of Amenophis III; fourteen letters from Rib-Adda [Rib-Hadda], governor of Byblos, eleven of which are addressed to the King of Egypt, and three to Amanappa, an Egyptian official; two letters from Ammunira of Beyrut; four letters from Abi-milki [Abi-Milku] of Tyre; fifteen letters from governors of towns in Phoenicia and Syria; twenty-seven letters from governors of towns in Palestine; eight letters from governors of towns the positions of which are unknown; and a part of a mythological text referring to the goddess Irishkigal.[2]

They then continued, saying "They [i.e., the tablets] give an insight into the nature of the political relations which existed between the kings of Western Asia and the kings of Egypt, and prove that an important trade between the two countries existed from very early times. They also supply information concerning offensive and defensive alliances between the kings of Egypt and other countries, commercial treaties, marriage customs, religious ceremonies, and intrigues, which has been derived from no other source."[3]

In the detailed sixty-page summary that followed, they then proceeded tablet by tablet, with a paragraph devoted to each one explaining the contents, but without actually providing a translation for any of them. Instead, they let the facsimiles of the tablets, which took up the rest of the volume, speak for themselves, at least to those who could read them, just as Winckler and Abel had done with their volumes for the Berlin and Cairo tablets.

A year later, Bezold followed this up with a single-authored "supplement" entitled *Oriental Diplomacy*, that included transliterations of the eighty-two tablets, rendering all of the cuneiform signs into English sounds. No actual translations were included. As he put it, "The object of this book is to supply to students and beginners . . . a transliteration and full concordance of the 'despatches' from Amarna that were now in the British Museum." Although the transliterations were completed in early September 1892 and probably could have been included in the initial volume, the supplement did not appear until 1893. For reasons that are now unclear but possibly because of the intended British audience, his name appeared as "Charles Bezold" rather than "Carl" on the cover and title page, and he signed the preface simply "C. Bezold."[4]

As to why he did not include any translations in the supplement, his explanation—or perhaps it should be seen better as an excuse—is that it would have been impossible to provide any that "would entirely satisfy the expert or general reader" because of "the present state of cuneiform research." This, he said, was because "No two scholars would agree as to any interpretation which might be placed upon certain rare grammatical forms and unknown words in the Babylonian text, and any literal translation in a modern language would not be understood by the general reader on account of the involved style and endless repetition of phrases common to a Semitic idiom and dialect."[5]

This is rather astounding but suggests that we should read between the lines. It seems quite likely that Bezold's statements about no two scholars agreeing on any particular interpretation and that it would be impossible to provide a translation "which would entirely satisfy the expert" may be a not-so-veiled reference to intractable arguments between himself and Budge on correct translations and may explain why it took so long for the initial volume to finally appear in 1892. Though that is admittedly sheer speculation, it would not be at all surprising. Regardless, for whatever reason, neither Bezold nor Budge ever provided any further transliteration or translation of the tablets in the British Museum.

———

In the same year that the British Museum volume finally appeared, Abel published a brief article in the 1892 volume of the *Zeitschrift für Assyriologie und verwandte Gebiete*, which was concerned with the very fragmentary tablet owned by Reverend Chauncey Murch, previously discussed by Budge. Abel now included a hand copy showing all of the signs on both sides of the tablet, as well as an attempted transliteration and translation of the contents. Although the names of both the sender and the receiver are unclear, Abel confirmed that it was part of the "Mittani series" of tablets and said that it had been sent by Tushratta to Amenhotep III; in fact, it seems to actually have been sent directly to Queen Tiyi.[6]

In the same volume of that journal, Alfred Boissier, a Swiss Assyriologist whom we have not met previously but who had received his PhD in 1890 at

Leipzig with Delitzsch, published a short note on some of the other Amarna Letters; it was one of the first publications in his distinguished career. He was concerned with the letter of Tarkhundarau, still identified as the "king of Arsapi," which Winckler and Abel had just published as letter number 10 in their first volume of the tablets in Berlin, but also commented on various cuneiform signs and their transliteration / translation on some of the other tablets.[7]

Meanwhile, over in the United States, an American scholar finally ventured into the Amarna arena. Morris Jastrow Jr., an American Assyriologist who had studied with Delitzsch in Leipzig, receiving his PhD in 1884, and who was now teaching at the University of Pennsylvania, published an article in the 1892 volume of the *Journal of Biblical Literature*. The article was derived from a paper that Jastrow had delivered at a meeting of the Society of Biblical Literature and Exegesis a few months earlier. It was on the same topic and had almost the same title as Zimmern's article that had appeared earlier in 1891 in *ZDPV*, though Jastrow's article was in English: "Egypt and Palestine, 1400 B.C." Since Jastrow only refers to Zimmern's article on the very last page and in the very last footnote of his own article, we may assume that the article only came to Jastrow's attention shortly before his own manuscript was published.[8]

Jastrow's article was meant to show "Old Testament students" the general importance of the Amarna tablets in understanding the relations between Egypt and Canaan ca. 1400 BCE. He praised the recent publication of the Berlin tablets by Winckler and Abel, joining the chorus of other scholars, but, like the others, lamented that the tablets in the British Museum had not yet been published when he was working on the paper.

He also condemned in no uncertain terms the efforts of Sayce in particular, writing in a footnote: "Sayce . . . published . . . transliterations of most of the Bulaq tablets, together with translations and short comments; in addition to this he has given transliterations and translations of 14 tablets in the possession of M. Bouriant . . . but none of his translations are reliable. The same criticism applies to Sayce's translations in *Records of the Past*, New Series, I and II." However, he praised the efforts of other scholars in the same breath: "Far superior, and full of most valuable suggestions, though to be accepted with the reserve inseparable from the present state of our knowledge, are Halévy's translations of the entire edition of Winckler and Abel, now appearing in instalments in [the] *Journal Asiatique*." He added that "Delattre has [also] published very good translations of a selection of the letters."[9]

Despite the title and stated intent, Jastrow spent by far the greater part of his article commenting on the occurrence of Jerusalem in the tablets, again giving credit to Sayce for having been the first to announce this. He also noted that the letters mentioning Jerusalem had recently been published by Winckler and Abel in their volumes and that both Zimmern and Halévy had weighed in already with their own transcriptions and translations.[10]

However, even in giving credit to Sayce for the initial identification, Jastrow pulled no punches, stating in a footnote: "Sayce in various articles . . . by falsely interpreting the 'mighty King' to refer to a deity, has drawn conclusions from these passages as to the religious ideas prevalent in Jerusalem at this period that are totally erroneous. The 'mighty King' can only refer to Amenophis IV. It is to be regretted that the distinguished English scholar should have been so hasty in spreading his conjectures through the medium of popular journals, thereby doing a mischief of incalculable extent."[11]

He also commented specifically on the lines in which Abdi-Heba described himself as a "ship in the midst of the sea," stating that these had given everyone trouble, including Halévy and Zimmern, as well as Sayce. Jastrow's attempt was no better, for he rendered it as "If any one were to see [my condition], he would see the tears of the King my lord at the hostility that is being carried on against me, as when a ship is [cast about] in the midst of the sea."[12]

Jastrow also devoted a fair amount of his article to a topic which has been much discussed ever since. Throughout a number of the Amarna Letters, including from Abdi-Heba in Jerusalem, mention is made of a group of people collectively known to the writers as the 'apiru or habiri, as we have seen. Sayce had been arguing for some time that the term should be translated as "confederates" or "allies" but others, including Zimmern, thought that this was none other than a reference to the "Hebrews" and that we should see here the first indication of the arrival of the Israelites in the land of Canaan.

Jastrow was of the belief that while the identification of the 'apiru as the Hebrews was tempting, he also warned that "the proposed identification would have to be received with the greatest caution." Indeed, while the association was deemed acceptable by a number of scholars right up until the 1970s, the majority no longer agree and instead now see the 'apiru more along the lines of a social class rather than an ethnicity or specific nationality, and do not identify them with the Hebrews.[13]

———

Thus, by the end of 1892, when Bezold and Budge published the British Museum's tablets just five years after the initial discovery of the archive in 1887, all three major collections—in Cairo, Berlin, and London—were now available to all scholars who knew cuneiform and Akkadian, whether they had access to the originals or not. This was amazingly fast, especially in comparison to today, when tablets can often lie undeciphered in museum and university collections for decades.

In the meantime, Delattre, who had just been mentioned by Jastrow as "the distinguished French *savant*," published four more articles transliterating, translating, and commenting on additional Amarna tablets that had caught his eye or his interest. These all appeared in the *PSBA* for 1892–1893; in actuality, they were one long article that had been broken up into four sections, each appearing in a different fascicle: November 1892, and January, May, and June 1893.[14] This time his efforts included tablets in the British Museum just published by Bezold. He included an attempt at translating Amarna Letter EA 1, sent by Amenhotep III to Kadashman-Enlil, king of Babylonia, though Delattre translated the Babylonian name as Kallima-Sin, just as Budge and Bezold had done.[15] He also continued to use "Burraburiyash" instead of Burna-Buriash, though he did switch to "Tushratta" instead of Dushratta, just as they had.

Jastrow also elaborated on the topics he had treated earlier, in two additional articles. One was entitled "The Letters of Abdiheba," which was published in the journal *Hebraica* in an issue that straddled the end of 1892 and the beginning of 1893. In it he presented his own interpretations of the Jerusalem / Abdi-Heba tablets at greater length, specifically addressing suggestions made by both Zimmern and Halévy in their articles.

The second article was published in the 1893 volume of the *Journal of Biblical Literature* and was entitled "'The Men of Judah' in the El-Amarna Tablets." In this, he debated at length a suggestion that had been previously made about a phrase found in the Amarna tablets that was thought to mention "the men of Judah." Jastrow felt that it was a reference to a group or clan.[16]

Less trustworthy publications also appeared in 1892 and 1893. Conder reappeared once again, like a bad penny, with an article in the *Journal of the Royal Asiatic Society of Great Britain and Ireland* in 1892. Fully a hundred pages long, the article addressed just two of the Amarna Letters. First was a brief consideration of the letter of Tarkhundaradu that Winckler and Sayce had first mentioned in 1888. Conder called him "Tarkondara" and identified him as a "prince of Reseph (not far from Palmyra)" rather than the king of Arzawa.

The greater part of the article continued Conder's discussion of the much longer letter of Tushratta, though he persisted in calling him Dushratta. Conder contended that Winckler had identified both letters in 1888 as having been written in Hittite, rather than Akkadian ("there are two letters in the collection in another language, clearly not Semitic; . . . Dr. Hugo Winckler . . . came to the conclusion in 1888 that they were in the Hittite language"). In fact, Winckler, with Abel, stated more specifically that the Tushratta letter is written "in the language of Mittani."[17]

Conder got some things correct in this article, including the fact that the letter had been sent by Tushratta to Amenhotep III and mentions both his own father, Shuttarna, and his own daughter Tadu-Heba (whom Conder calls Tadukhepa), because those lines were written in Akkadian at the beginning of the letter. It is also clear that Conder was aware of the viewpoints that had appeared in print to that point, including what appears to have been an unpublished manuscript by Sayce, for Conder says at one point: "As far as I am aware, no attempt has yet been made to determine the character of the language, or to translate the contents of Dusratta's Hittite letter. Dr. Sayce kindly sent me a short printed paper, which contains his preliminary remarks on the text, which are very valuable . . . ([but] where published is not stated)."[18]

Conder then continued his discussion as to whether the language is "Aryan or Mongolic." He concluded that it was "of Mongolic speech" and even included a "grammatical treatise and index" at the end of the article. He then attempted a translation that leaves much to be desired, but at the same time is to be admired to some degree, since the letter after the opening lines was written in Hurrian, "the language of Mittani," which had not yet been deciphered. Conder was attempting to join the big leagues of scholars who had successfully translated and discussed a previously unknown written language. In this attempt, however, he failed rather spectacularly.

18

Facts and Alternative Facts

IN 1893, Conder doubled down on his efforts and published an entire volume, *The Tell Amarna Tablets*. To say that it was a mess is to put it mildly, but to give him credit, he did follow the general outline and the details of the history of the period as it was then understood. However, the opening lines from his preface show just how far off course he was in terms of the accuracy of his translations and understanding of the material. He wrote there: "Those tablets under present consideration date about 1480 B.C., and are written to the King of Egypt and to certain of his officials by Amorites, Phænicians, Philistines and others. The names of Japhia, King of Gezer; of Jabin, King of Hazor; and, probably, of Adonizedek, King of Jerusalem—contemporaries of Joshua—occur among those of the writers. The events recorded include the conquest of Damascus by the Hittites, that of Phænicia by the Amorites, and that of Judea by the Hebrews."[1]

Unfortunately for Conder, he was incorrect in virtually every aspect of these declarations. Not only do the tablets date to a century later, ca. 1380–1350 BCE, but the names Japhia, Jabin, and Adonizedek do not occur anywhere and there is no mention at all in the tablets of the conquest of Damascus by the Hittites, of Phoenicia by the Amorites, or of Judea by the Hebrews.

Interestingly, a note dated January 1893 and signed by James Glaisher, Chairman of the Executive Committee of the Palestine Exploration Fund, was placed at the beginning of the volume, on an unnumbered page. It says: "After two years' study of the published texts of the tablets found at Tell Amarna, Major Conder has completed a translation of them, which the Committee of the Fund have undertaken to publish." That would mean Conder was finished with his translations by January 1893 and would further imply that he had been working on them in 1891 and 1892; in fact, he signed and dated the preface as 17 October 1892. If he indeed finished his translations by January 1893, and perhaps as early as October 1892, he would have begun soon after Winckler and Abel's volumes on the Berlin and Cairo tablets appeared in 1889–1890. It would also mean that Bezold and Budge's 1892 volume on the British Museum tablets would have appeared while Conder was nearing completion of his translations, implying that he didn't actually have two full years to study the British Museum tablets. Moreover, his work was written before Bezold's supplement with the transliterations appeared later in 1893, though he did, of course, also have the preliminary attempts at translation by both Budge and Sayce, which had been done four and five years earlier.

To be fair, we have seen that Conder had been publishing articles on the Amarna Letters in scholarly journals since 1889. By 1892, he apparently felt that he had pretty much everything needed to do his translations, assuming that he could read the original cuneiform. By default, we must assume that he could, and, in fact, he says as much in the preface to the volume: "The present translations, from the cuneiform characters, are based on the copies published by Dr. H. Winckler at Berlin, and Dr. C. Bezold of the British Museum, which include the whole of the letters now in Cairo, Berlin and London."[2]

What is unclear, however, is where and how he learned to read cuneiform, for we have no evidence that he had been trained in any type of philology. Was he taught by someone during his time at UCL? Who would that have been? He may have even been self-taught, though that seems a stretch. Far more likely is that he took part in what were essentially adult education classes, described as "semi-formal classes in cuneiform and Egyptian hieroglyphs conducted in London through the Society of Biblical Archaeology (SBA)." These were offered by Sayce and other leading academicians from 1875 onward; we know that William St. Chad Boscawen, another Amarna translator, initially took such classes, and it seems quite possible that Conder did so as well, either while a student at UCL or after his return from his activities overseas.[3]

Conder had learned the Arabic of Ottoman Palestine while he was conducting the survey of Western Galilee. He believed that his knowledge of a modern Semitic language, albeit quite distant in time, function, and culture from the Amarna Letters, allowed him to undertake his translations of the tablets. He said specifically, "I may at least claim that the language in which they are written is the mother-tongue of that Syrian dialect which became known to me by speaking it daily for seven years. In dialectic pronunciation, in idiom, and in the peculiar meaning of many expressions the common speech of the Palestine peasantry is perhaps one of the best possible guides to an understanding of the writings of their Canaanite ancestors."[4] However, he continued, "The language is Aramaic, resembling Assyrian. . . . The language of the letters is very like the Aramaic of the Talmud . . . and is like Arabic in many particulars rather than like Hebrew. It is the same language in an archaic condition which is now spoken by the peasantry of Palestine."[5] Every detail of this is, of course, completely incorrect.

Conder's book was split into six chapters: "Introduction"; "The Hittite Invasion of Damascus"; "The Amorite Treachery"; "The War in Phoenicia"; "Northern Palestine"; and "Southern Palestine." However, it was not written as a general history of the era and the specific regions, as the chapter titles would imply. Instead, each of the chapters, after the introduction, consisted of Conder's translations of specific tablets from the Berlin, British, and Cairo Museums that he deemed relevant to the topic indicated in the title of that chapter. The translations were presented one after the other, with a minimum of commentary and discussion, and only a few footnotes. The choice of tablets in each instance appears to have been made entirely at Conder's discretion and in some cases were only summarily linked to the topic at hand.

In addition, Conder tended to choose the translation that he preferred rather than the one that most scholars accepted. Or he randomly provided his own. Conder's translations in this volume are not to be trusted. For example, concerning the king of Hazor, who was specifically identified by name in one letter, we read the following buried in a footnote: "The king of Hazor's name is unfortunately not quite clear in the text, but seems to be either *Abdebaenu*, or more probably *Iebaenu* (Jabin)." Conder, of course, proceeded to identify the king as Jabin, so that he could link the letters from Hazor to the biblical account. We now know that the king was named Abdi-Tirshi (or Abdi-Shullim), which is not even close to Jabin (see Amarna Letter EA 228). Similarly, the king of Jerusalem, whom Conder acknowledged in a footnote was probably to be rendered Abdi-Heba according to Winckler, was nevertheless presented by Conder in his translations as Adonizedek, again simply because he wished to link the tablets to the biblical account. In these attempts, he was worse even than Sayce.[6]

———

At the same time as Conder's book appeared, a leading Dutch theologian and influential professor of comparative theology named Cornelius Tiele mounted the dais at Leiden University in early February 1893 to deliver a "Rectorial Address" as part of the celebrations surrounding the 318th anniversary of the founding of the university.

Clad in his full academic regalia, he spoke at length on the recent discovery of the Amarna Letters and the light that they shed on the ancient Near East. The transcript of his address was published the next year (1894) as a pamphlet entitled *Western Asia, According to the Most Recent Discoveries*. In just over thirty printed pages, which must have taken the better part of an hour to read aloud to the assembled faculty members and other guests, Tiele presented a dramatic account of the tablets, beginning, "The discovery, to which I would draw your attention, is one of the most important concerning ancient history."[7]

He proceeded to discuss at length the contents of the tablets, almost as if he were able to read the cuneiform and translate the Akkadian himself, though he never claimed to be able to do so. In fact, he said specifically at the beginning of his talk that the tablets were now all published and accessible to all and noted that he had "mentioned the sources from which I have drawn." He continued, "With full recognition of my indebtedness to various learned writers, I now proceed to go my own way."[8] In fact, he did not mention any of his sources nor include any footnotes or bibliography to indicate from where he had derived his information.

Nevertheless, we can probably discern who some of these sources were, for at one point during the presentation, Tiele referred to one of the letter writers as the Babylonian king "Burraburiyash." This is the same spelling for Burna-Buriash II that Budge used in his 1888 article in the *Proceedings of the Society of Biblical Archaeology*, in which he provided his initial transliterations and translations of the tablets that he had purchased for the British Museum, and that he and Bezold continued to use in their final 1892 publication of the tablets.[9]

At another point, Tiele referred to an earlier Babylonian king, Kadashman-Enlil, as "Rish-Kulimma-Sin." This is very similar to Sayce's rendition of the name as "Ris-takullimma-Sin," which he presented in the same journal, the very next year, as part of his efforts at translating the Frénay / Bouriant tablets.[10] However, Tiele either ignored or was not aware of the fact that by this point Budge had changed his translation of the name to Kullimma-Sin (though that was, of course, still incorrect). Similarly, Tiele discussed a man named "Dudu" who was serving as an Egyptian governor in Canaan; again, we find that it is Sayce in his 1888 and 1889 articles who discusses this "Dûdu," who was actually the royal vizier Tutu.[11]

It is obvious that these five-year-old Budge and Sayce articles, which had been superseded by much more sophisticated translations in the interim, constituted at least part of Tiele's sources. In fact, this comes as no surprise, once one realizes that he had been a corresponding member of the Society of Biblical Archaeology since 1878 and could have read the publications of both Sayce and Budge in the *Proceedings* published by that society.[12]

Thus, we seem to have here a clear instance of a scholar who may or may not have been able to read the tablets in their original language(s) but was fully content, and indeed extremely excited, to present the results as published by others—accurate or not—to a general (and captive) audience.

———

Winckler finally published both his transcriptions *and* his translations of the Amarna Letters in the Berlin and British Museums three years later, in 1896. Somewhat surprisingly and without explanation, he did not include those in the Cairo Museum. This new volume was meant to go hand in hand with the earlier volumes that he and Abel had published in 1889–1890 but that had included only the hand copies of each of the tablets, not translations. Winckler made arrangements for this volume to be published simultaneously in German and English editions, so that it could reach a wider audience.[13]

In both versions, Winckler presented a total of 296 tablets in just over 400 pages, plus appendices. In the preface to the volume, he noted that he did not intend to "give the final exposition, but only the beginning of such exposition" for the letters. He said further that he had solved many difficulties, especially when it came to reading the signs on the "crumbled clay" of the tablets, and then transcribing and translating them, but that much more still remained to be done and that a revised edition was already needed. He reminded his readers once again: "Accordingly, let him who discovers where I have fallen into these snares, remember that his surer progress is made possible only by the clearing away of innumerable obstacles, the existence of which can scarcely be at all suspected, now that they are removed."[14]

His book began with a very brief line-by-line summary for each tablet, in a slightly different order than he had done back in 1889, starting with the royal letters sent between the kings of Egypt and Babylonia, followed by those sent from Assyria to Egypt, Mittani to Egypt, and Alashiya (Cyprus) to Egypt, and then continuing with the letters from the Canaanite petty rulers. He then went tablet by tablet, with a complete transcription of the contents on the left-hand page and a translation on the right-hand page, along with some lengthy indices.[15]

His translations were vastly superior to those of Conder; in fact, they remained the best translations in English for several decades. They also brought order to the earlier efforts of both Budge and Sayce, and took into account the contributions by other scholars, especially Zimmern, whom Winckler cited in particular in the opening pages and in footnotes throughout the volume.

One thing that Winckler did not do was to include the letters from Arzawa in his volume, for some reason. He also did not attempt to create a continuous narrative based on the letters—to write a history of the period based on the correspondence. Since there were now translations, transliterations, hand copies, facsimiles, and photographs available of virtually every tablet in the archive, that latter omission left the door wide open for other scholars to attempt their own narratives.

Conder had already tried to do this in 1893, but badly. Petrie's effort, in contrast, was a well-received book published five years later, entitled *Syria and Egypt from the Tell El Amarna Letters*. In addition, an independent German scholar and journalist named Carl Krug, writing under the pen name Carl Niebuhr, published a brief volume of approximately sixty pages entitled *The Tell El Amarna Letters* in 1901. This, however, had a decidedly racist and colonialist aspect to it: "In the beginning of 1888 some fellahin digging for marl not far from the ruins came upon a number of crumbling wooden chests, filled with clay tablets closely covered on both sides with writing. The dusky fellows must have been not a little delighted at finding themselves owners of hundreds of these marketable antiquities, for which a European purchaser would doubtless give plenty of good gold coins."[16]

———

Eventually, Jørgen Knudtzon, the Norwegian Assyriologist and linguist (Fig. 14), decided to pick up where Winckler had left off and created a comprehensive two-volume set, reuniting the groups that had obviously been split up among the various museums, such as the letters from and to Tushratta of Mittani and those relating to Rib-Hadda of Byblos. Written in German, the first volume appeared in 1907, and the second in 1915.[17]

In the opening pages, Knudtzon first attempted to reconstruct the path of acquisition that each group of tablets had followed, from initial discovery until their deposition in each of the various major museums. He then not only presented translations and transcriptions of each of the tablets, but also reordered and renumbered them according to the status of the author / sender and the geographical and then chronological origin for each letter.

FIGURE 14. Jørgen Knudtzon. Illustration by Glynnis Fawkes.

The letters between the Great Kings were given first, followed by those from the lesser Canaanite rulers, thereby essentially following what Winckler had done back in 1889. This system is still observed today, so that each tablet now has an "EA" number, standing for "El Amarna," as identified by Knudtzon, and as mentioned in the introduction.[18]

At almost the same time as Knudtzon's second volume appeared in 1915, another volume devoted to the tablets in Berlin was also published. Written by Otto Schroeder (Fig. 15), an Assyriologist who had studied with both Delitzsch and Winckler in Berlin, the book contained updated hand copies of some of the tablets, just as Winckler had suggested needed to be done. It also contained a few new discoveries that had recently come to light, thereby rendering Knudtzon's volumes instantly out of date. Knudtzon's original volumes contained tablets numbered from 1 to 358, but Schroeder's additions and other subsequent discoveries over the years added 22 additional tablets. There are now a total of 349 actual letters within the Amarna archive and related discoveries.[19]

FIGURE 15. Otto Schroeder. Illustration by Glynnis Fawkes.

Following Knudtzon's magisterial attempt, no new compilations were made for nearly twenty-five years. In 1939, Samuel Mercer published what was essentially an English version of Knudtzon's volumes, but with the new tablets added. It was almost half a century after that before a better version of the full corpus was undertaken by William Moran of Harvard University, after he had published a number of individual articles that appeared in various scholarly journals over the decades from 1948 onward. Moran first published a French version of the complete corpus in 1986, with an English translation following in 1992.[20]

Moran's volumes then reigned supreme until 2015, when a new compilation appeared as a two-volume work by Anson Rainey, who—incidentally—was mentored by Moran. Rainey passed away before finishing his magnum opus, so it was seen to completion posthumously by William Schniedewind and Zippora Cochavi-Rainey. Even more recently, Jacob Lauinger and Tyler Yoder posted their translations of the vassal letters online (open access as of 2022) and are now reportedly working on the letters of the Great Kings.[21]

———

The Amarna Letters in particular offer us an insight regarding the problems involved when translating ancient texts, especially in unknown languages and / or scripts that are in the process of being translated for the first time. For Sayce and Budge, as well as for the Young Berliners who were working on these letters in the years immediately following their discovery, this holds true not only for the means of writing, i.e., cuneiform, but also for the dialect of Akkadian being used, especially in the letters sent by the vassal kings, for neither the Egyptians nor the Canaanite petty kingdoms spoke the same language as standard Assyro-Babylonian.

But the language question is even more subtle than that. Alice Mandell of Johns Hopkins University and others who represent the most recent generations to work on these letters have dubbed the language used in the vassal tablets not just "Amarna Akkadian" but specifically "Canaano-Akkadian," in order to reflect "the Akkadian based scribal code used in the southern Levant in the Late Bronze Age" (as opposed to the Middle Babylonian cuneiform that appears more frequently in the royal letters exchanged between the Great Kings).[22]

As Mandell has noted, the decipherment of the Amarna Letters, and particularly the vassal letters, was challenging not just because Assyriology was a relatively new field, but because these letters defy norms and expectations as a result of the Canaanite influence on the language. "Scholars still debate how to read and classify the letters," she says, "and they argue about the varied orthographies [the conventional spelling system] and the Canaanite influence in the letters."[23]

Another problem for the early translators was that not every tablet in the Amarna archive is written in the same language, though they used a common writing system (cuneiform). The letters in Hurrian and Hittite caused endless problems for the scholars because they were so singular among the hundreds of other letters. What is therefore also striking, as Amanda Podany, emerita professor at California State Polytechnic University, Pomona, has noted, is just how far the early scholars got in understanding these very difficult, and often incredibly broken, documents in such a short period of time.[24]

In any event, as a result of all this work, especially the newest translations, plus studies published by many other scholars in the interim, including by those who work in both Assyriology and Biblical Studies / Northwest Semitic,[25] we are now in a position to understand more fully, and recreate in greater detail, the world of Egypt and the ancient Near East during the Amarna Period.

In the next chapters, we will explore additional examples from the remaining letters sent by the petty rulers in Canaan. Among these are the ones concerned with the aggressive rulers of Amurru in northern Canaan; the dozens of missives sent by Rib-Hadda of Byblos in central Canaan; and the letters concerned with the actions of Abdi-Heba of Jerusalem in southern Canaan, which had so excited Sayce, Lehmann, and the other early translators.

PART VI

Amurru, Byblos, and Jerusalem

19

The Dog of His House

AT ABOUT the same time that the Lab'ayu Affair was taking place in southern Canaan and the conflicts involving Biryawaza were taking place in central Canaan, a similar regional conflict was beginning in northern Canaan. Here, Abdi-Ashirta, the ruler of a region known as Amurru, located just to the south of Ugarit, attempted to expand his holdings and influence across the area. Like Lab'ayu, his actions created a legacy, and his conflicts were continued by his sons after his death.[1]

The entire episode could be summed up in a single sentence or two—"Although he denied it to the Pharaoh, Abdi-Ashirta was caught dead to rights fomenting rebellion in Amurru, aided by the Hittites, according to letters sent to Egypt by Rib-Hadda, the ruler of Byblos. The same could be said of his sons, especially Aziru." However, since the devil, and the joy, is in the details, it is worth taking a look at the actual letters and trying to reconstruct the situation in northern Canaan during the mid-fourteenth century BCE.

We must bear in mind that the letters themselves do not contain any indication of when they were written and so the order of events is a matter of discussion. I present here what seems to me to be the most logical scenario, although it is quite possible that I have some things slightly out of order.

Abdi-Ashirta's first letter to Amenhotep III (EA 60) begins cordially: "Look, I am a servant of the king and a dog of his house. I guard all the land of Amurru for the king, my lord." Abdi-Ashirta then noted all that he had been doing for the pharaoh to protect the region of Amurru, and its capital city Sumur (Tell Kazel), and requested to be officially recognized by the Egyptian pharaoh as its legitimate ruler.[2]

A second letter sent by Abdi-Ashirta (EA 61) is too broken to be able to read much, apart from the opening greetings, which is what alerts us to the fact that it is from him,[3] but a third letter (EA 62) is of interest, for it is not sent to the pharaoh, but rather to Pahanate, the Egyptian commissioner who was based in the city of Sumur. In it, Abdi-Ashirta protested his innocence against charges that he had been acting against Egyptian interests. Instead, he said that he had actually been protecting Egyptian interests, specifically rescuing the city of Sumur from an attack by troops from the city of Shehlalu:

> What are your words, my lord, to me [that you] are speaking? Why do you speak as follows, my lord? "You are an enemy of the land of Egypt. You committed a crime against men of Egypt." My lord should listen! There were not men in Sumur to guard it [in accordance with] his (the Pharaoh's?) command, and Sumur was fearful of the troops of Šehlalu. There were not men in it to guard it, so I myself came to assist from Irqata. . . . If I myself had not (happened) to be present in Irqata—if I had been present in a place where a house is peaceful—then the troops of Šehlalu [indeed] would have burned Sumur and its palace with flames.[4]

However, Abdi-Ashirta was guilty of the charge that he had been acting against Egyptian interests. He had not, in fact, been protecting Egyptian interests; instead, he had been fomenting rebellion and generally creating havoc, aided by the Hittites, who had a vested interest in undermining Egyptian affairs and control in the region.

We know this from a plethora of letters—more than sixty—written by Rib-Hadda, the ruler of Byblos. He wrote to the pharaoh and assorted high-ranking officials more often than any other single ruler, Great King, or vassal prince, during the Amarna Period. Rib-Hadda's letters paint a much different picture of Abdi-Ashirta's activities.[5]

In one of his letters (EA 71), sent to Haya, the vizier of the pharaoh, Rib-Hadda complained that Abdi-Ashirta was on the offensive, supported by the *'apiru* men. "Why are you silent and not speaking to the king so that he can dispatch the regular troops, and they can capture Sumur? Who is Abdi-Ashirta, the slave, the dog, that he is capturing the land of the king for himself? Who is his auxiliary force that he is strong? Because of *'apiru* his auxiliary force is strong. So dispatch fifty pairs of horses and two hundred foot soldiers to me so that I may take a stand in Šigatu before him until the campaigning of the regular troops."[6]

At about the same time, Rib-Hadda also wrote to a highly placed Egyptian official named Amon-appa [Amanappa] (EA 73). Here he explained that Abdi-Ashirta was attempting to start rebellions in Amurru against rival local rulers and was encouraging the local townsmen to join the *'apiru* men.

"To Amon-appa, my father," he began his letter, "the message of Rib-Hadda your son." He then proceeded to ask Amon-appa the same question that he had asked Haya: "Why are you silent and not speaking to the king, your lord, so that you will campaign together with the regular troops and attack the land of Amurru?" He also asked Amon-appa for support against Abdi-Ashirta: "So speak to the king, your lord, so that auxiliary troops may be dispatched to me as quickly as possible."[7]

Having apparently gotten nowhere with these two officials, Rib-Hadda then wrote directly to the pharaoh. "All of my cities that are in the mountains or on the coastline have allied with the *'apiru* troops," Rib-Hadda told the Egyptian king. "[Only] Byblos together with two cities remains to me. Look now, Abdi-Ashirta has captured Šigatu for himself and . . . has sent a message to the troops in the temple of NINURTA: 'Gather so that we may attack Byblos! Now see, there is not a man who can rescue it from our control.'"

According to Rib-Hadda (EA 74), Abdi-Ashirta had exhorted local citizens to rise up in rebellion against Egypt: "We should drive the city rulers out of the lands," he told them, "so that all of the lands will ally with the *'apiru*, and an alliance should be made for all of the lands so that sons and daughters will be at peace for everlasting days. And if, moreover, the king campaigns, then all the lands will be hostile to him, and what will he do to us?"

Rib-Hadda noted that Abdi-Ashirta and his allies "have established an oath among themselves, and, consequently, I am very fearful, since there is not a man who can rescue me from their control. Like birds that are placed inside a bird-snare, so am I in Byblos." He informed the pharaoh that he had sent earlier messages to the palace, probably meaning to Haya, the vizier, as well as to Amon-appa, and said that the pharaoh should ask Amon-appa about the situation. "Now, Amon-appa is with you. Ask him! He himself knows, and he has seen the dire straits that I am in. The king should hear the words of his servant and give the provisions to his servant and keep his servant alive so that I may guard his loyal city, together with our Lady (and) our gods, for you. The king should pay attention to his land and his servant and show concern for his land."[8]

In another letter (EA 75), Rib-Hadda made it clear that things were getting worse, for the local citizens of the various cities were now rising up in rebellion and killing their rulers. "The king should listen to the words of his servant . . . all of the lands of the king, my lord, have abandoned me. As for 'Aduna, the ruler of Irqata, *'apiru* troops killed him, and there was no one who said anything to Abdi-Ashirta. They captured Miya, the ruler of Arašni; the city of

Ardatu has been seized. And, look now, the men of Ammiya killed its lord, so I, myself, am fearful."

Rib-Hadda warned that Abdi-Ashirta had the backing of the Hittites, who were now also threatening Mittani. "The king, my lord, should be informed that the king of Hatti has seized all of the lands of . . . the king of the land of Mittani, the land of great kings. Abdi-Ashirta, the slave, the dog, is capturing the king's lands, so dispatch regular troops. Hostility towards me is severe."[9]

In another letter (EA 76), probably sent almost immediately after, Rib-Hadda recapped the ongoing events with Abdi-Ashirta and asked again for horses and troops to be sent:

> The king, my lord, should know that the hostility of Abdi-Ashirta towards me is severe. Now, he desires to capture for himself the two cities that remain to me. . . . Who is he, Abdi-Ashirta, the dog, that he desires to capture all the cities of the king, the Sun god, for himself? Is he the king of the land of Mittani or the king of the land of Kassites that he desires to capture the land of the king for himself? Here now, he gathered all the 'apiru together against Šigatu and Ambi. If he captures these two cities, then he will become strong. There is nowhere people can take refuge. He seized the mountain for himself. So dispatch to me 400 guardsmen and 30 pairs of horses as quickly as possible.[10]

He then complained about the lack of Egyptian response to his letters:

> Now, I sent a message to the palace in this fashion, but you do not send back (any) word to me. All the lands of the king are not like before. For years, the regular troops were campaigning in order to inspect the lands. But, look now, a land of the king and Sumur, your garrison city, have allied with the 'apiru, and you are silent. Dispatch abundant regular troops so that they can drive the enemies of the king out of his land. Then all of the lands will be allied with the king. . . . You are a great lord. You should not at all keep silent about this report.[11]

Rib-Hadda repeated nearly all the above in a subsequent letter (EA 79), though he added that Amon-appa had finally appeared with some Egyptian troops—most likely the horses and infantry Rib-Hadda had been requesting. However, as a result, "since Amon-appa reached me, all the 'apiru have turned against me on account of the command of Abdi-Ashirta!" He repeated his plea: "So my lord should hear the words of his servant and dispatch guardsmen to me in order to guard the king's city until the campaigning of the regular troops. If there are not regular troops, then all the lands will ally with the ʿapiru. Listen! Since seizing Bit-arha on account of the command of Abdi-Ashirta, in this manner they desire to conquer Byblos and Baṭruna, so that all of the lands will be allied with the ʿapiru."

He concluded by repeating that only two cities remained to him and that he was in his city of Byblos "like a bird which is placed within a bird-snare." He also warned: "If the king is unable to take me away from the power of his enemies, then all of the lands will be allied with Abdi-Ashirta. Who is he, the dog, that he is capturing the king's lands for himself?"[12]

Matters worsened in Rib-Hadda's next letter (EA 81). Abdi-Ashirta and his men, including the ʿapiru, continued to press their advantage and to foment rebellion. "May the king, my lord, be apprised that the hostility of Abdi-Ashirta is severe and he has taken all of my towns for himself," said Rib-Hadda again. "[Only] the city of Byblos and the city of Baṭruna remain to me and [now] he is seeking to take the two cities."

Moreover, Abdi-Ashirta was actively encouraging political assassinations. Rib-Hadda himself had been targeted, he said in the same letter. "A man took a stand against me with a bronze dagger, but I killed him. . . . This deed was done to me by his [i.e., Abdi-Ashirta's] command. Now, as a result, I stayed, and I was silent within my city. I was unable to go out to the open country, so I sent a message to the palace, but commands were not returning to me. I was beaten nine times, consequently, I was fearful for my life."

Once again, Rib-Hadda begged for Egyptian troops. "If within two months regular troops do not campaign, then Abdi-Ashirta will come up and capture the two cities (Byblos and Baṭruna). . . . What can I do on my own?"[13]

In a letter (EA 82) sent at the same time from Rib-Hadda to Amon-appa, the Egyptian official, he repeated the same information. However, he now clarified that by saying he was beaten nine times, he meant that he had been stabbed that many times: "He [i.e., Abdi-Ashirta] commanded a man, so that he [i.e., the man] took a stand against me with a bronze dagger, and I was struck nine times. . . . If in two month(s) there are not regular troops, then I must abandon the city and go away so that I stay alive in order to do what I want."[14]

Rib-Hadda grew increasingly frustrated with his precarious situation and eventually threatened to align himself with Abdi-Ashirta, as others had already done, including his neighbor Zimri-Haddu of Sidon. He wrote directly to the pharaoh again (EA 83), saying: "Listen to me, why are you silent, so that your land is taken away? It should not be said in the days of the commissioners:

'The *'apiru* captured all of the lands.' Not so. It will be said in the days (of the commissioners): 'They were not able to capture it.'"

He continued:

I sent a message for guardsmen and for horses, but they are not given. Send back word to me, or I, myself, will make an alliance with Abdi-Ashirta like Yapa'-Ba'lu / Haddu and Zimri-Haddu, so that I may live. . . . Since, moreover, Sumur and Bit-arha have now gone away, you should give me into Yanhamu's control so that he may give grain for me to eat and I may guard the king's city for him. . . . If you do not send word back to me, then I will abandon the city, and I will go away, together with the men who are loyal to me.[15]

It is unclear whether the subsequent events took place over days, weeks, or months. In one letter (EA 84), Rib-Hadda denied the rumor that his city of Byblos has been captured but said that most of the officials had fled. "Inasmuch as men are saying about me in the presence of my lord: 'Byblos has been seized, its ruler is distraught,' my lord should know, they did not capture Byblos, but all the *qiptu*-officials went away, so it is very difficult for the lands of my lord. . . . The king, my lord, should dispatch his commissioner, who is strong, together with troops, and he should guard the city of my lord so that I, myself, may go away and serve my lord, the Sun god of the lands."[16]

In another letter (EA 85), Rib-Hadda said that he had been attacked by Abdi-Ashirta and requested that both grain and troops be sent to him:

Now, he [i.e., Abdi-Ashirta] took a stand against me three times in this year, and I am being robbed of my grain for two years. There is no grain for us to eat. What will I say to the men of my *hupšu*-citizens? Their sons, their daughters, (and) the wood of their house are used up in consequence of paying (them) into the land of Yarimmuta in exchange for obtaining provisions for our life. . . . The king, my lord, should hear the words of his loyal servant so that he may dispatch grain within ships and furnish provisions for his servant and his city. He should give 400 men (and) 30 pairs of horses, as was given to Surata, so that they may guard the city for you.[17]

Rib-Hadda sent additional letters, including several to the pharaoh and one to Amon-appa. In one letter to the pharaoh (EA 88), he noted that some towns had gone over to the side of Abdi-Ashirta and that others were threatened. Furthermore, the enemy troops were now at the city gate of Byblos. "The king, my lord, should listen to the words of his servant [i.e., Rib-Hadda]. He should make chariots and troops hasten here as quickly as possible so that they may guard the city of my lord and his servant until the arrival of the king, my lord. As for me, I have not abandoned my lord's command, but if the king, my lord, does not listen to the words of his servant, then Byblos will ally with him [i.e., Abdi-Ashirta], and all of the king's lands, as far as the land of Egypt, will ally with the *'apiru*."[18]

His letter to Amon-appa (EA 87) reiterated that various cities had been taken and Byblos itself was under attack "He [i.e., Abdi-Ashirta] heard that there were no troops with him, so Baṭruna allied with him. He put *'apiru* troops and chariots inside (it), and they have not departed from the entrance of Byblos's city gate."[19]

Rib-Hadda updated the pharaoh in his next letter (EA 90). "Know that the hostility towards me is severe! He [i.e., Abdi-Ashirta] has captured all of my cities; Byblos on its own remains to me." He also reported that Abdi-Ashirta had traveled to Mittani, for unknown reasons, and requested that reinforcements be sent:

> Now, that dog is in the land of Mittani, and his intention is regarding Byblos. But what can I, myself do on my own? You were silent concerning your cities when the *'apiru*, the dog(s) captured them, but I turned to you. . . . Like a bird that is placed within a bird snare, so am I in Byblos. . . . The king, my lord should hear his loyal servant and dispatch [n]+100 troops and 30 pairs of horse(s) so that I may protect the city for you. As for your messengers, dispatch them here. And as for my request, if you do not dispatch guardsmen and do not furnish provisions for the city, then I am fearful for my life.[20]

Rib-Hadda complained in a follow-up letter (EA 92) that although the pharaoh had written to the rulers of Beirut, Sidon, and Tyre and asked them to send auxiliary troops to help Rib-Hadda, they had not done so. "The action of the king, my lord, was good when the king sent a message to the king of Beirut and to the king of Sidon and to the king of Tyre: 'Look, Rib-Addi will send a message to you for auxiliary troops, so go, all of you!' This was good in my opinion, so I sent my messenger, but they did not go, and they did not send their messenger to send greetings to us." Moreover, as Rib-Hadda wrote, Abdi-Ashirta had heard that the pharaoh had not sent any assistance himself and so "he [i.e., Abdi-Ashirta] is now rising up against me."[21]

Rib-Hadda wrote continuously (EA 93–95, 121, 127), reiterating that he had no garrison troops with him and asking for reinforcements and troops to be sent, including requesting foreign warriors, from Meluhha and Cush, probably Nubia and East Africa. He sent his pleas out widely, to Amon-appa, to the pharaoh, and to a "senior Egyptian official," but all apparently to no avail.[22]

Rib-Hadda also had additional related "Abdi-Ashirta problems" closer to home. He had previously made a marriage alliance with the ruler of nearby Tyre, as he noted at the outset of one letter (EA 89), and had sent his sister and nieces to live there, where he thought they would be safe from Abdi-Ashirta. However, now the people of Tyre had risen up and killed their ruler, along with Rib-Hadda's sister and her children, just as he himself had been previously attacked.

He stated plainly: "As for me, I made a marriage alliance with Tyre; they were friendly with me. Look, they killed their city ruler together with my sister and her sons (and) daughters. I dispatched my sister's daughters to Tyre, away from Abdi-Ashirta, and they killed him [i.e., the ruler of Tyre] together with his sons (and) daughters." He then beseeched the pharaoh to investigate the death of the ruler of Tyre, which he believed was related to the activities of Abdi-Ashirta.[23]

Rib-Hadda does not mention the name of the ruler of Tyre who was killed. It is possible that it was Abi-Milku, whom we have seen mentioned in related letters, but this seems unlikely since we have additional letters written by Abi-Milku during the time of Abdi-Ashirta's son Aziru, as we will see below, so we are left wondering who it might have been.

Finally, Rib-Hadda's pleas, and Abdi-Ashirta's further actions, persuaded the Egyptians to act. A letter (EA 97) from Yapah-Hadda, the ruler of Beirut, to a fellow ruler named Shum-Hadda (apparently being detained in Egypt at the time) said plainly that Abdi-Ashirta had caused the loss of the lands of the king.[24] Finally admitting that the situation was getting out of control, Amenhotep III sent troops to the region under the leadership of Haya, an Egyptian vizier and commander.

We know that Abdi-Ashirta was killed, from one letter (EA 101) which was most likely sent by Rib-Hadda to the Egyptian pharaoh. In it, he said: "Because the ships of the men of the [Egyptian] army were not entering the land of Amurru, they [i.e., the land of Amurru] killed Abdi-Ashirta. . . . They [i.e., the land of Amurru] killed Abdi-Ashirta."[25]

Some scholars have suggested that Abdi-Ashirta was assassinated at the order of the Egyptian pharaoh, but the most recent translation of these lines would seem to indicate that it was more likely a local uprising during which he lost his life. Regardless, Abdi-Ashirta's son Aziru soon took over rulership of Amurru and continued the policies of his father, as we shall see in the next chapter.

20

Triple-A Roster

THE DEATH of Abdi-Ashirta did not change the politics of the region, for his son Aziru's friendship with Egypt ebbed until he completely embraced Hittite overlordship, turning against the Egyptians and their local vassal rulers.[1] Or at least, that is the story to be told if we can believe the gossip, scuttlebutt, and complaints in the letters sent by others, such as Akizzi, the ruler of the city of Qatna in what is now modern Syria.

As was the case for Abdi-Ashirta, we wouldn't know any of this if we had only the letters of Aziru that he sent to Egypt, of which there were more than a dozen. Their contents are at complete odds with the story presented in letters by other rulers.

In all of his letters, Aziru protested his innocence and described his fear of the Hittites, who were supposedly encroaching on nearby territory. We have mentioned two of these letters in previous chapters, for Sayce attempted to translate the tablets that are now known as Amarna Letters EA 157 and 158. He thought that the former mentioned Pharaoh Necho, which it does not, and that the latter mentioned someone named Dûdu, whom Sayce connected to the biblical King David, though we now know it is a reference to an Egyptian vizier named Tutu.[2]

Now in control of Amurru after the death of his father, Aziru claimed in one letter (EA 157) that he had been wanting to fulfill the pharaoh's desires, but that "the senior officials of Sumur [his capital city] were not permitting me." Somewhat out of the blue, he added: "I did not commit a crime—nothing against the king, my lord." He then hinted that the king of the Hittites might soon be coming against him and requested, if that transpired, the pharaoh should send troops to defend him: "If the king of the land of Hatti . . . comes against me for hostility, the king, my lord, should give me the regular troops and the chariotry for my help so that I may guard the land of the king, my lord."[3]

In a subsequent letter (EA 171), Aziru said again that he wanted to serve the king, but Yanhamu (the Egyptian commissioner, whom we have met previously) would not permit him to do so. He had tried to send messengers directly to the king, "but Yanhamu detained them on the journey, and they have not departed."[4]

Aziru also wrote to Tutu, the Egyptian chief minister, invoking the formal father-son relationship of an inferior (Aziru) writing to a superior (Tutu), as if Tutu were actually the pharaoh (EA 158). "To Tutu, my lord, my father, a message from 'Aziru, your son, your servant. I fall at the feet of my lord. May it be well for my father." His request was that Tutu not allow lies to be told about Aziru in the Egyptian court. "Look," he said, "you are present before the king, my lord. May it not be that dishonest men can speak a bad word about me before the king, my lord. You should not permit them. . . . You should not permit bad words about me."

He concluded by saying: "I am a servant of the king, my lord, and I do not ever deviate from the commands of the king, my lord, or from the commands of Tutu, my father. If the king does not love me, but (instead) hates me, as for me, what can I say?"[5] We are not told what "bad words" might have been being told to the pharaoh about Aziru. We suspect that there may have been some truth to them based on other correspondence.

––––––––

Several additional Amarna Letters from Aziru concerned rebuilding his capital city of Sumur. Although it is never explained what happened to it, such that it needed to be rebuilt, initially Aziru said in one letter (EA 161) that "the kings of the land of Nuhašše [a small city-state located to the north of Qatna] were hostile with me, and they captured my cities . . . so I have not [yet] rebuilt it. I will now rebuild it at once."[6]

Letters written by the other Canaanite rulers help fill out the picture, including some written by Rib-Hadda of Byblos, Abi-Milku of Tyre, Addu-nirari of Nuhašše, and particularly Akizzi of Qatna. These mention not only Aziru but at least two other sons of Abdi-Ashirta, as well as Aitukama, the ruler of Qadesh, who were all interwoven in these activities.

We have a single letter in the archive sent by Addu-nirari of Nuhašše (EA 51). He reported pressure being exerted by the Hittites. We know from other sources that this was during the reign of Hittite king Suppiluliuma I,[7] who would eventually conquer this area, although the Hittite king is not mentioned by name. Addu-nirari is at pains to express his loyalty to the Egyptian pharaoh, as had been the case in his family for generations, back to the time of Thutmose III in Egypt and Addu-nirari's grandfather Tagu. He wrote as follows:

> Thutmose (III), the king of the land of Egypt, your father's father, invested Tagu, my father's father, with kingship in the land of Nuhašše and placed oil upon his head. . . . Now, our lord, as for the tablets and treaties that the king of the land of Hatti sent to me, my lord, I rejected the tablets and treaties. I am a loyal servant of the king of the land of Egypt. . . . Now, our lord should campaign to us, so that we may return the lands to his control, and we may [. . .] to our lord. Our lord should make an appearance here (this) year; do not be neglectful! Indeed, they are loyal to my lord; you will see them. But if my lord does not consent to campaign (in person), my lord should send one of his counselors together with his troops and together with his chariots.[8]

More detailed information comes from Akizzi, the ruler of Qatna. There are six letters from him in the Amarna archive, all sent to Akhenaten.

In the badly broken first letter (EA 52), Akizzi reported an attack of some sort and something being stolen, perhaps by the Hittites. He also mentions Biryawaza of Damascus by name: "I came here. [. . .] of my lord [. . . the king of the land of Ha]tti [. . .] stole them . . . (It was) three year(s) [a]go, my lord, that I was trying to depart to my lord, but I did not know of messengers or a caravan, my lord. . . . [Ma]y I not go away [from] my lord [or] from Biryawaza!"[9]

The second very detailed letter from Akizzi (EA 53) discusses Aitukama, the prince of Qadesh, who allied with Suppiluliuma I and the Hittites rather than with the Egyptian pharaoh:[10]

> (Speak) to Akhenaten, the son of the Sun god, my lord, a message from Akizzi, your servant. . . . I, myself, am now your very servant, the one who belongs to my lord, but the king of the land of Hatti is now causing Aitukama to campaign against me, and he [i.e., Aitukama] has been desiring my head. But now Aitukama has sent a message to me and said: "Come with me to the king of the land of Hatti!" I said: "How can I go to the king of the land of Hatti? I belong to my lord, king of the land of Egypt."

Akizzi also reported that Aitukama had attacked an area known as Apu, located in the region of Damascus, and had even plundered Biryawaza's palace in Damascus itself. "My lord, Aitukama came, and he seized the land of Apu, lands of my lord. And he captured the house of Biryawaza. He captured 200 ingots of . . . he captured 300 ingots of . . . and he captured 100 ingots of . . . everything from the house of Biryawaza." He also reported that Aitukama was being helped by several other rebellious leaders and that together they were "burning the land of Apu, lands of my lord, with flames."

Even though the Egyptians had allies in the area, including "the king of the land of Nuhašše, the king of the land of Niya, the king of the land of Zinzar, and the king of the land of Tunanab," Akizzi described the situation as dire and beseeched the king to send assistance. "My lord, if this land is a concern for my lord, my lord should dispatch the regular army so that it comes here. (Only) my lord's messengers have arrived here."[11]

Akizzi sent another similar letter to the pharaoh (EA 54), but it is very fragmentary. It mentions the same people, specifically Aitukama, ruler of the city of Qadesh, Tiwate of Labana, Arzawya of Ruhizu, and "the king of the land of Hatti" (i.e., Suppiluliuma I), all of whom were planning to seize Akizzi's land (or so he said).[12] Yet another fragmentary letter from Akizzi (EA 56) mentions Aitukama and the others again and says that "they repeatedly attack me."[13]

Another letter from Akizzi (EA 55) describes a different threat, for Aziru of Amurru was also causing problems. Akizzi begged once more for assistance from Akhenaten, writing:

> My lord, all of the lands are afraid before your troops and before your chariots. If my lord would seize these lands for his own land, in this year my lord should dispatch his troops and chariots. It (the army) should come here so that all of the land of Nuhašše will belong to my lord. If, my lord, the troops campaign and stay for (only) six days, they will certainly capture Aziru away from the land of Amurru. But if in this year my lord's troops and chariots do not campaign and do not arrive here, the land will be afraid before Aziru.

The same letter reports that both Aziru and the king of the Hittites had attacked his cities, taken away some of the inhabitants of Qatna for ransom, and stolen venerable statues sent by previous pharaohs:

> My lord, the men of Qatna are my servants. . . . Aziru . . . has captured them and assigned them to work outside of the land of my lord, so now they are situated outside of the land of my lord. May my lord desire to show concern. My lord should dispatch the ransom for the men of Qatna so that he may set them free. . . . My lord, your forefathers fashioned (a statue of) the Sun god, the god of my father, and they became renowned because of it.

Now, as for the Sun god, the god of my father, the king of the land of Hatti captured it.[14]

———

At some point Pharaoh Akhenaten seems to have gotten fed up. He sent out a letter to many, if not all, of the vassal rulers, telling them to be ready to commit troops for the campaign that he was about to commence in the region. There are a tremendous number of replies to this letter in the Amarna archives—approximately seventy—from a variety of rulers across the entire area.[15]

One of these (EA 141) was sent by Ammunira, the ruler of Beirut, who reported that he was "prepared, together with my horses and together with my chariots and together with all of my possessions that are with the servant of the king, my lord, for the arrival of the regular troops of the king, my lord." He added, for emphasis, "May the regular troops of the king, my lord, my Sun god, my god, flood the head of his enemies, and may the two eyes of your servant look upon the life of the king, my lord."[16]

Another (EA 147) was sent by Abi-Milku of Tyre, who wrote, "Now, I am guarding Tyre, the foremost city, for the king, my lord, until the strong right arm of the king comes forth over me in order to give water for me to drink and wood for me to keep warm." He then added, almost as an afterthought, "Something else: Zimri-Haddu, the king of Sidon, sent messages day after day to the criminal, Aziru, son of Abdi-Ashirta, regarding every command that he had obeyed from the land of Egypt. Herewith I have sent a message to my lord, and it is good that he knows."[17]

Thanks to this reporting by Abi-Milku, we know that Zimri-Haddu of Sidon was working in league with Aziru and passing on all relevant news of the upcoming campaign to him. This should not be a surprise, given that we already knew that Zimri-Haddu had previously been working with Abdi-Ashirta, Aziru's father.

Abi-Milku stated from the outset (EA 146) that he was having problems with Zimri-Haddu: "There is much hostility towards me! Now look, (it is) the ruler of Sidon, Zimri-Haddu. Daily he does not allow me to draw water. I cry out: '(He is) a criminal against the king!'"[18] We might remember that this is the letter that Sayce had mangled in his 1888 *PSBA* publication when he thought that it was one of the letters that mentioned Pharaoh Necho (which it does not).

Abi-Milku reported in a later letter (EA 149) that things were not going well for him or for the region. He blamed this on both Aziru and Zimri-Haddu of

Sidon: "Listen, my lord, Aziru, the son of Abdi-Ashirta, the criminal against the king, has captured Sumur. Ḫaʿip brought up the traitors, my enemies; he has given Sumur to Aziru. . . . Zimri-Haddu captured Usu from his servant; I have abandoned it, so there is no water, there is no wood for us, and there is nowhere (that) we can put the dead." He continued:

> The king, my lord, sent a message to me by tablet: "Send a message to the king about whatever you hear!" Zimri-Haddu of Sidon and Aziru, the criminal against the king and the men of Arwada repeatedly swore an oath among themselves, and they have gathered their ships, their chariots, (and) their foot soldiers in order to seize Tyre, the maidservant of the king. . . . As for Tyre, they are unable to seize (it), but they have seized Sumur at the command of Zimri-Haddu, who sends the king's word to Aziru. So I sent a tablet to the king, my lord, but he has not sent back word to me, his servant. . . . There has been hostility towards me [s]ince last year! There is no water, there is no wood.[19]

In another letter (EA 154), Abi-Milku reported that Zimri-Haddu was preventing him and his men from gathering either wood or water and that they were also charging him an exorbitant tax. "Since the troops of the king, my lord, went away from me, the ruler of Sidon does not allow me (or) my men to go ashore onto land in order to acquire wood (or) to acquire water for drinking. He killed one man and captured another. Zimri-Haddu, ruler of Sidon, and the criminal, Aziru, have (also) captured 80 (shekels) as interest for my men."[20]

Elsewhere (EA 148), Abi-Milku complained again about Zimri-Haddu's hostility. He also notified the pharaoh that the ruler of Hazor, whose name he doesn't give, "abandoned his house and stationed himself with the ʿapiru. The king should know about other treacherous foot soldier(s). He conquered the king's land for the ʿapiru."[21]

In some of these letters, Abi-Milku also claimed that he would like to come plead before the king in person, but that Zimri-Haddu was preventing his ship from sailing. In one letter (EA 151), he said specifically: "My intention is to go in order to see the face of the king, my lord, but I am unable because of the power of Zimri-Haddu of Sidon. He heard about me that I was entering (Egypt), so he waged war against me. The king, my lord, should give 20 men to me in order to guard the city of the king, my lord, so that I may enter into the presence of the king, my lord, in order to see his pleasing face."[22] It is interesting that he felt it would only take twenty men, a very small number, to help guard the city.

In this same letter, in response to an earlier request from the pharaoh for information, Abi-Milku also reported on events that were taking place further afield, including up in northern Canaan and even beyond. We have mentioned this letter previously, but it is worth quoting from it again. "The king, my lord, sent a message to us: 'As for that which you hear from the land of Canaan, send a message to me!'" Abi-Milku therefore relayed the news that "the king of the land of Danuna is dead, his brother [rules] after him, and his land is peaceful." Furthermore, "Fire consumed the house of the king of Ugarit; it consumed half of it, so half of it is not there (any more). There are no troops from the land of Hatti present." He added that Aitukama, the prince of Qadesh, and Aziru were now fighting Biryawaza: "Aitukama is the magnate of Qadesh. Aziru is at war; the war is against Biryawaza."

This, and similar letters, confirms that Aziru, Aitukama, Abi-Milku, Akizzi, and Biryawaza were all ruling contemporaneously in their various cities and territories. The very next sentence of this letter verifies that we can add Zimri-Haddu of Sidon to this list: "I experienced acts of violence from Zimri-Haddu when he gathered ships (and) troops from Aziru's cities against me."

Zimri-Haddu himself also sent two letters found in the Amarna archive. One (EA 145) was addressed to the Egyptian commissioner Pahanate and complained that "the king, our lord, has neglected his lands and the breath of his mouth does not reach his servants whom he has in the lands of the Canaan-ite open country."[23] The second, subsequent letter (EA 144) stated how happy Zimri-Haddu was that the pharaoh was sending regular troops in the near future. Like Rib-Hadda, he reported that "The king, my lord, should know that the hostility towards me is very severe. All of the cities that the king gave in to my control have allied with the *'apiru.*"[24]

It is not hard to conclude that life in these small petty kingdoms was never peaceful for long. Many of the Canaanite rulers seem to have spent their days in contention with one another, rather than living together in harmony. It is likely that the letters from both Abi-Milku of Tyre and Zimri-Haddu of Sidon were from the earlier part of these conflicts, before the end came for Rib-Hadda, while at least one if not two of the letters from Ammunira of Beirut comes from near the end of Rib-Hadda's tale, as we shall see next.

21

Gaslighting the Pharaoh

IF WE return to his sad story, the hostility against Rib-Hadda of the coastal city of Byblos continued to grow, as did his problems with Aziru, at least from his point of view. In one letter (EA 91), Rib-Hadda writes to the pharaoh: "I sent a message to you: 'Why do you stay there, and you are silent, while the *'apiru*, the dog, captures your cities?'" He then began to enumerate his woes, city by city: "When he [i.e., Aziru] captured Sumur, I sent a message to you: 'Why are you silent?' And then Bit-arha was captured. When he saw that there was no one who said anything to him about Sumur, he gained courage, so that (now) he desires to capture Byblos. It [i.e., Byblos] has fallen down upon me."

He offered further details: "My orchards and my [field]s have been cut down. As for my grain, I have been robbed. So would you not pay 1,000 (shekels) of silver or 100 (shekels) of gold so that he [i.e., Aziru] would go away from me? He has captured all of my cities. Byblos on its own remains to me, and he desires to capture it. . . . What can I, myself, do on my own? Now, as a result, I send messages for regular troops or auxiliary troops, but my words are not heard."[1]

In several other letters to the pharaoh, Rib-Hadda listed the cities and areas that had fallen to Aziru and other sons of Abdi-Ashirta (including a son named Pu-Ba'lu, whom we haven't met before). It seems that they had conquered the land of Amurru, their home territory, and had killed Pawura, one of the Egyptian commissioners.[2] Eventually Aziru and his brothers reached Damascus (EA 107), forcing Rib-Hadda to beseech the pharaoh to send the regular army "so that it may capture him [i.e., Aziru] and the land of the king may be at peace!"[3]

This is confirmed by Yapah-Hadda of Beirut. In one letter (EA 98), sent to the Egyptian commissioner Yanhamu, Yapah-Hadda related that all the lands were hostile, from Byblos to Ugarit, and that they were now following Aziru. He then asked specifically, as many others had, why there was no action on the part of the pharaoh.[4]

It is unclear whether Yapah-Hadda was gaslighting the pharaoh or if this letter was from earlier in the conflict, for in yet another letter (EA 116), Rib-Hadda said that this very same man, Yapah-Hadda of Beirut, had joined forces with Aziru and was actively opposing him (i.e., Rib-Hadda). "Aziru and Yapah-Haddu have conspired against me," he wrote, "and I am unable to do anything. Their actions are hostile to me."[5]

In subsequent letters, Rib-Hadda noted that more and more of his neighbors were allied with Aziru. In one (EA 114), he wrote: "The ships of the men of Tyre, Beirut, and Sidon are in Wahliya. As for everyone in the land of Amurru, they are peaceful. Only I, myself, am at war. Look now, Yapah-Haddu is now, with Aziru, hostile to me. You see, he seized my ship. You see, in this manner he is moving out into the sea in order to seize (more of) my ships."[6]

Moreover, he said in another letter (EA 130) that the citizens of the various towns and cities were now actively killing their own rulers: "Now, as for the city rulers, their cities are killing them like dog(s), and there is no one who will investigate them."[7] This must have felt like déjà vu to Rib-Hadda, for he had written much the same during the time of Abdi-Ashirta.

Things continued to get worse. Although the names are broken off in one letter (EA 67), so we don't know either the sender or the recipient, mention is made specifically of Aziru and the fact that "he has taken an oath with the ruler of Byblos."[8] Since it is unlikely that Rib-Hadda had suddenly changed his mind and signed a treaty with Aziru, Moran thinks that this is most likely a reference to Rib-Hadda's brother, for we know from other texts that this brother, probably named Ilu-rapi, did take over Byblos at some point, eventually allying himself with Aziru, while Rib-Hadda was sent into exile, first to Beirut and then elsewhere.

———

In fact, we know from subsequent letters, sent by Rib-Hadda from Beirut rather than Byblos, how this exile came about. It seems that Rib-Hadda had gone to Beirut to make an alliance with the new king there, Ammunira, whom we have met previously and who appears to have suddenly succeeded Yapah-Hadda. As Rib-Hadda wrote in one letter (EA 136): "The men of Byblos and my household and my wife were saying to me: 'Follow the son of Abdi-Ashirta so that we may make peace between us!' But I, myself, refused. I did not listen to them." He continued, "So, I went to his house [i.e., Ammunira's] because I made an alliance between us." However, upon returning home, Rib-Hadda found that his own brother had staged a coup in his absence and "had shut me out of the house. . . . Now, day and night I await the regular troops of the king, my lord, so the king, my lord, should show concern for his servant." And, to add to his misery, and perhaps in his absence, he says also: "They handed over my two son(s) and (their) two wives to the criminal against the king [i.e., to Aziru]."[9]

In another letter (EA 137), Rib-Hadda expanded on what had happened. "I, myself, went to 'Ammu-nira, and my young brother made Byblos hostile to me in order to give the city to the sons of Abdi-Ashirta. When my brother saw that my messenger came forth empty-handed, (since) there were no guardsmen with him, he despised me. Consequently, he committed a crime and drove me from the city. The king, my lord, should not keep silent concerning the deeds of this dog."

He spent much of the letter asking the pharaoh to find him a new place to settle down. He was unable to travel to Egypt to beseech the pharaoh in person, he said, for he was old "and a severe illness is in my own flesh." Instead, he was sending his son in his place: "Now, I dispatched my son, a servant of the king, my lord, to the king, my lord, so the king should heed the words of his servant."

He asked again for the pharaoh to send "regular" troops, "so that they may seize Byblos and treacherous troops and the sons of Abdi-Ashirta may not enter inside it." He claimed that the Egyptian troops would find ready support within the city, writing: "Look, the men who are loyal to me inside the city are many; traitors inside it are few. If the regular troops campaign, they will hear (about them) on the day of their arrival, and the city will be restored to the king, my lord." As he explained, "My lord should know that I will die on his behalf. When I was in the city, I guarded it for my lord, and my heart was proper regarding the king, my lord; it did not give the city to the sons of Abdi-Ashirta. Consequently, my brother made the city hostile in order to give it to the sons of Abdi-Ashirta."[10]

A letter (EA 142) sent by Ammunira, the ruler of Beirut, confirms Rib-Hadda's story. "Now, I am very much on my guard," said Ammunira, "and I am guarding the city of Beirut for the king, my lord, until the arrival of the regular army of the king, my lord. . . . Concerning the ruler of Byblos, who is with me now, I will guard him until the king gives advice about his servant. (And) something else: The king, my lord, should be informed of the deed of his [i.e., Rib-Hadda's] brother, who is in Byblos, that he handed over the sons of Rib-Hadda, who were with him, to criminals against the king who are in the land of Amurru." Ammunira's letter confirms what we know about Rib-Hadda's fortunes: he had taken refuge with Ammunira in Beirut; his brother Ilu-rapi had taken over Byblos; and Rib-Hadda's sons had been taken hostage to Aziru and the other rebels in Amurru.[11]

Another long letter from Rib-Hadda (EA 138), sent from Beirut a year later, confirmed that the situation had not changed: "Have I not dwelled in Beirut for twelve month(s)?" He reminded the pharaoh of what had happened previously, during the time of Aziru's father: "When Abdi-Ashirta seized Sumur, I guarded the city on my own. There was not a garrison with me, so I sent a message to the king, my lord, and troops campaigned and captured Sumur and Abdi-Ashirta." This was new information, that Egyptian troops had captured Sumur and Abdi-Ashirta at some point in the past. But history was repeating itself, for Rib-Hadda continued that when Aziru captured Sumur again, just as his father had done, the people of Byblos grew anxious. "So I, myself, went to Beirut to speak to 'Ammu-nira, and we made an alliance."

Rib-Hadda then repeated his tale of the previous year: the new alliance had come to naught and when he returned home to Byblos, "They did not allow me to enter. The criminal against the king [i.e., Rib-Hadda's own brother] acquired the troops of Aziru. He put (them) inside the city." But he still insisted, "as for the city, half of it is loyal to the sons of Abdi-Ashirta and half of it (is loyal) to my lord."

He did now say that, immediately upon being exiled to Beirut, he had sent his son with a message for pharaoh. However, four months later, that son was still waiting for an audience with the Egyptian king: "After ten seconds of my reaching Beirut, I dispatched my son to the sovereign's palace, (yet) after four month(s), he has not seen the face of the king."

He concluded: "Here now, I am dwelling in Beirut like a dog; my word is not heard. If the king had listened to his servant and troops had been given to me, the city would have returned to the king. So the king should give troops so that we may seize the city. The troops of the sons of Abdi-Ashirta must not capture it for themselves so that its people change allegiance. . . . Look, the criminal [i.e., his own brother] did a very significant thing in order to give (the city) to Aziru. He captured property [and] he expelled me."[12]

———

Most surprising of all, however, is that his supposedly treacherous brother, Ilu-rapi, sent two letters of his own to the pharaoh. Ilu-rapi does not even discuss Rib-Hadda but plunges right into his own story of defending Byblos and the lands of the pharaoh against Aziru. In the first letter (EA 139), he began with the same type of opening as would any other vassal king: "To the king, my lord, my Sun god, a message from Ilu-rapi, your servant, a message from Byblos, your maidservant. I fall at the feet of the lord, the Sun god, seven (times and) seven (times)." He then continued:

> Do not keep silent, O king, concerning Byblos, your city and a city of your forefathers since time immemorial! . . . Look, as for Byblos, like Memphis, in this way is Byblos to the king, my lord. Do not keep silent concerning Aziru, the slave. He acted according to his desire in the lands of the king. Look, as for the crime that Aziru committed against the king: He killed the king of the land of Ammiya and the king of the land of Ardatu and the king of the land of Irqata, and the commissioner of the king, my lord, and he breached Sumur. Here now, he desires to commit a crime against the king.

Moreover, "I am his [i.e., the king's] loyal servant, so he should dispatch a garrison into his city—30 men or 50 men—as far as Byblos. The king should not pay attention to anything that Aziru dispatches to him. Anything that he dispatches is a matter of Sumur. He dispatches to you the property of royal city rulers whom he killed. Look, Aziru is a criminal against the king, my lord."[13]

In the second letter (EA 140), Ilu-rapi repeated the same message:

> The king, my lord, should not keep silent regarding Byblos, his maidservant, a city of the king since time immemorial. . . . Why did the king permit (it), regarding Aziru, so that he acts according to his desire? Look, Aziru killed 'Aduna, king of the land of Irqata. He killed the king of the land of Ammiya, and the king of the land of Ardatu, and the senior official, and he captured their cities for himself (and) Sumur for himself. . . . Look, with respect to the crime that Aziru committed against you when he entered, the crime was against us. He dispatched his men to Aitukama, and he defeated all of the lands of 'Amqu, the king's lands, and now he has dispatched his men in order to seize the lands of 'Amqu and (their) territories.[14]

Neither letter mentions his exiling Rib-Hadda nor that Ilu-rapi was himself now allied with Aziru. However, this barrage of messages about Aziru's actions produced the desired result. The Egyptian pharaoh wrote a lengthy letter to Aziru (EA 162), telling him that either he needed to come to Egypt or else should send his son in his place. He began the letter by referring to the recent activities concerning Byblos, Rib-Hadda, and Ilu-rapi (though not mentioning them specifically by name), instructing his messenger: "Speak to Aziru, the ruler of (the city of) Amurru, a message from the king, your lord."

The message itself was plain and straightforward:

The ruler of Byblos spoke to you, the one whose brother threw him out from the gate, saying: "Take me away and bring me into my city! There is much silver (there), so let me give it to you. Look, there is much of everything, but it is not (here) with me." In this manner he spoke to you. Were you, yourself, not sending messages to the king, your lord, saying: "I am your servant like each of the loyal city rulers [who] is inside his city?" But you are committing a crime on account of capturing the city ruler whose brother threw him out from the gate, outside of his city.

He also noted Aziru's friendship with the ruler of Qidšu (Qadesh), who is unnamed but probably Aitukama, and complained: "You are at peace with the ruler of Qidšu. You were eating food (and) beer with each other! And (the words) are true! Why were you acting in this manner? Why are you at peace with a ruler with whom the king has quarreled? . . . You are not reliable concerning the matters that you were doing previously. What was done to you in their midst so that you are not with the king, your lord?"

He then got to the heart of the matter, issuing a direct threat: "If you do your service for the king, your lord, what is that which the king will not do for you, yourself? If because of possessions, you desire to do these things, and if you plan these things, dishonest matters, then you, together with all your family, will die by the king's axe. Do your service for the king, your lord, so that you will live! You, yourself, know that the king does not desire that he become angry with the entire land of Canaan."

The pharaoh ended his letter by listing eight specific men, as well as a few of their sons, all of whom he said were enemies of the king. He gave instructions to Aziru, telling him to send the men to Egypt to face the pharaoh, and adding with emphasis, "and do not leave out one from among them! Bronze chains should be placed on the ankle(s) of their feet."[15]

Most likely as a response to all of this, in one very short letter, Aziru reported to the pharaoh that he has sent two of his sons to Egypt, in order to carry out whatever wishes the king might have. However, Aziru also requested that he himself should be allowed to stay in Amurru.[16]

Aziru then wrote both to Tutu and to the pharaoh. In two separate letters sent to Tutu (EA 164 and 167), Aziru wrote that the Hittite king had come to the land of Nuhašše and that he needed to wait until after the Hittite threat had passed. At that point, he said, he would come to Egypt.[17] He elaborated a bit more in his letter to the pharaoh (EA 165): "The king of the land of Hatti is present in the land of Nuhašše, and I am fearful of him. May it not be that he comes here into the land of Amurru, into the land of the king, my lord. So, because of this matter, I am staying. Let him go away and return into his land, and then I will come." In fact, he said, the danger was dire, for "He [i.e., the king of Hatti] is now present in the land of Nuhašše, two one(-day) march(es) into Tunip, and I am fearful of his attacking Tunip. Let him go away!" He ended by beseeching the pharaoh not to listen to any lies and reassuring him of his own loyalty: "Oh my lord, do not listen to dishonest men. I and my brothers and my sons are servants of the king, my lord, in perpetuity."[18]

We do have what seems to be a final letter from Ammunira of Beirut (EA 143), which appears to confirm that the pharaoh had finally taken some action, for Ammunira acknowledged that Egyptian ships had arrived and were anchored in the harbor at Beirut.[19] However, since we have no further letters from the pharaoh, or from anyone else involved in this conflict, we do not know the final outcome of the situation in Byblos.

We do know that at some point Aziru made good on his promise to go to Egypt (EA 168).[20] He remained there long enough to receive at least one letter (EA 170), sent to him by two men, Ba'luya and Beti-'ili, who may have either been his actual brothers or simply close friends or colleagues. They wrote to tell him that he should return home soon, for the Hittites were causing trouble: "Troops of the land of Hatti (under) Lupakku have captured the cities of the land of 'Amqi by force, and with the cities they have captured Haddumi by force (also). Our lord should know. . . . Something else: We have heard as follows: 'Zidana came, and (there are) 90,000 foot soldiers who came with him.' But we did not confirm the report." But, they hastened to assure him, "If they are truly (there) or they are reaching Nuhašše," then they would quickly send a messenger, "so that he may send back a report to you whether it is so or whether it is not."[21]

It was not easy for Aziru to leave Egypt. Eventually his son, whose name is not preserved, wrote a letter directly to the pharaoh (EA 169), beseeching him to let his father go. "We belong to the king, our lord," he wrote. "You can keep me alive, and you can put me to death. I belong to you: You are my lord, and my lord should listen to his servants. Do not delay Aziru, your servant, there. Dispatch him quickly so he may guard the lands of the king, our lord."

In the same letter, he also addressed a note to Tutu:

> To Tutu, my lord: Hear the words of the men of the land of Nuhaššе: They said to me, "As for your father, you sold him to the king of the land of Egypt for gold. So, when will he dispatch him from the land of Egypt?" And all of the lands and all of the Sutuean troops spoke thus: "Aziru is not going to come out from the land of Egypt." So the Suteans are now changing allegiance from the lands, and they keep alerting me: "As for your father, he is present in the land of Egypt, so we are going to wage war against you." . . . listen to me, Tutu, my lord: Dispatch Aziru quickly![22]

In the end, his son had to pay a ransom to get Aziru released, after which he was able to return home to Amurru. Amarna scholar Anson Rainey suggested that Aziru may even have been considered by the pharaoh to be a royal hostage and that "The payment of the gold was meant to convince the authorities that Amurru and its ruler (and his sons) were determined to remain loyal to Egypt."[23]

Unlike his father, upon his return to Amurru, Aziru lived to fight another day. In fact, we know that he subsequently left the Egyptian orbit and allied himself firmly with the Hittites, for in the archives at Hattusa, we have a copy of a treaty that he signed with Suppiluliuma I. In it, Aziru pledged allegiance to the Hittite king and promised to visit each year, bringing an annual tribute of three hundred shekels of refined gold. Within the introductory section of the treaty, Suppiluliuma wrote: "Aziru, king of the land [of Amurru], came up from the gate of Egyptian territory and became a vassal [of] My Majesty, [King] of Hatti. And I, My Majesty, Great King, [accordingly rejoiced] very much."[24]

———

I have tried to put the relevant letters, and the events, in the order that seems most logical to me. Unfortunately, there are still scholarly debates swirling around the proper chronological order and so we have no real sense as to when Aziru was called to Egypt and had to be ransomed by his son. Was that before or after his troops began fighting with those of Akizzi of Qatna and others? I think that it would make sense for Aziru to have been summoned to Egypt by the pharaoh precisely because of such fighting and because of the expulsion of Rib-Hadda from Byblos, which means that we should place those events prior to the summons to Egypt.

It would certainly make sense that the time he spent in Egypt, where he was essentially a royal hostage until he was ransomed, as Rainey has pointed out, would have solidified his decision to make an alliance with the Hittites following his return to Amurru, specifically because of the way he had been treated by the Egyptian pharaoh. However, it is likely, as one can infer from the various letters from other kings, that he had already been in at least a shadow alliance with the Hittites during his earlier activities.[25] It was, to be sure, a very complex situation, made even more so by the Byzantine machinations of the various petty rulers, their occasional gaslighting of the pharaoh and fellow vassal rulers, and the fact that we can only make educated guesses at the proper chronological order of these various letters.

22

If I Forget Thee, O Jerusalem

WE HAVE seen the power plays between different kingdoms in the northern
Levant, largely in what is now modern Syria and Lebanon, driven by super-
power competition between Egypt and Hatti. In the southern part of Canaan,
where Hittite influence was much less, the local conflicts continued during
the time of Akhenaten too. They now involved the infamous sons of Lab'ayu
again, also Milkilu of Gezer, Shuwardata of Qilti, and, perhaps most interestingly, Abdi-Heba of Jerusalem. We have met both Shuwardata and Milkilu
previously, as well as the sons of Lab'ayu. Abdi-Heba is new to our narrative in
these chapters, but we have mentioned him previously in earlier sections, for
readers will remember that the letters that mention his name caused much
excitement when scholars first translated them and saw that the name "Jerusalem" was mentioned.[1]

Abdi-Heba was the ruler of Jerusalem but uniquely described himself as
"a soldier of the king" rather than as a city ruler. He claimed further to have a
special status, saying that he had been appointed to his position by the pharaoh
himself. "Look," he said in one letter (EA 288), "I am not a city ruler (but) a
we'u-soldier of the king, my lord. Look, I am a friend of the king, and I am a
bearer of the king's tribute. It was not my father; it was not my mother; the
strong arm of the king appointed me in my father's house."[2]

We can learn about Abdi-Heba and his role by first reading the letters of the
kings who subsequently interacted with him. The correspondence with
Milkilu of Gezer, a city on the first hill above the coastal plain, is a good place
to start. One letter (EA 369, which is now in Brussels) is particularly useful,
but it was also extremely rare, because it was actually sent *by* the pharaoh,
Akhenaten, *to* Milkilu, rather than the other way around; this tablet at Amarna
must be a copy of the one that went to Milkilu. It reads:

165

To Milkilu, ruler of Gezer, thus (says) the king: Herewith he is sending this tablet to you in order to command you. Herewith the king is dispatching to you Hanya, stablemaster of the regular troops, along with everything (needed) in order to acquire beautiful female cupbearer(s): Silver, gold, linen garments, carnelian, all (types of precious) stones, an ebony chair; likewise, all of these things are high-quality. A total of 160 deben (in weight). Total: 40 female cupbearer(s). 40 (shekels of) silver is the purchase price of the female cupbearers. So send very beautiful female cupbearers with not a bad one among them so that the king, your lord, may say to you, "That was good," in accordance with the instructions that he sent to you.[3]

This letter is not only one of the extant few sent by the pharaoh to a vassal Canaanite king, but it is also one of the very few in which we see the pharaoh make such a specific request of that vassal king. In response, Milkilu sent not one but two letters back to the pharaoh.

In the first one (EA 267), he indicated that he was preparing to satisfy the request: "As for the command that the king, my lord, my god, my Sun god, sent to me, now, I am preparing it for the king, my lord, the Sun god from the heavens."[4] In the second (EA 268), he noted that he had fulfilled the request: "I have obeyed the command that the king, my lord, sent to me, and, I am preparing (it) for the king, my lord. Herewith I have dispatched via Haya 46 female servants and five male servants—the five men are *aširu*-personnel—to the king, my lord."[5]

A third letter (EA 269) may also be related to this exchange, for in it Milkilu reported that he had fulfilled an unspecified request from the pharaoh and was now asking for a favor in return: "I have obeyed the message of the king, my lord, to me. So may the king, my lord, dispatch regular troops to his servants, and may the king, my lord, dispatch myrrh for healing."[6]

A fourth letter (EA 270), however, is concerned with a different matter, for in this one Milkilu complained to the pharaoh about the actions of an Egyptian administrator or commissioner named Yanhamu, also mentioned in numerous other Amarna Letters. According to Milkilu, Yanhamu was attempting to extort him, demanding to be given 3,000 shekels of silver as well as Milkilu's wife and sons (perhaps as hostages): "The king, my lord, should know the deeds that Yanhamu has been doing to me since my departure from the king, my lord, (namely) that he desires three thousand (shekels) of silver from me and saying to me: 'Hand over your wife and your sons, and let them act as guarantor!' The king should know this deed. May the king, my lord, dispatch chariots and take me away to him, lest I perish."[7]

Unfortunately, we have no more letters concerning this situation, so we do not know how it was resolved, but in another letter (EA 271), Milkilu tried to bring Yanhamu to the attention of the pharaoh again. This concerned a local conflict involving both himself and Shuwardata—they were now allied against the *'apiru* men and perhaps other unnamed opponents. He wrote: "The king, my lord, should know that the hostility towards me and against Shuwardata is severe, so may the king, my lord, rescue his land from the might of the *'apiru*. If not, send chariots, O king, my lord, in order to take us away lest our servants attack us. . . . The king, my lord, should ask Yanhamu, his servant, about what is being done in his land."[8]

———

Shuwardata, ruler of Qilti, also wrote to the pharaoh, sending a total of seven letters in all. One of them (EA 278) is a mundane acknowledgment of receiving a request from the pharaoh,[9] but all the rest are concerned with hostilities and conflicts with other rulers, together with requests that the pharaoh send troops.

Some of these are generic and cannot be further identified. For instance, one letter (EA 282) simply says, "The king, my lord, should be informed: I am alone. The king, my lord, should send a very large regular army so that he may rescue me. May the king, my lord, be informed."[10]

Another similarly nondescript letter (EA 281) is a bit more detailed in painting the reason for the request:

> The king, my lord, should be informed that all of my cities are hostile to me. So the king, my lord, should dispatch the regular troops so that they [i.e., the cities] may be captured in accordance with the command of the senior officials concerning them. The king, my lord, should capture them. The soldiers should be on guard so that these ones [i.e., the cities] may be captured and writhe before the king, my lord. . . . the king should know of the hostilities towards me. Who would commit a crime against the king? But these ones [i.e., the cities] are dogs, so they have committed a crime against the king. So the king should dispatch the regular army so that he may capture them.[11]

Shuwardata still did not provide further details in his letters as to who was set against him but at one point (EA 283) specified that fully thirty cities were at war with him. He asked the pharaoh to send Yanhamu, the same Egyptian commissioner about whom Milkilu of Gezer had complained, to investigate the situation. Shuwardata wrote:

> Now, Yanhamu is with you, so speak with him! If there is no regular army (available) at this time, may the king, my lord, rescue me! May the king, my lord, be informed that 30 cities are waging war against me. I am (but) a single city. The hostility towards me is severe. The king, my lord, has cast me from his hand. May the king, my lord, dispatch the regular troops. May the king, my lord, rescue me. Now, Yanhamu is a commissioner of the king, my lord. The king, my lord, should speak with him, (asking) "Is the hostility towards Shuwardata severe or not?"[12]

It is unclear when this hostility and antagonism toward Shuwardata lies within the general timeline of this period, for various Amarna Letters make it clear that Shuwardata was involved in at least two separate conflicts, perhaps also separated in time. The first of these letters, and these conflicts, concerned an unnamed *'apiru* man whom Shuwardata defeated. In this conflict, Shuwardata said, he was aided by Abdi-Heba of Jerusalem, who makes his appearance in these letters for the first time at this point. Two other rulers were involved as well, Surata of Acco and Intaruta of Achshaph, both of whom we have already met.

Since Surata of Acco was involved in the events surrounding Lab'ayu's death, we can probably date this conflict and this letter (EA 366) to the same approximate period. Though there is no mention here of Lab'ayu, at the very least we know that the letter dates to the time of Surata's rule rather than that of his successor Satatna. In the letter, Shuwardata requests that Yanhamu be sent to assess the situation:

> The king, my lord, should be informed that the god of the king, my lord, handed over to me the *'apiru* who was elevated in rank in the lands, and I defeated him. May the king, my lord, be informed that all my brothers have abandoned me, so only I and Abdi-Heba were hostile to the *'apiru*. But Surata, ruler of Akko, and Intaruta, ruler of Akšapa, the two of them, came to me to assist in 50 chariots. Now, they are with me in the hostility. May it be pleasing before the king, my lord, so that he may send Yanhamu, so that all of us may wage war, so that you may restore the lands of the king, my lord, to its borders.[13]

The second conflict must have taken place sometime later, for it is clear from additional letters that Shuwardata's previous ally, Abdi-Heba of Jerusalem, was now an opponent. Several letters relate to this second conflict.

In one sent to the pharaoh (EA 279), Shuwardata said simply: "The king, my lord, should know that the land of the king, my lord, is no more . . . has gone out to Qilti to the traitors. So may the king send the regular army. The king must listen to his city rulers so that we may take a stand against them and drive away the traitors from the land of the king, my lord."[14] Apparently Shuwardata meant that Qilti had gone over to, or been taken over by, unnamed "traitors."

A subsequent letter (EA 280), which is essentially an "after action report," related that Shuwardata had retaken the town from the rebels, after receiving permission from the pharaoh to do so. He wrote: "The king, my lord, permitted me to wage war against Qilti. I waged war. My city is intact for me and has been returned to me."

Of immediate interest is that he further reported that the "traitors" had apparently been bribed and were acting on the orders of Abdi-Heba, though Shuwardata professed not to know why: "Why did Abdi-Heba send a message to the men of Qilti: 'Bring silver and follow me!'? The king, my lord, should know that Abdi-Heba has captured my city from my control." Shuwardata then compared Abdi-Heba to Lab'ayu, noting that Lab'ayu was now dead but that Abdi-Heba was acting in a similar manner: "Lab'aya is dead—he who used to capture our cities—but, now Abdi-Heba is another Lab'aya, and he is capturing our cities!"[15]

This places the conflict between Shuwardata and Abdi-Heba after the period in which they had been allies, since it occurs after the death of Lab'ayu. Now Abdi-Heba was causing similar problems.

———

Contemporary letters in the archive sent from Abdi-Heba himself confuse the issue, because they explain the situation from his point of view. Once again, we are speculating as to the order of the various events and the proper chronology of the letters themselves.

In his letters, Abdi-Heba offers a completely different view of the events. He asserts that he is the victim, rather than the oppressor, just as had Lab'ayu before him and, for that matter, both Abdi-Ashirta and Aziru. It is unclear whether he is gaslighting the pharaoh or is telling the truth in these letters.

Abdi-Heba addressed in one letter (EA 286) what appears to have been a complaint lodged against him regarding his activities: "Speak to the king, my lord, a message from Abdi-Heba, your servant. I fall at the two feet of my lord, the king, seven times and seven times. What have I done to the king, my lord?

They are slandering me in the presence of the king, saying 'Abdi-Heba has changed allegiance from the king, his lord.'"

Abdi-Heba further protested his innocence, writing in the same letter that he owed everything to the king:

> Look, as for me, neither my father nor my mother appointed me in this place. The strong arm of the king brought me into the house of my father. Why would I commit a crime against the king, the lord? Indeed, as the king, my lord, lives, I was saying to the commissioner of the king, my lord: "Why do you love *'apiru*, but you hate city rulers?" Consequently, I am slandered in the presence of the king, my lord. When I was saying, "the lands of the king, my lord, are out of (his) control," consequently I am slandered to the king, my lord.[16]

He then attempted to lay the blame partially at the feet of Yanhamu, the Egyptian commissioner who seems to have been everywhere at this time. He also blamed some unknown man named Ili-Milku. Some scholars, like Moran, accept this as a misspelling of Milkilu (of Gezer), which makes much more sense.[17]

Abdi-Heba claimed that Yanhamu had sent the entire garrison of thirty Egyptian soldiers back home to Egypt from Jerusalem. As a result, Abdi-Heba said, "The king, the lord, should know: There is not a garrison." Moreover, he said, because of the departure of the garrison, "'Ili-milku [= Milkilu] is causing the entirety of the king's land to go out of (the king's) control."

Abdi-Heba continued by blaming the *'apiru* men for causing problems and beseeching the pharaoh to come to his aid by sending troops. Perhaps in an effort to gain both sympathy and the attention of the pharaoh, he stated bluntly that "the hostilities towards me are severe" and that "*'apiru* [have] plundered the entirety of the king's lands!"

The letter ends in an unusual manner, which seems to have been unique to Abdi-Heba but is found in several of his letters. His concluding words were aimed not at the pharaoh, but as a postscript meant for the scribe who would be reading the letter out loud to the Egyptian king: "To the scribe of the king, my lord, a message from Abdi-Heba, your servant. Bring loyal words to the king, my lord: 'The entirety of the lands of the king, my lord, are out of (his) control!'"

These final words seem to indicate that the scribe(s) reading the letter to the king would have used discretion at times and would not always have read the entire letter to the king, especially if there were notes such as this which were meant for the scribe rather than the pharaoh. We see this in another instance, where the scribe writing from Arzawa included a postscript at the bottom of the letter (EA 32), which was addressed to the scribe at the Egyptian court who would be responding: "Always write in Hittite." Interestingly, such examples are few and far between; Abdi-Heba is the only vassal ruler in southern Canaan to do this.

———

It is unclear when the events, and the accusation against Abdi-Heba, had taken place, but chances are extremely high that they are related to the discussion in another letter (EA 287) in which Abdi-Heba specifically fingers Milkilu of Gezer, as well as the rulers of Ashkelon and Lachish, as conspiring with the sons of Lab'ayu and the *'apiru* men and helping them to take over the town of Qilti (Keilah). "All the lands are peaceful," said Abdi-Heba, "(yet) there is hostility towards me." As evidence, he reported that Milkilu had given bows and bronze arrow(s) to the sons of Lab'aya and to someone named Tagi, who is identified elsewhere as Milkilu's father-in-law and ruler of his own city (Gath-Carmel, also recorded in other letters as Ginti-kirmil), and that "the land of Gezer, the land of Ashkelon, and Lachish gave bread, oil, and everything else to them" (i.e., to those assaulting Qilti). "Look," he said, "this is the deed, the deed of Milkilu and the deed of the sons of Lab'aya, who gave the king's land to *'apiru*."[18]

Readers will remember that Shuwardata had claimed that exactly the opposite had taken place and that it was actually Abdi-Heba who had taken over the town of Qilti / Keilah.[19] We can also now say, with a fair degree of confidence, that these letters were all referring to the same incident involving Qilti / Keilah and that it took place after the death of Lab'ayu and during the time that his sons were continuing their father's efforts at conquering or controlling neighboring city-states. This would also explain why Shuwardata said that Abdi-Heba had become another Lab'ayu.

In this same letter (EA 287), Abdi-Heba also repeated that he had been left high and dry, abandoned by the departure of the Egyptian garrison troops from his city. He gave additional details, however, saying that they had left under the command of an Egyptian commissioner named Haddaya, and that he was presently awaiting the arrival of a different Egyptian commissioner, named Piwuru, hopefully with more troops and other support. He also reported that he himself had been nearly assassinated "by the hand of the men from Cush [ins]ide my own house!" and specifically reminded the pharaoh that it was the pharaoh's responsibility to protect him because of his unique status: "Look, as for this land of Jerusalem, neither my father nor my mother gave (it) to me; the strong hand of the king gave (it) to me."

Abdi-Heba brought up similar topics again in another letter (EA 288), where he took a page out of Shuwardata's playbook and claimed once more that he was all alone and surrounded by hostile enemies. We have already discussed the opening lines of this letter, where Abdi-Heba describes himself as "placed like a ship in the middle of the sea." He continued to itemize the rampant hostility and the assassinations of other rulers and travelers that had recently taken place:

> Look, as for Turbazu, he was killed inside the gate of Silu; the king was silent. Look, as for Zimri-Haddu of Lachish, servants allied with 'apiru attacked him. As for Yaptiḥ-Haddu, he was killed inside the gate of Silu; the king was silent. Why did the king not ask about them? The king should show concern for his land. He should turn his attention to it so that the regular troops campaign to his land. If there is not a regular army this year, the entirety of the lands of the king, my lord, will be out of (his) control.[20]

It is possible that some of these assassinations may have been targeted and approved by the pharaoh, for in one letter (EA 333), Zimri-Haddu of Lakiša (Lachish) is named as one of two men who were reportedly plotting against the pharaoh (the other being Shipti-Ba'lu, also of Lakiša), despite Zimri-Haddu's apparent loyalty attested in other Amarna Letters.[21]

Abdi-Heba gave an even more detailed explanation in another letter (EA 289), blaming everything once more on Milkilu and the sons of Lab'ayu, as well as on Tagi. He also once again requested aid from the pharaoh, this time saying that the newest Egyptian representative to the city, the commissioner named Piwuru for whom he had been waiting and who had apparently replaced Yanhamu, had already abandoned them.[22]

He then elaborated on the abandonment of the city by the Egyptian troops. "Haddaya took away the garrison that you dispatched via Haya, son of Miya-Re. He placed (them) in his house in Gaza and dispatched twenty men to the land of Egypt. The king should know: There is no royal garrison with me. Consequently, as the king lives, indeed, his *irpi*-official, Piwuru, left me. He is in Gaza. The king should remember (this) on his arrival, and he should dispatch a garrison of 50 men in order to guard his land. All of the king's land has deserted. Dispatch Yanhamu here so that he may take care of the king's land."

He concluded his letter in his typical fashion, addressing the pharaoh's scribe directly once again: "To the scribe of the king, my lord, a message from Abdi-Heba, your servant. Give loyal words to the king: 'I would truly die for you! I am your servant!'"[23]

We see that Abdi-Heba offered further explanations in additional letters sent to the pharaoh, in which he again blamed everything on Milkilu and Shuwardata. For example, in EA 290, which is the same letter originally mangled in translation by Sayce in his 1888 *PSBA* article, we now know that Abdi-Heba claimed that "Milki-'ili and Shuwardata assembled troops from Gezer, troops from Gath, and troops from Qilti against the land of the king, my lord." Moreover, he said, "a town of the land of Jerusalem—Bit-'Anat, a city of the king—has deserted (to) where the men of Qilti are." He ended on a strong note, daring to lecture the pharaoh: "The king should listen to Abdi-Heba, your servant, and dispatch the regular troops and return the king's land to the king. If there is not a regular army, the king's land will desert to the *'apiru*. This deed was on account of a command of Milkilu and on account of a command of Shuwardata. . . . So the king should care for his land!"[24]

———

It is quite possible that we have things slightly wrong, or out of order here, and readers will be forgiven if they are unable to easily follow the various twists and turns of the above events with full comprehension, especially since it is not completely clear who was really telling the truth in these tablets. Was Abdi-Heba describing the reality and it was Milkilu and others, including Shuwardata and the rulers of Ashkelon and Lachish, who were rebellious against the Egyptians? Or was Shuwardata telling the truth and it was Abdi-Heba who was the one causing problems? Who was gaslighting the pharaoh, Abdi-Heba or Shuwardata? Or did alliances shift from day to day, moment to moment, conflict to conflict, seizing opportunities as they arose? We may never know the answers to any of these questions. In fact, we may never know how this episode ended, for there are no other letters relating to this situation in the Amarna archive, and, for that matter, no other references to any of this anywhere else apart from the Amarna archive.

One thing is clear, however, from the details provided in the letters. Life during the Amarna Period, whether in the city or the countryside—or whether in northern, central, or southern Canaan—does not seem to have been particularly peaceful for the smaller petty kings, regardless of how well things were going at the higher level of the Great Kings. In some ways, it's still not much different in this region today, especially in terms of neighboring countries or states being more often in conflict or at war than they are at peace.

PART VII

The Social Networks and Globalized World of the Late Bronze Age

23

It's a Small World After All

BY NOW it is clear that we can harvest a lot of historical information from the contents of the Amarna Letters. It is also clear that the Bronze Age Great Kings, vassal rulers, merchants, and messengers of the day optimized the existing diplomatic, mercantile, and communication networks for maximum efficiency.[1]

However, since we have almost four hundred letters in the archive, it can be difficult to keep track of all the social ties, or social information, including who wrote to whom, traded with whom, sent gifts to whom, intermarried with whom, got in quarrels with whom, and complained to the pharaoh about whom. It is a complex web of interactions, to say the least, especially if we think of the trade routes and roads between them as communication channels. But, if we turn to Social Network Analysis (SNA), we can get some help with this. It will entail us changing gears fairly rapidly, from our previous descriptions and discussions of the facts that we have gleaned from the Amarna Letters to statistical analyses of that same data, but the end results offer an additional, and different, way of examining these texts, which have been studied in traditional ways for almost 150 years.

Social Network Analysis has its roots in the combination of mathematics and graph theory with sociology. It uses sociograms (aka network diagrams) created from the data to look for patterns. Researchers in dozens of fields use SNA, with a shared language and common tools and methods. It has been used, for example, in sociology, business, and international security since at least the 1970s in many cases, but is now also beginning to be applied in many more fields in the humanities and social sciences, including in archaeology and ancient history.[2]

In our case, it provides a way to record and visually display the social relations between and among the people in the Amarna Letters. It allows us to think about how the people mentioned in the letters, as well as the people who sent and received them, interacted and formed a network, for it is, quite specifically, a method designed to map relationships and transactions between people or groups, understanding them collectively through data visualization.

For instance, we can measure a person's importance or position relative to others in the network and describe who should be seen as part of the core and who is peripheral. We can also note that social networks are not necessarily local or geographically bound, for people who live a long distance apart can be very close, and people who live close by can be quite distant or even absent from one's social network.[3] (We should also note, however, that the writers did not always completely understand the geographical distances that were involved, as is clear from the letter of Burna-Buriash II of Babylonia, when he wrote to Akhenaten in Amarna Letter EA 7 and asked him why the pharaoh had not inquired about his health.)

What we should also emphasize is the very high quality of evidence that we have in these Amarna Letters about the social relationships between individuals. Not only do we know who wrote to whom and how often, but we also have wonderfully detailed evidence within the correspondence of efforts to be close to one another, as well as feelings of anger at each other or even tension and mistrust. This is their social world, and it is clear from these letters that the Bronze Age Eastern Mediterranean was actually a measurable "Small World," according to terminology used by Social Network Analysis, despite covering thousands of square miles of often-rugged terrain.

Such a Small World is not necessarily physical but is rather measured by the presence of connected clusters of people. For instance, the Bronze Age Great Kings formed a cluster with their close relations—all either knew each other directly or knew of each other, so that they were connected through one, two, or three degrees at most (i.e., the friend of my friend). Such a phenomenon is commonly referred to as "six degrees of separation" today, but the network of the Amarna Letters was so tightly knit that the average number of "hops" to get from one person to another was just over three, meaning that it was a very Small World indeed.

Two caveats are in order, however. The first is that we are entirely dependent on the extant letters for our data. If we had the entire original corpus of Amarna Letters, including those that were accidentally destroyed during their transportation to Luxor, Cairo, and elsewhere in the first days and weeks after their discovery, as well as the others that were presumably taken to Luxor when the court moved back there following the death of Akhenaten, then our findings might be entirely different. Second is that the scribes themselves are not included in the following sociograms and social network analyses, but in part this is because we do not have their names, and only have hypotheses about how many were involved, though there has now been some preliminary work done to identify them.

We cannot do anything about the first problem, unless additional letters are discovered in Luxor. However, it might be possible to do something about the second problem and eventually add the individual scribes into the network. If so, we would be able to show the links between them and the major players who either ordered the letters to be written or received the letters, as well as the locations from which the letters were sent. For the present purposes, however, it will suffice to simply note that the scribes will help to fill in the gaps and that they provided the invisible glue that made Amarna diplomacy possible.[4]

Along those lines, we are making progress. In recent articles, Francesco De Magistris, currently at the University of Lausanne in Switzerland, discusses a number of the Amarna Letters in terms of "focal points" and what he calls the "Proximity Principle," in which he links specific local Canaanite petty rulers both to scribes working at specific Egyptian centers, such as Beth Shean and Sumur, as well as to Egyptian commissioners. This is, to my mind, an example of using a variation of Social Network Analysis (though without calling it such) in which he is able to include the scribes in addition to everyone else.[5]

———

While keeping the above caveats in mind, we can begin by examining the relationships or ties to be found in the royal letters sent between the Great Kings (EA 1–49), as opposed to the vassal letters that make up the larger part of the archive. We can see these relationships in the sociogram shown in Figure 16. Here each person or "node" (known as an "actor" in SNA terminology) is shown as a triangle, square, or circle, while each line or "edge" connecting the various nodes represents a relationship of some sort between two members of the network. The different shapes are used to identify the various connected members of each cluster, though some individuals can belong to more than one cluster (and therefore can serve as a bridge or link between different clusters). Note that the size of the node increases according to the number of ties that each person has.

From this, we can see that the four people who have the most connections or ties to other members of the network and who serve as hubs of the

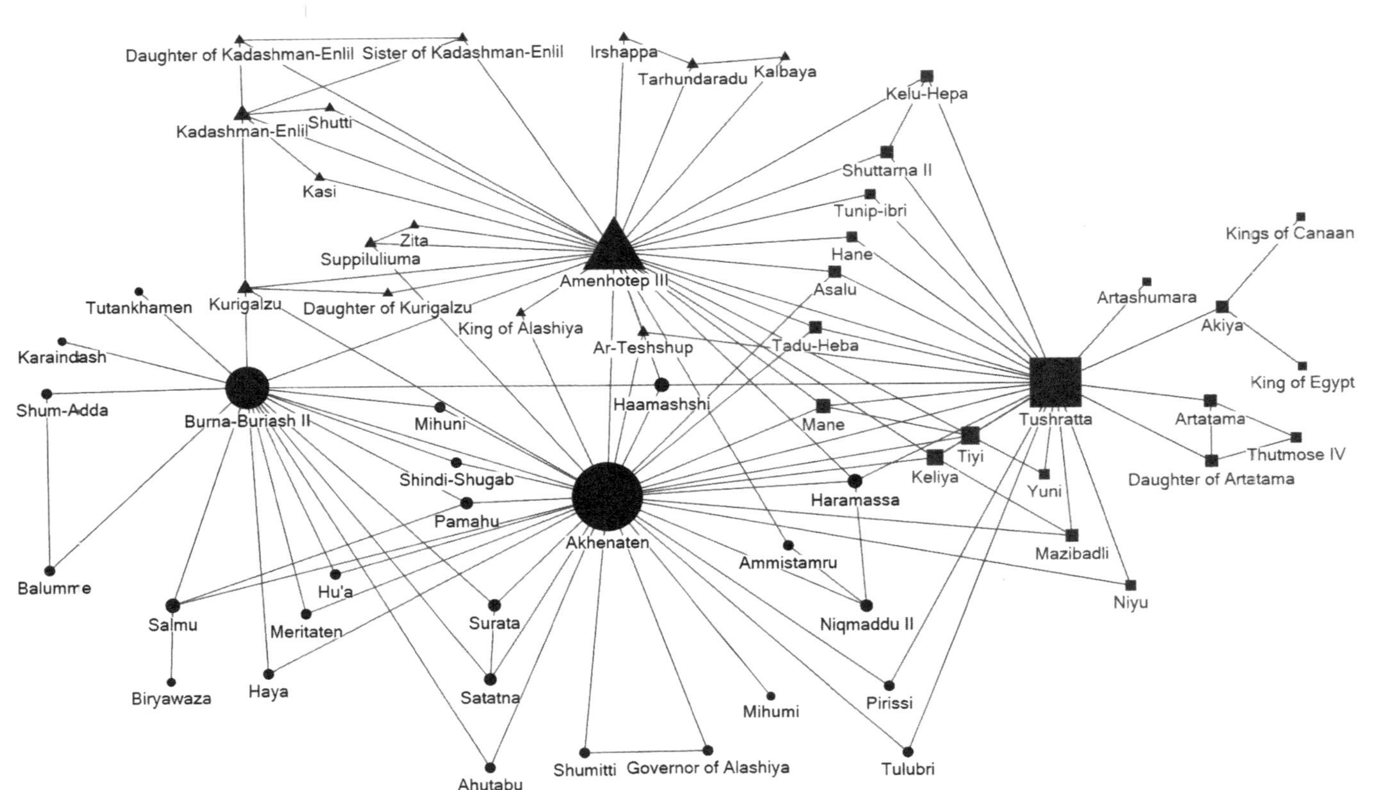

FIGURE 16. The network of the royal letters in the Amarna archive (EA 1–49) (after Cline and Cline 2015, fig. 3).

clusters are Amenhotep III, Akhenaten, Burna-Buriash II, and Tushratta. This is perhaps not surprising, since they are the ones writing most of the royal letters. However, what is notable is that we can also see a significant relationship specifically between Akhenaten and Burna-Buriash II. Although at initial glance this relationship looks about equal in terms of lines or connections between them, as do both Akhenaten's and Amenhotep III's relationships with Tushratta, a quick count of the edges shows that Akhenaten and Burna-Buriash II have more friends / actors in common than they have with anyone else, and more than any other pair of actors, for that matter. The letters sent back and forth, and their content, tie them together in a way that is significantly more cohesive than those two men's relations with others in the network.

For example, in looking at the sociogram (see Fig. 16), one sees many people whom these two kings have in common, forming elbow-like patterns that connect them. These include Satatna and his son Surata, who both served as ruler of Akko, and Ahutabu and Salmu, who were Babylonian envoys / messengers sent to Akhenaten by Burna-Buriash II. These individuals are part of a shared social network, whom both kings knew, wrote about, met with, or sent as messengers. This closeness between the king of Egypt and a king of Babylonia is quite remarkable, given the physical distances between them. It is also of interest to note that Tushratta, the king of Mittani, obviously knows both Egyptian pharaohs, Amenhotep III and Akhenaten, but is not so close to either one that he gets absorbed into their clusters.

Much of Amenhotep III's cluster is made up of the Babylonian king Kadashman-Enlil and his family, including the latter's unnamed sister and his father Kurigalzu. This gives us a good idea of the content of those letters, especially the marriages arranged between Amenhotep III and the daughters of these two Babylonian kings.

On the other hand, we can see that Tushratta, king of Mittani, has ties to both Amenhotep III and Akhenaten, as just mentioned, but it is with his father, Artatama, and his sister (i.e., Artatama's daughter) that we see a "kite formation" with Thutmose IV. Such a formation refers to a group of people with a closed set of relationships. In this case, it is the result of a previous dynastic marriage that is mentioned in the letters. From the combination of the sociogram and the actual contents of the letters, we get the idea that the social network here, at least among the royals, concerns marriage proposals and fathers trading their own daughters for either gold, as we have seen in earlier chapters, or a chance to be socially closer to a king of Egypt.

This is not surprising, of course, for royal marriages were frequently arranged in an effort to create tighter relations between families or even states at a social level, as we have seen in the chapters above. The sending of gold, and gift exchange in general for that matter, was also part of the effort to strengthen social ties at the same time as acquiring much-needed raw material.[6]

———

Having demonstrated that SNA works with the letters sent between the Great Kings, in that it corroborates some of what we already knew and provides further insights into the strength of relationships in visual form, we can expand the sample size and add in the correspondence from the petty Canaanite rulers, in order to get a look at the entire archive. This results in a picture that is much more interesting and complex.

For instance, in Figure 17 we can see the overall view; namely, the structure of the entire social network of the Amarna Letters. We have a total of 246 people (actors) who are named in the letters, with 464 ties or connections between them, since for every pair of actors there exists a social relationship of some kind. In the sociogram, once again, the actors are the points (or "nodes") in the chart, and the lines ("ties" or "edges" in SNA terms) are the relationships between them.

Inside such a large network, there are, of course, smaller units. Identifying these groups and mapping their relations with each other is an essential part of what Social Network Analysis can do.[7] This particular network has as many as eleven subsets or clusters, but some of those are simply families who have ties to each other, making a dense little unit or "clique."

Of greater interest is that we have at least five large clusters of relationships in this particular network. Again, different shapes are used to represent members of each cluster: solid square, solid triangle, open circle, solid disk, open diamond.

Our first observation is that in one cluster the royals are all together, represented by solid squares toward the upper left of the chart in an umbrella-like shape. If one were to try to find pathways from the royal cluster down to the other clusters, there are only two main gateways, via Amenhotep III and Akhenaten. The people below them in the network diagram serve as connecters, tying the royals to the vassals. We can see, in particular, Akizzi of Qatna directly beneath Amenhotep III, while Satatna and Surata of Akko are in that position for Akhenaten. People in the "open diamond cluster" like Satatna and

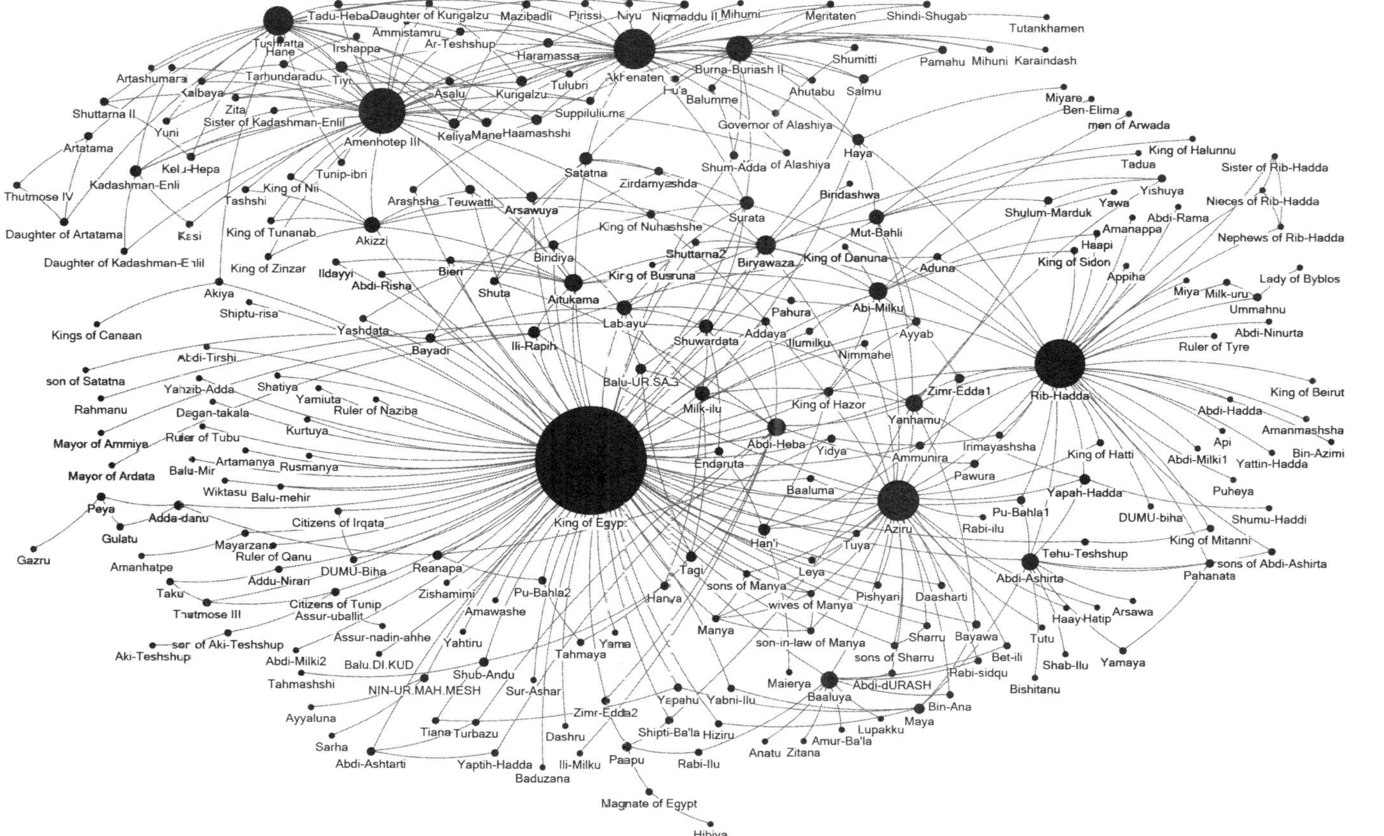

FIGURE 17. The entire Social Network of the Amarna Letters with four clusters (after Cline and Cline 2015, fig. 4).

Abi-Milku occupy structurally similar positions along these pathways and therefore have become a cluster unto themselves.

A second cluster—the solid triangles on the far right—has as its focal point Rib-Hadda of Byblos, while a third, smaller, cluster centered on Aziru is represented by open circles. A fourth cluster, represented by solid disks in the lower part of the chart, is centered on the unnamed "King of Egypt" since so many of the Amarna Letters are not addressed specifically to either Amenhotep III or Akhenaten but instead simply to the "King of Egypt." Clearly, the unnamed king of Egypt is the focal point of the graph, with the most ties or connections of all, though if the actual name of the pharaoh had been given on these tablets, our diagram would change substantially and dramatically, as we will see below.

The final group is not so much a "cluster" as it is a group of "in-betweeners," which is a fascinating list unto itself. These are represented by open diamonds on the chart, filling the spaces and bridging the other clusters.

However, this is where it can get especially interesting, for frequently the SNA computer program being employed (in this case, a program called NodeXL) will cluster the relationships differently than might have been anticipated, which in turn can sometimes lead to new observations. The same data can also be visualized or laid out in many other ways via the SNA program, by using different algorithms, for example, or arranging the results in different shapes, such as a circle, sine wave, or spiral.[8] These can also lead to new observations.

For instance, if we want to break down the network into as many clusters as we can, to see all of the subcommunities, we can ask the computer program that we are using to automatically put each cluster into its own box (Fig. 18).[9] In this experiment, we essentially split the data into its smallest possible denominators. Since, in the sociogram, the relative size of the nodes corresponds to the number of ties that each individual has, we can quickly see that the largest nodes appear in four of the ten clusters.

The sociogram that we looked at above with just the royal letters (see Fig. 16) now can be seen in its larger context, fitting almost entirely into the lower left cluster of this new figure (see Fig. 18). Inside the royals cluster, we find the same four large nodes—Amenhotep III, Akhenaten, Tushratta, and Burna-Buriash II—as we saw in Figure 16, followed by a number of smaller ones in decreasing size.

The largest node of all, however, is found in the upper left box. This is again the unnamed "King of Egypt" of the vassal letters, which is perhaps not surprising. This box contains many people who only have ties to the king and to

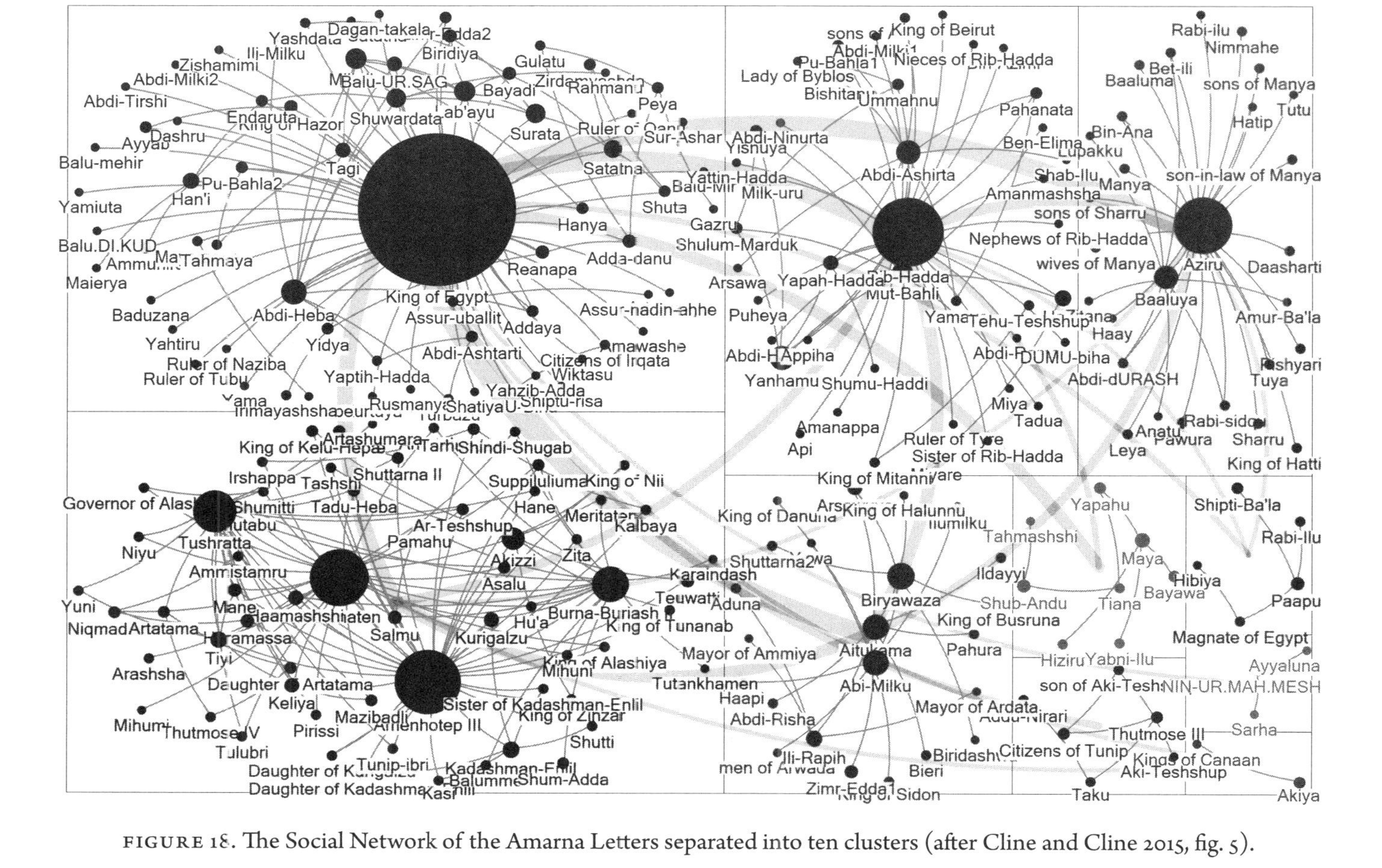

FIGURE 18. The Social Network of the Amarna Letters separated into ten clusters (after Cline and Cline 2015, fig. 5).

no one else. In this box, the other larger nodes include Surata of Akko, Abdi-Heba of Jerusalem, Lab'ayu of Shechem, Milkilu of Gezer, and Shuwardata of Qilti, all of whom are figures familiar to us from our discussions of the vassal territories in Canaan.

As we have seen in the previous chapters, many of these men sent, or are mentioned in, letters requesting help from the Egyptian king. Asking an ally or an overlord for military assistance against one's enemies is, of course, evidence as well for a social tie or relationship, even at the vassal level. Remember that Biridiya of Megiddo wrote to the Egyptian pharaoh that Lab'ayu had been waging war on him (EA 244), while Abdi-Heba of Jerusalem reported to the pharaoh that there was hostility all around him and that he was "like a ship in the middle of the sea" (EA 288). Thus, each of our discrete examples is actually part of a larger context, namely all of their social relationships.

Moving to the right and looking at the box in the center of the upper row, we see that the program's algorithm has discovered a cluster that has Rib-Hadda, the ruler of Byblos, as the largest node. Abdi-Ashirta, the ruler of Amurru, is the second largest node. This makes sense, as we have seen in the chapters above, especially given the sheer number of letters sent by Rib-Hadda, particularly in response to the larger-than-life roles played by Abdi-Ashirta and his son Aziru in northern Canaan (although Aziru merits his own cluster, in the upper right box).

———

What is surprising is that in this sociogram (see Fig. 18), the pharaohs dominate only two of the ten clusters in the network. Although virtually all the letters were excavated in Egypt within the royal archive at Amarna (with just a few exceptions such as the letter found at Tell el-Hesi), the contents of these letters indicate that eight of the ten clusters in the Amarna social network were not intimately tied to the pharaoh. The majority of these clusters were more local than global, concerned with nearby activities and actors.

So, if we look at the individual actors, we can measure each one's position using one or more specific measures used in Social Network Analysis, such as Degree Centrality, Betweenness Centrality, and Eigenvector Centrality. These focus on the value of a person's position within the network, such as the contribution that they make to the overall structure.[10]

For instance, the simplest centrality measure to understand is Degree, which simply counts up the number of ties, or relationships, that an actor or

TABLE 2. The top actors in the social network of the Amarna Letters in terms of Degree Centrality (after Cline and Cline 2015, fig. 6)

Vertex	Degree
King of Egypt	97
Rib-Hadda	41
Amenhotep III	38
Aziru	36
Akhenaten	32
Tushratta	23
Burna-Bariash II	18
Baaluya	14
Abdi-Ashirta	13
Biryawaza	13
Abdi-Heba	12
Abi-Milku	12
Aitukama	12
Yanhamu	11
Akizzi	10
Lab'ayu	9
Milk-ilu	9
Mut-Bahli	9
Shuwardata	8
Surata	8
Satatna	7

person has, as can be seen in Table 2.[11] As one might imagine, this doesn't always mean that the person is the most important—think of Rib-Hadda, the ruler of Byblos, for example, who wrote nearly sixty of the letters found in the Amarna archive and may have been more prolific than important.

In our case, as it happens, the unnamed king of Egypt has the highest number of ties or relationships—nearly one hundred—with other individuals. This is more than double that of the next closest person, namely Rib-Hadda of Byblos. If we knew who that unnamed king was, we could add this number, or a portion of it, to either Amenhotep III or his son, Akhenaten, who have thirty-eight and thirty-two ties respectively.

Note also that Aziru, the ruler of Amurru, has thirty-six ties, giving him a place on the list in between Amenhotep III and Akhenaten. Biryawaza, the ruler of Damascus, and Aziru's father Abdi-Ashirta are also high on the list, tied for ninth place at thirteen ties each. Such high placement for all three men might initially come as a surprise, since—as we have seen—they were trouble-makers who caused disruption in Egyptian-controlled Canaan. However, their high ranking comes about precisely *because* they are written about frequently and repeatedly by other Canaanite vassal rulers who are complaining about them. Their notoriety makes them infamous—everyone knows them, so they are in many social networks, even if they are regarded negatively.

Aziru's family members are also mentioned (e.g., his father Abdi-Ashirta, one brother Baaluya, and two unnamed brothers, who are mentioned only as

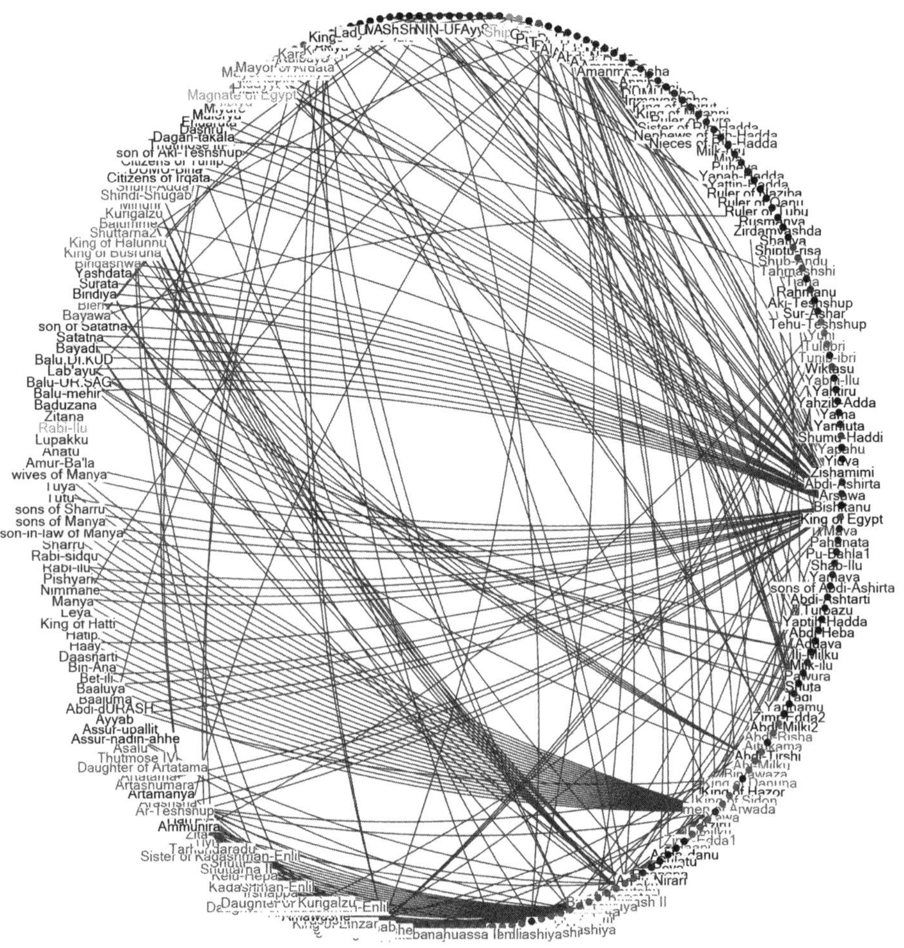

FIGURE 19. The "Small World" of the Amarna Letters
(after Cline and Cline 2015, fig. 10).

"sons of Abdi-Ashirta"), which also enhances his scores. Other actors with high numbers of ties include Tushratta, king of Mittani, and Burna-Buriash II, king of Babylonia, which comes as no surprise, but also Abdi-Heba, the ruler of Jerusalem, and other Canaanite rulers.

In Small World networks, we typically also find that there are a few actors with a lot of links and a whole lot of others with only a few or even just one, which is certainly the case here (Fig. 19). One only needs a few people serving as brokers or bridges between clusters to make introductions between strangers from different clusters in a Small World; such would certainly have been the case in the Eastern Mediterranean during the fourteenth century BCE.

24

Three Degrees of Separation

WHAT MIGHT be of additional importance in our particular network is the Eigenvector Centrality score. A high score here means that the actor is connected to central, rather than peripheral, people. It is a way of identifying highly connected individuals within highly interconnected clusters. Thus, it is often thought of as a measure of influence or prestige for identifying strategically connected people.[1] Being linked to a highly connected person increases one's Eigenvector Centrality. In most cases, it may be simply another way of saying that important people usually know other important people,[2] but in some circumstances the score can indicate an actor's importance, which might not otherwise be so obvious.

This can be seen in Table 3, which shows that the people around Amenhotep III and Akhenaten have higher Eigenvector Centrality scores than they do; the two kings do not even rank in the top twenty people within the social network and are not shown in this table. With scores of 0.009 and 0.007 respectively, Amenhotep III ranks twenty-fifth and Akhenaten forty-eighth. On the other hand, with an Eigenvector Centrality score of 0.060, the unnamed king of Egypt is first on the list, and if either Amenhotep III or Akhenaten could be identified as that king, their numbers would merge and their ranking would rise accordingly.

How can we interpret the puzzlingly low Eigenvector Centrality scores for these two pharaohs in this network? If we look at the data visualization, we find our answer. As we have seen above, the pharaohs named in the royal Amarna Letters are represented in just one cluster out of the ten shown back in Figure 18—in the lower left corner—as well as at the very top in Figure 17. While that cluster has some cohesion and density, it is not well connected or integrated with any of the other nine clusters. In viewing the network as a whole, it seems that the two pharaohs could be construed as relatively

190

TABLE 3. The top actors in the social network of the Amarna Letters in terms of Eigenvector Centrality (after Cline and Cline 2015, fig. 7)

Vertex	Eigenvector Centrality
King of Egypt	0.060
Aziru	0.028
Rib-Hadda	0.021
Biryawaza	0.014
Abdi-Ashirta	0.013
Aitukama	0.013
Abi-Milku	0.012
Baaluya	0.012
Lab'ayu	0.011
Milk-ilu	0.011
Pu-Bahla(1)	0.011
Surata	0.011
Abdi-Heba	0.010
Manya	0.010
Shuwardata	0.010
wives of Manya	0.010
Zimr-Edda(1)	0.010
Han'i	0.009
son-in-law of Manya	0.009
sons of Manya	0.009
Yanhamu	0.009

peripheral figures in terms of overall activity and connections with others in the network, surprising as that may seem. Looking back to Figure 17, notice how they are perched on the top edge of the whole social network, rather than being centrally located. It is, in fact, the Canaanite petty rulers who dominate the data set of the Amarna Letters and it is this situation that is reflected in these Eigenvector scores.

In contrast, the third type of measure, known as Betweenness Centrality, is an indication of how often a given actor lies along the shortest path connecting otherwise disconnected nodes (Table 4).[3] That is to say, it measures the relative importance of a person's position in the overall structure of the network, especially in terms of being positioned on the shortest pathway for others to get to different parts of the network. It thus measures the extent to which the actor or person can connect or mediate between any two other actors.

TABLE 4. The top actors in the social network of the Amarna Letters, in terms of Betweenness Centrality (after Cline and Cline 2015, fig. 8)

Vertex	Betweenness Centrality
King of Egypt	19696.013
Rib-Hadda	6574.707
Amenhotep III	4798.716
Akhenaten	3609.507
Aziru	3063.697
Surata	1857.723
Tushratta	1748.936
Burna-Buriash II	1549.281
Baaluya	1489.025
Akiya	1379.457
Aitukama	1327.613
Akizzi	1305.232
Biryawaza	1299.165
Haya	1244.337
Abdi-Ashirta	1242.219
Satatna	1235.608
Abi-Milku	952.366
Mut-Bahli	886.696
Adda-danu	729.000
Abdi-Heba	710.469

Do people have to pass information through him or her to get it to others? Would a branch of the network be cut off if he or she weren't there? A high Betweenness Centrality score is an indicator that the individual might have a role that involves gatekeeping, brokering, controlling the flow, or liaising otherwise separate parts of the network. Actors with high Betweenness Centrality tend to behave as brokers, bridges, hubs, connectors, liaisons, and mavens. In the world of the Amarna Letters, they might be messengers, traders, raiders, or diplomats.

We should note that in some ancient social networks, women frequently have high Betweenness Centrality scores, since they bring together two families through marriage and frequently communicate through back channels with others.[4] However, apart from the various royal marriages with which quite a few of the letters sent between the Great Kings were concerned, few other women are mentioned in the Amarna Letters, and therefore the actors with the highest Betweenness Centrality scores listed in Table 4 are all men. These include the kings of Egypt, along with Burna-Buriash II of Babylonia and Tushratta of Mittani, but also some rebels like Aziru of Amurru and Biryawaza of Damascus. These latter two, as we have seen above, are on the list in a negative way; they are both people who link many nodes to each other because they are so troublesome to so many, including a number who reported their nefarious activities to the Egyptian pharaohs in various letters.

However, a comparison can be made with Haya, who also appears on the list. Although we have not mentioned him often in the previous chapters, and although there may be more than one person named Haya among those mentioned in the Amarna Letters, it is fairly clear that this Haya was an ambassador and emissary of the Egyptian king and thus served as a connector or bridge in a positive way. The Betweenness Centrality scores show Haya ranked in fourteenth place out of 264 and reinforces the observation that it is an indicator of the manner in which the individual behaves in bringing the network together, either positively as in the case of ambassadors, messengers or merchants, and wives, or negatively as a common threat.

Rib-Hadda, the ruler of Byblos, scores even higher than Amenhotep III and Akhenaten in Betweenness Centrality, because in his sixty letters he mentions people who otherwise would not be in our database, and thus in the social network, if it were not for him alluding to them. They each have one tie or relationship, which is to Rib-Hadda alone. Each of them is dependent upon him and must go through him to reach any other part of the network.

However, this brings us to a known problem in Social Network Analysis; namely, the issue of the nature of our evidence. If we had additional tablets written by or mentioning those individuals, that is, if we had more of the Amarna corpus, and if we were able to more closely examine their social networks, it might well transpire that Rib-Hadda played only a marginal or peripheral role in their lives. But given the data set that we have, he is everything to them, and that raises his score. As to how much of a power broker he actually was, we shall see in a moment.

Let us now use what we have just learned to look specifically at a few vassals. By examining their various scores, we can see who might have been considered the real power brokers within the Amarna network—was Rib-Hadda really among them or is that just an illusion? These measures can help us to understand the positions that actors hold in the structure of the network, for people who fill equivalent structural roles often hold the same jobs in real life or behave in similar ways.[5] In many cases, it can be interesting to look at the less well-known actors, because their scores can lead us to look in directions that we might not normally have gone or get us to pay more attention to people that we might not have usually thought about.

For example, if we turn back to Aziru and his ties in the upper right-hand box of Figure 18, we can see that he is connected to many of the actors whom we have discussed in the previous chapters—Biryawaza of Damascus, Abi-Milku of Tyre, an unnamed king of the Hittites, Ilu-rapi of Byblos, and Yan-hamu (the Egyptian commissioner), among others. Aziru is one of the two principal actors in the square cluster, second only to Rib-Hadda in Figure 17. (To find Aziru in the network diagram as a whole, locate the node of the unnamed king of Egypt and then look to the right. Aziru is the closest large node, within a sizeable cluster of people.) He is also second in Eigenvector Centrality, behind only the unnamed king of Egypt. And he comes in fourth (out of 248 people) in Degree Centrality, with 33 ties or relationships, and fifth in Betweenness Centrality. We can conclude, therefore, that Aziru was quite important in the Amarna network. This is not particularly surprising given our earlier discussions, but it is nice to see it confirmed visually.

What about Biryawaza of Damascus, seen in the center box of the lower row in Figure 18? He scores fourth in Eigenvector Centrality, ninth in Degree Centrality (with thirteen ties), and thirteenth in Betweenness Centrality. It is clear, from having discussed the letters in the previous chapters, that here we see an example of someone who figures prominently in the social network, but in a negative way, for he was a troublemaker. Recall that numerous people wrote to the pharaoh asking him to do something about Biryawaza and that one letter from Burna-Buriash II to Akhenaten (EA 7) even names Biryawaza specifically as having robbed a caravan sent from Babylonia.

Thus, while Biryawaza is positioned at the very center of the entire network, with connections to Rib-Hadda of Byblos, Aziru of Amurru, and many other petty rulers, it is only because all of them are complaining about his aggressive and uncollegial behavior. (To find Biryawaza on the network chart in Fig. 17, locate Aziru and follow an arc in the direction up toward Akhenaten; Biryawaza is between them.)

Another thing to consider in terms of Social Network Analysis is that individuals with similar scores are often considered to perform similar roles in a network. This is a principle called "regular equivalence" or "structural equivalence," particularly when they share the same neighbors in the network.[6] If we look closely at both Aziru and Biryawaza, for instance, we can certainly detect a similarity in their position and roles within the structure of the network. Both are tied to actors from different clusters, spread like an octopus across clusters. What they have in common besides their structural similarities only becomes clear from the texts, however—they are two of the "bad boys" of the Amarna Letters.

What about Rib-Hadda of Byblos? He is represented by the largest triangle on the right side of Figure 17. He is, of course, overrepresented in the Amarna Letters relative to his actual status, since he is responsible for about sixty of them. He has a Degree Centrality score of forty-one, meaning that he has ties with forty-one unique people, which puts him in second place, sandwiched between the unnamed king of Egypt and Amenhotep III. His Betweenness Centrality score takes second place as well, again between the unnamed king of Egypt and Amenhotep III. And at 0.021, his Eigenvector Centrality score is also very high, in third place, this time just below the unnamed king of Egypt (0.060) and Aziru of Amurru (0.028). So, we should expect to see numerous lines emanating out in a star pattern around him for the forty-one ties (high Degree) and expect him to be quite centrally located and to connect one or more clusters in the network to each other (high Betweenness), as well as to know important people (high Eigenvector), all of which can be seen and confirmed in Figure 17.

Just for interest, let's look at one last vassal with slightly higher than average scores. This is Akizzi, the ruler of Qatna, who is featured in Amarna Letters EA 52–56. (To find him in the whole network sociogram, Fig. 17, find Amenhotep III near the top and look straight below.) We may recall that Akizzi was ruling at a time when Hittite raids were common and tensions in the region were high, in part because of the actions of Aziru of Amurru (see, e.g., EA 55, discussed above).

Akizzi has ten ties (Degree Centrality), which puts him in fifteenth place. He also has a high Betweenness Centrality score of 1305.232, which puts him in twelfth place; and a pretty good but not great Eigenvector Centrality score of 0.009, which puts him in twenty-second place. From a purely social network perspective, we can also observe that he is embedded inside the "Royals" cluster in the lower left-hand box within Figure 18.

It is in Figure 17 that we see his role within the network, however, insofar as it is clear that he serves as a hub or bridge on a number of paths leading to both the unnamed king of Egypt and Amenhotep III. In fact, as Jana Mynářová has noted,[7] he is the only Canaanite vassal ruler to ever address Akhenaten, the Egyptian pharaoh, directly by his prenomen (*nam-hur-ia*) in several letters (EA 53 and 55), which is something that usually only the Great Kings do.

Whereas the other people who have structurally equivalent roles belong to the open diamonds cluster—for instance, the group of "in-betweeners" seen in Figure 17—Akizzi is one of the few located that far "south" in the network to still belong to the "Royals" cluster, represented by a solid square. Thus, a number of his fellow actors would have to go through him to get a message either to the pharaoh or to other important people outside their immediate neighborhood within the network.

However, these are just a few examples; we can learn something from every one of the 246 nodes, or actors, within the network—working to understand to whom they are connected; to which clusters they are assigned; what structural roles they play inside their neighborhoods, both within the clusters and within the structure of the network as a whole; and then looking at their ranking in the Centrality measures to learn more about them. Akizzi and the others are just several among many in the Amarna Letters whom future researchers might profitably investigate at greater length using Social Network Analysis.

———

There is, of course, one big elephant in the room, which is the problem of the unnamed Egyptian pharaoh. By now we are all well aware that many of the Amarna Letters are simply addressed to the "King of Egypt" without actually naming him. In most of these cases, it is impossible to decide whether the letter was meant for Amenhotep III or Akhenaten, if not Tutankhamun or some other pharaoh, like Ay. Thus, we might well wonder what the network would look like if we experimented with making either Amenhotep III or Akhenaten be the generic, unnamed king of Egypt, which would be the most likely scenarios.

It is easy enough to make a global change in the spreadsheets, substituting first one, then the other—Amenhotep III and Akhenaten—for the unnamed king of Egypt, and then to run the SNA software using the new data. In Figure 20, we show the network diagram for the hypothetical situation that would result if Akhenaten were the unnamed king of Egypt, simply as an experiment.

We can see a tight core for the first-degree associates of the king, with a clear periphery emerging as an outer ring of second and even third-degree

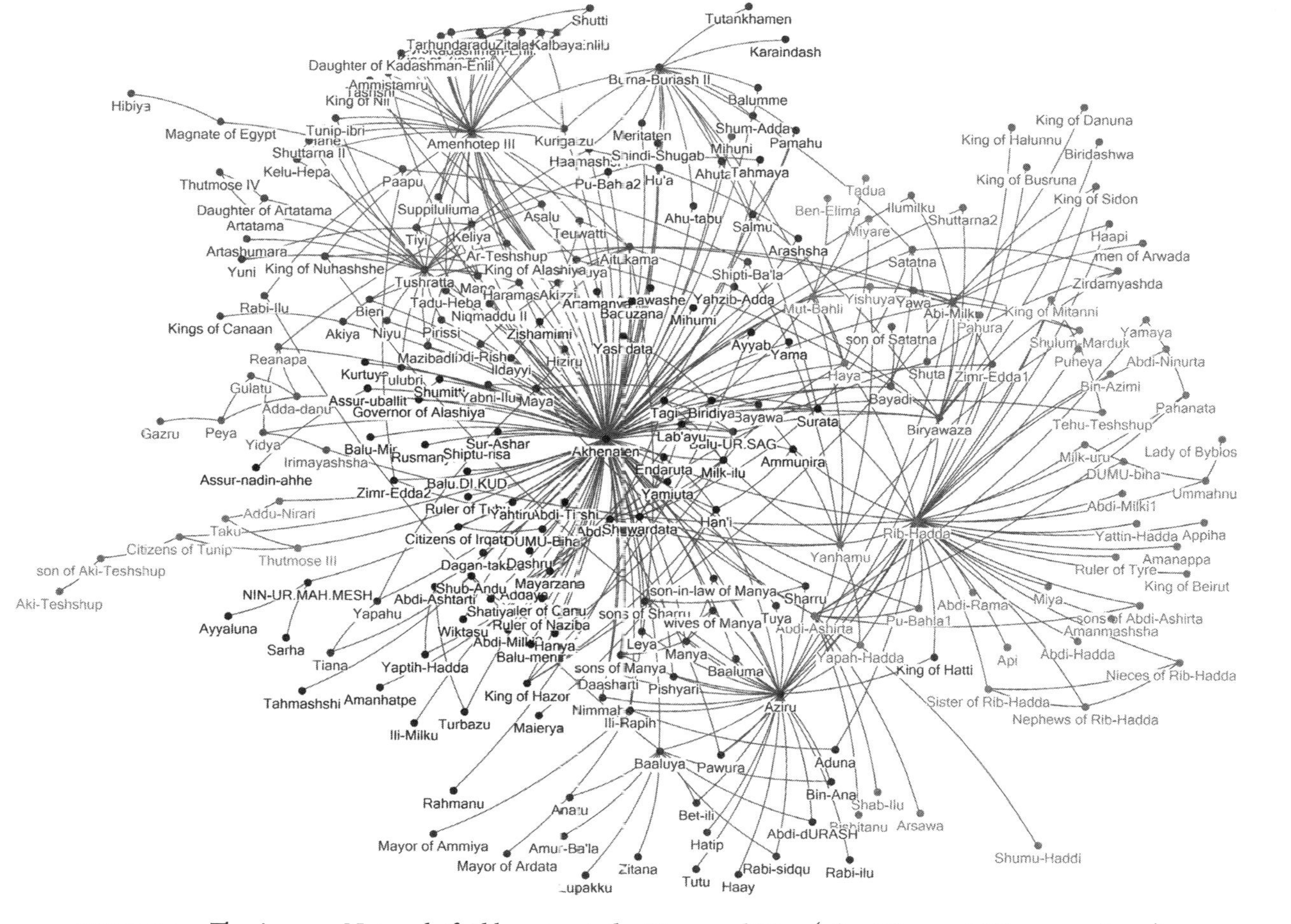

FIGURE 20. The Amarna Network if Akhenaten is the Unnamed King (after Cline and Cline 2015, fig. 13).

relations. There are several prominent hubs visible in the graph—the un-named king of Egypt / Akhenaten is in the center, while Tushratta and Amenhotep III are at the top left. Down and to the right of the king / Akhenaten are two noticeable hubs; the larger one is Rib-Hadda, while slightly below and to the left of him is Aziru.

And, of course, making such changes impacts the overall network data. For example, if we combine Akhenaten and the unnamed king of Egypt into a single node, as we have done in Figure 20, we find that the average path length between individuals comes down from 3.21 to a very healthy and respectable 2.84, which means that we can feel comfortable declaring that it's a Small World after all.

Unfortunately, we cannot determine whether the unnamed king of Egypt in the various Amarna Letters is actually Amenhotep III or Akhenaten in each case. It may be that some letters were written and sent without the sender knowing precisely to whom they were sending their letter(s), simply sending them to whoever was in charge in Egypt at the time. It also may be the case, as in the single letter that might have been sent to Tutankhamun by Burna-Buriash II (EA 9), or the letter sent from Tushratta to Queen Tiyi (EA 26), that the recipient was neither Amenhotep III nor Akhenaten. What the Social Network Analysis indicates is that conflation of the unnamed king of Egypt with one of the known pharaohs makes the network look more realistic and draws attention away from Canaanite vassal interrelations and back toward Egypt, which reinforces the tried-and-true axiom that such an analysis is only as good as the data fed into it.

———

One final thought is relevant here: as we study ancient lives, historians tend to label and categorize people; as we describe them, we frequently pigeonhole them and put them into boxes and discrete groups. The SNA charts remind us that group boundaries are actually fluid, and that humans tend to live in social neighborhoods inside networks; that is, we live in clusters connected by ties to other clusters.[8]

Thus, rather than thinking of a trade route between Amarna and Babylon, perhaps we should think of it instead as the way that two individuals like Akhenaten and Burna-Buriash II might have been able to reach each other. Since they couldn't travel personally, they sent messengers bearing gifts and letters written on tablets. Moreover, we should also keep in mind that the trade routes followed specific roads, meaning that the roads or trade routes themselves are thus also the conduits or flows for social ties; they are the edges that link the nodes, carrying the diplomats, the trade embassies, and the activities that tied people to each other in a social way.

We have examined such social ties here, as seen through the lens of the Amarna Letters, by generating sociograms that allow us to graphically depict such relationships. Data visualization is one part of the digital humanities that involves seeing our data sets in new ways. Such visualizations, like the sociograms, can sometimes point researchers in unanticipated directions, perhaps uncovering relationships or individuals that seem unusual or unexpected, and can launch whole new directions of research, simply by providing a new way to see old and familiar data, such as the Amarna Letters. Viewing our data through the sociological framework of SNA reframes the research focus to look at relationships and the structure of communities that we study.

Thus, Social Network Analysis can be a useful tool for mapping and analyzing social relationships in the Bronze Age world of the Eastern Mediterranean and a fresh way of looking at the Amarna Letters and the information that they contain. And, just as the writing on tablets facilitated social relations in their lives 3,400 years ago, so too can the digital humanities enhance our understanding of them today. We might suspect that Sayce and Budge would approve of such experimentation, and that Winckler and the other Young Berliners would have been intrigued as well.

Epilogue

AFTER AMARNA

THE END of Akhenaten's reign also brought an end to the full-time occupation of the city that he had built in Middle Egypt at Amarna / Akhetaten. The Egyptian court moved back to Karnak / Luxor in Lower Egypt, most likely taking with it part of the royal archives, the communications that were still ongoing and relevant. The letters from days gone by were left at Amarna, in "The House of the Letters of the Pharaoh—Life, Prosperity, Health," to be discovered more than three thousand years later, either by a woman searching for fertilizer or a nefarious antiquities dealer.[1]

Unfortunately, the archive(s) that must have existed in Karnak / Luxor have not yet been discovered, but we know from other sources that the end of Akhenaten's rule did not also spell the end of Egypt's relations with the other Great Powers or with the vassal kings in Canaan. Those interactions continued for another century and a half, until the globalized network of interconnections, their "Small World," came crashing down because of the collapse at the end of the Late Bronze Age in the decades after 1200 BCE.[2]

Thus, such written communications with the other Great Kings and lesser rulers must have continued as well, and there are undoubtedly other archives to be found from the kings who followed the Amarna Period pharaohs, from ca. 1330 BCE to 1177 BCE, but we simply don't have any yet from Egypt. Fortunately, there are such archives known from Hattusa in Anatolia and at the city of Ugarit in northern Canaan. It is from the Hittite archives that we know, for instance, about the so-called Zannanza Affair, in which the widowed Egyptian queen—perhaps Nefertiti but possibly Ankhsenamen—wrote to Suppiluliuma I, asking to marry one of his sons, with unfortunate results, as we have seen.

This is how we also know that Aziru of Amurru, the troublemaker in northern Canaan, eventually realigned his loyalties and became a Hittite vassal, answering directly to Suppiluliuma I. Subsequently, Aziru's successors signed similar treaties with the Hittites thereafter, including his grandson, Tuppi-Teshshup of Amurru, who declared allegiance to the Hittite king Mursili II. Similarly, Benteshina of Amurru subsequently aligned himself with Hattusili III, with such alliances continuing right down until the end of the thirteenth century BCE, when Shaushgamuwa of Amurru signed a treaty with one of the last Hittite kings, Tudhaliya IV.[3]

And it is from these Hittite archives, as well as records carved on Egyptian monuments, that we know the proxy clashes between the Hittites and Egyptians eventually flared into an open war between the two Great Powers, starting with the First and Second Syrian Wars of Suppiluliuma, which took place already during the time of Akhenaten, and culminating in the Battle of Qadesh, fought in 1274 BCE. The latter, ending in a draw, resulted in what is possibly the world's first recorded peace treaty, of which a portion is now on display at the United Nations in New York City. It also apparently resulted in yet another royal marriage, this time successful, in which Pharaoh Ramses II wed an (unnamed) daughter of Hattusili III, and which may have included a visit to Egypt by the Hittite king.[4]

We also have additional Egyptian records, inscribed either upon stelae or upon the walls of temples and other constructions, which document campaigns to southern Canaan conducted by various pharaohs of the Nineteenth Dynasty, including Seti I and Ramses II. Most famously, in 1207 BCE, at approximately the same time as sending relief ships to the Hittites and Ugarit, Pharaoh Merneptah recorded his military campaign to southern Canaan: "Plundered is . . . Canaan with every evil; carried off is Ashkelon; seized upon is Gezer; Yanoam is made as that which does not exist; Israel is laid waste, his seed is not . . ."[5] Leaving aside the whole question of whether the Israelites were actually in Canaan by this point, which I have discussed elsewhere, including in *1177 BC* and *After 1177 BC*, note the mention here of two of the petty vassal kingdoms that we have been discussing in the previous chapters—Ashkelon and Gezer—so we know that they continued to function during the century after the Amarna Period.[6]

We also hear of some of the other individual petty kingdoms in central Canaan during these years, for the archives found at Ugarit, belonging to the merchants who were working for both themselves and the palace, record specific examples and precious details of commercial interactions right up until just before the end came for Ugarit in the years after 1200 BCE. These letters and other records specifically name sites such as Tyre, Sidon, Byblos, and Beirut with whom the Ugaritic merchants were interacting, and give us the name of at least one additional ruler during this period—Adad-Yashma, the king of Sidon.[7]

We also know, however, from both the archives at Hattusa and those at Ugarit, that when push came to shove at the end of the Late Bronze Age, when drought and famine were stalking the populations, and enemy ships were sighted at sea, the Egyptians attempted to help both their former enemy (the Hittites) and the former "Lesser Great Power" (Ugarit) by sending ships full of grain, dried fish, and the like. It was, alas, to no avail, for the Hittites fell, Ugarit was burnt to the ground by invaders, and the globalized network that had flourished during the time of Amenhotep III and Akhenaten collapsed in the years around 1177 BCE.[8]

———

I would like to bring this book to a close by briefly addressing the proverbial question that ancient historians and other academicians should be continually asking themselves: "Why does any of this matter?"

That is a relatively easy question to answer in this case, I believe, for I see the Amarna Letters as a further indication of the interconnectedness of the Eastern Mediterranean area during the Late Bronze Age, giving us insight into a specific thirty-year period. Susan Sherratt of the University of Sheffield has referred to this situation as the "globalized Mediterranean," a description with which I agree and have attempted to illustrate elsewhere. More recently Federico Zangani and others have argued even more strongly that the Late Bronze Age not only "represents an unprecedented phase of large-scale interconnectedness that closely resembles our notion of globalization" but also that it is perhaps the earliest example of such globalization in world history. If they are correct, which might very well be the case, that would be an extremely good reason why we should care about this period and this particular archive.[9]

One major problem that remains unresolved, however, is the lack of any mention of the Mycenaeans or Minoans in this archive, especially given the obvious connections between Egypt and the Aegean during this period.[10] This remains a question and a problem for those of us who see the Aegean region as part of this interconnected world. It may be as simple as the fact that the royal letters, of which there are less than fifty, represent only a small portion of the correspondence in this archive—perhaps as little as 11 percent (according to a recent estimate by Zangani)[11]—and that it is simply an accident that we have no letters to or from the Aegean.

Remember that we also have only a few letters to and from the Hittites, and that only two were sent to and from Assyria, and only two sent to and from Arzawa. If any of these had been lost, or accidentally destroyed, then we would be left wondering at the lack of missives from those countries as well. And indeed, remember how many tablets from the original discovery were reportedly damaged or destroyed entirely in the early days when they were being transported by antiquities dealers before ending up in various museums, including possibly being dropped on the platform of a train station in Cairo. It may be that one or more of these were those sent to or from the Aegean, and thus are now lost to us.

Another interesting point to note is that the letters we do have clearly establish the fact that Akhenaten was taking an active interest in the events taking place in Canaan during this period, contrary to suggestions by previous Egyptologists that he was more preoccupied with the religious revolution that he was fomenting in Egypt itself. Whether or not the Egyptians maintained a firm control on Canaan can be debated, just as we can also debate how to best describe the way that they viewed their presence in the various parts of Canaan. Did they view it as an empire, for instance, or simply as an area over which they exercised some degree of control, otherwise staying out of day-to-day affairs? The discussions will be ongoing.[12]

———

So, as is my wont in writing such books about the ancient world, and as I mentioned briefly at the beginning of this book, I am left wondering if this is all just ancient history or whether there are any modern, or reasonably modern, parallels?[13] One could certainly suggest a comparison to the recent civil war in Syria and to the proxy conflicts that have been instigated in recent years by Iran against Israel in the Levantine regions, from Hezbollah in Lebanon to Hamas in Gaza and the Houthis in Yemen. But even that could be considered trying too hard to make ancient history relevant to today, even if there are similarities to be noted.

Instead, perhaps there are better parallels to the Late Bronze Age world that one could use for comparisons. For example, Niels Peter Lemche, emeritus professor at the University of Copenhagen, has suggested that we might successfully compare the small polities of Late Bronze Age Canaan to the similarly small polities that dotted the landscape during the Ottoman occupation of the region in the centuries prior to World War I.[14]

One could certainly make the case that the balance of superpowers, aka the Great Kings, during the heyday of the Late Bronze Age was not unlike the situation in nineteenth century (CE) Europe. At that time in Europe, not unlike the Amarna Period, the system held together for about a century in part because of all the complex personal alliances, until World War I was triggered by the assassination of Archduke Ferdinand, just as the murder of Zannanza touched off the Egyptian-Hittite wars. Throughout the nineteenth century CE, just like in the fourteenth century BCE, there were several major powers but no single primary dominant state, and many of the kingdoms were related and allied through the process of trading princesses to each other and cementing relationships through dynastic marriages. And, just like the petty Canaanite kings, the various alliances of the rulers in nineteenth-century Europe constantly shifted. Moreover, in what should probably be regarded as simply an interesting coincidence, the apex of this more recent period was at approximately the same time that the Amarna Letters were discovered, in 1887; one wonders if any of the British and German scholars pondered on the similarities of their world and the world that their decipherments were revealing.

And finally, but not to put too fine a point on it, the proxy wars fought by the petty rulers in northern Canaan during the Amarna Period, which culminated in the eventual confrontation between the two Great Powers of Egypt and Hatti at the Battle of Qadesh in 1274 BCE, could be construed to have parallels to the US–Soviet tensions from the 1940s through 1989 (or even today).

Some of the above topics and thoughts have been explored by previous scholars, especially in the volume *Amarna Diplomacy* edited by Cohen and Westbrook, and now more recently by scholars such as De Magistris and Zangani. But perhaps we should also simply understand and appreciate the Amarna Letters for themselves and enjoy the light that they shed on the complex interactions of the fourteenth century BCE, without asking them to do too much else. It is not hard to see why Sayce said in 1923 that "Next to the historical books of the Old Testament, the Tel el-Amarna tablets have proved to be the most valuable record which the ancient civilized world of the East has bequeathed to us."[15]

DRAMATIS PERSONAE

Amarna Period Great Kings, Queens, and Others

Akhenaten, pharaoh of Egypt; ruled ca. 1353–1334 BCE

Amenhotep III, pharaoh of Egypt; ruled ca. 1391–1353 BCE

Ammistamru I, king of Ugarit; ruled ca. 1360 BCE

Assur-nadin-ahhe II, king of Assyria; ruled ca. 1400–1391 BCE

Assur-uballit I, king of Assyria; ruled ca. 1363–1328 BCE

Burna-Buriash II, king of Babylonia; ruled ca. 1359–1333 BCE

Eriba-Adad I, king of Assyria; ruled ca. 1391–1364 BCE

Kadashman-Enlil I, king of Babylonia; ruled ca. 1374–1360 BCE

Niqmadu II, king of Ugarit; ruled ca. 1350–1315 BCE

Shuttarna II, king of Mittani; ruled ca. 1380 BCE

Suppiluliuma I, king of the Hittites; ruled ca. 1350–1322 BCE

Tarkhundaradu, king of Arzawa; ruled ca. 1360 BCE

Tiyi, queen of Egypt and wife of Amenhotep III; ruled ca. 1391–1353 BCE

Tushratta, king of Mittani; ruled ca. 1360 BCE

Tutankhamun, king of Egypt; ruled ca. 1333–1323 BCE

Relevant Canaanite Vassal Rulers

Abdi-Ashirta of Amurru

Abdi-Heba of Jerusalem

Abdi-Tirshi of Hazor

Abi-Milku of Tyre

Addu-nirari of Nuhašše

Aitukama of Qadesh (Qidsi / Qidšu) [also spelled Atak(k)ama,
    Etak(k)ama, Itak(k)ama]

Akizzi of Qatna

Ammunira of Beirut (probably ruled after Yapah-Hadda)

Aziru of Amurru (son of Abdi-Ashirta)
Ba'lu-meher of Yoqne'am (?)
Ba'lu-[UR.SAG] of Rahabu or Rehob
Biridiya of Megiddo
Biryawaza of Damascus
Ilu-rapi of Byblos (brother / usurper after Rib-Hadda)
Intaruta of Achshaph
Lab'ayu of Shechem
Milkilu of Gezer
Satatna of Acco (ruled after Surata)
Shuwardata of Qilti (Keilah)
Surata of Acco
Tagi of Gath-Carmel (father-in-law of Milkilu of Gezer)
Yapah-Hadda of Beirut
Yashdata of Taanach
Yidya of Ashkelon
Zimri-Haddu of Lachish
Zimri-Haddu of Sidon

Egyptian Commissioners and / or Other High Officials
[with Alternate Spellings]

Amon-appa [Amanappa]
Haddaya [Addaya]
Pahanate [Pahamate]
Piwuru [Pawuru / Pawura]
Yanhamu [Yanhanu]

Assyriologists, Egyptologists, Archaeologists, Museum Curators, and Librarians

AMERICAN

Brünnow, Rudolph—German American Orientalist who was eventually appointed to a chair of Semitic Languages at Princeton

Jastrow, Morris, Jr.—Assyriologist; professor at the University of Pennsylvania

Wilbour, Charles Edwin—Egyptologist; sent numerous letters to friends / colleagues commenting on happenings in Egypt at the time

BELGIAN

Delattre, Alphonse J.—Jesuit priest based in Belgium

BRITISH

Bond, Sir Edward A.—principal librarian at the British Museum; recipient of letters from Budge

Boscawen, William St. Ch.—Assyriologist; Budge's immediate predecessor at the British Museum

Budge, E. A. Wallis—assistant keeper of the Department of Egyptian and Assyrian Antiquities at the British Museum; obtained the first set of Amarna tablets during his second trip to Egypt and Mesopotamia, in 1887–1888

Conder, Claude R.—surveyor; led survey of the western Galilee in the 1870s; published on the Amarna tablets and prepared a translation into English of many of them in 1893

Petrie, William M. F.—Archaeologist; dug at Amarna in 1891–1892 and found a few additional tablets

Renouf, Sir Peter Le Page—keeper of Oriental Antiquities at the British Museum

Sayce, Archibald H.—Assyriologist; appointed professor of Assyriology at Oxford in 1891

DUTCH

Tiele, Cornelis P.—professor of Comparative Theology at Leiden University

FRENCH

Bouriant, Urbain—director of the French School in Egypt

Grébaut, Eugène—director of the Antiquities Service and Mission Archéologique in Cairo

Halévy, Joseph—Orientalist and biblical scholar originally born in Turkey; based in Paris

Maspero, Gaston—Egyptologist; gave a tablet to the Louvre (the first of their collection)

Oppert, Jules—Assyriologist, Collège de France; was sent tablet by Bouriant but declared it a forgery

GERMAN

Abel, Ludwig—Assyriologist; responsible for drawing hand copies of the tablets published by Winckler

Bezold, Carl—Assyriologist; published British Museum tablets with Budge

Erman, Adolf—Assyriologist; associate professor of Egyptology at the University of Berlin and director of the Egyptian department at the Royal Museum

Jensen, Peter—Assyriologist who held the first professorial chair in Assyriology at the University of Marburg

Lehmann, Carl Friedrich—former lawyer turned Egyptologist; then a research assistant in the Egyptian department at the Royal Museum in Berlin

Niebuhr, Carl—pen name of Carl Krug; published a book on the Amarna Letters in 1901

Schrader, Eberhard—Assyriologist at the University of Berlin; considered one of the founders of the field of Assyriology

Schroeder, Otto—Assyriologist who studied with both Delitzsch and Winckler in Berlin

Winckler, Hugo—Archaeologist and expert on ancient Near Eastern languages; published the first corpus of Amarna tablets that were in Berlin; later known for excavations at Hattusa

Zimmern, Heinrich—Assyriologist; eventually the first official professor of Assyriology at University of Leipzig

NORWEGIAN

Knudtzon, Jørgen A.—Assyriologist; produced a publication of the entire corpus of Amarna Letters and renumbered the tablets

RUSSIAN

Golénischeff, V. S.—Egyptologist; gave his tablets in 1922 to the Pushkin Museum of Fine Arts in Moscow

SWISS

Boissier, Alfred—Assyriologist; had a distinguished career based primarily in Geneva; donated his large collection of cuneiform tablets to the museum there

ANTIQUITIES DEALERS

Bénedict, G.—French; probably antiquities dealer; handled the purchase enlarging the Louvre's collection

Boulos, Todrus—Egyptian; antiquities dealer in Luxor

El-Hajj, Ali Abd—Egyptian; antiquities dealer in Giza

"Elias" or "Sidrak"—Egyptian; antiquities dealer in Ekhmim; sold thirteen tablets to Frénay, according to Sayce (Elias) or Wilbour (Sidrak)

Graf, Theodor—Austrian; antiquities dealer; owner of a prosperous carpet business, but also good at antiquities dealing; bought 160 tablets and later sold them to the Vorderasiatisches Museum in Berlin

Ismain / Ismail, Farag—Egyptian; antiquities dealer in Giza, who likely dug illicitly at Amarna and then sold some of the tablets to the authorities

Kyticas, Panayotis—probably Greek; antiquities dealer; possibly handled the tablets donated by Rostovitch Bey; also sold one to the British Museum in 1925

Mohassib, Mohammad—Egyptian; antiquities dealer in Luxor

Philip—unknown last name and nationality; antiquities dealer who sold the first two tablets to the Bulaq Museum in Cairo

Tano, Marius Panayiotis—Cypriot, but of Greek origin; antiquities dealer in Cairo

COLLECTORS

Daninos, Albert—Egyptian Egyptologist; worked with Mariette in the Antiquities Service; had large collection of Amarna tablets; sold them to the Vorderasiatisches Museum in Berlin

Murch, Rev. Chauncey—American; important collector of antiquities; sometimes involved in acquisitions and financial dealings for / with the British Museum

Rostovitch, Alexandros—Greek expatriate living in Cairo; gave four tablets to the British Museum

Simon, James—German; textile magnate and friend of the Kaiser; underwrote the purchase of Amarna tablets for the Vorderasiatisches Museum in Berlin

AGENTS

Frénay, Mr.—French; owner of a flour mill in Cairo; acting agent for the Louvre

Niemeyer, Felix von—German; diplomat ("Dragoman") at the German consulate in Cairo; donated one tablet to the Vorderasiatisches Museum in Berlin, purchased from Todrus

Shipping Merchants and Agents Messrs. Buwater, Tanqueray & Co.— British; middlemen for sale of tablets to the British Museum

ACKNOWLEDGMENTS

I am, as always, heavily indebted to the work done by other scholars on whose shoulders I have stood while writing each of the parts of the current book, especially the recent publications by Jana Mynářová, Jacob Lauinger, and Tyler Yoder. I am particularly grateful to the former also for her advice throughout and to the latter pair for permission to quote so extensively from their new translations. I am also grateful to Jana Mynářová and the other coeditors for permission to present here an abbreviated and updated version of a paper that my late wife, Diane Harris Cline, and I gave at a 2014 conference in Prague (published as Cline and Cline 2015). I am very pleased to be able to discuss it again here in the full context of the Amarna Letters as a whole.

Beyond all of the above, I am also very grateful to the two anonymous peer reviewers and to several other colleagues, who called my attention to various relevant publications, provided answers or information, and / or who read and commented on some or all of this manuscript while it was in draft form. With apologies in advance to those whom I may have unintentionally omitted, these include Rachel Hallote, Daniel Lacoretz, Jacob Lauinger, Alice Mandell, Jana Mynářová, Amanda Podany, Christopher Rollston, Tyler Yoder, and especially Mitchell Allen of Scholarly Roadside Assistance—to all of whom I am most grateful. I am also indebted to Billie Jean Collins, of Lockwood Press, for providing me with an advance copy of the book by Lauinger and Yoder (2025).

Finally, particular thanks go to Glynnis Fawkes for her marvelous images and maps, which illustrate the above pages, and, as always, to the team at Princeton University Press, especially Rob Tempio, Chloe Coy, Maria Whelan, Carmen Jimenez, and the director Christie Henry.

NOTES

Introduction: An Unexpected Discovery

1. Translation following Lauinger and Yoder 2025, 373–74. See also Rainey 2015, 1001, 1003, 1561; previously Moran 1992, 298. In the following chapters, all translations from the vassal letters, unless otherwise noted, are by Jacob Lauinger and Tyler Yoder, whose translations are posted online as open access (http://oracc.museum.upenn.edu/aemw/amarna/; CC BY-SA 3.0 license) and are now available in hard copy (2025). I am most grateful to them for permission to quote so extensively from their translations. A few of the translations of the vassal letters, and all of the translations from the great kings' letters, follow Rainey 2015 or Moran 1992 instead, but appropriate reference is made in such instances. I have also taken the liberty of occasionally omitting the various scholarly apparati, such as brackets or parentheses, in cases where it seems clear that the restorations and / or readings are most likely correct, and have also upon occasion changed the spelling of a personal or place name so as to be consistent throughout (for instance, Lab'ayu rather than Lab'aya). In all cases, however, the original publication should be consulted as needed or desired.

2. The story has been repeated many times, sometimes with embellishments (i.e., the tablets were found in a wooden box, or in "an earthenware vessel," according to some later discussions). See, e.g., Campbell 1964, 32–36, with references; Rainey and Notley 2006, 87–88; Thompson 2020, 36.

3. See Mynářová 2007, 11–33, esp. 13–15; 2015, 38–39, both with references for a discussion of where, when, and by whom the tablets might have first been found; also Campbell 1964, 33–36; Mandell 2015, 32–35; Artzi 1985, 8–9; Mandell forthcoming-a. See also, e.g., Budge 1888, 540; Sayce 1888e, 488; 1889b; Bezold and Budge 1892, I; Knudtzon 1907 / 1915, 4–7.

4. On the original name of the building, I have followed Moran 1992, xvi; and Bryce 2003, 223; see also Mynářová 2014, 16–17. On the origins of the tablets that came in from abroad, see, e.g., Goren, Finkelstein, and Na'aman 2004, 1, and their very important discussions throughout the volume, looking at the petrography of each of the tablets in order to identify where it was actually made; also Podany 2010, 186–87, 191–92.

5. Knudtzon 1907 / 1915; see Campbell 1964, 31; Artzi 1985, 4–6.

6. Mandell 2015, 45n99; Rainey 2015, 1–2, 9. See also the various itemizing lists in Moran 1992; Rainey 2015; Mynářová 2007; 2014; 2015; and Goren, Finkelstein, and Na'aman 2004, 1.

7. I have discussed this time period briefly elsewhere, most recently in chapter 2 of *1177 BC: The Year Civilization Collapsed* (revised edition, 2021). This book represents a deep dive specifically into the material found on pages 49–55 of that book, where the Amarna archive and the Amarna Letters are briefly discussed.

1. Dealers and Destructions

1. See, i.e., Mynářová 2007, 15n12, citing previous publications.

2. On his birth, see ruminations in Wilkinson 2020, 289–91, who says that the birth certificate names Budge's father as "Mr. Vyvyan" but with no further details and that "the name looks to have

been hastily added and it has been suggested that it was a decoy, masking the true identity of Budge's father to protect the reputation of a public figure." On his education and other matters, see Budge 1920, 67–68; Thompson 2020, 167; also Wilkinson 2020, 290–91, who says that "the personal interest taken in Budge's education and upbringing by . . . Gladstone is certainly unexpected, given the boy's modest, provincial origins." See also previously Mynářová 2007; 2015.

3. Budge 1920, 133; also Thompson 2020, 37; Wilkinson 2020, 296.

4. Budge 1920, 128–29.

5. Robinson 2012; Buchwald and Josefowicz 2020.

6. Rawlinson et al. 1857; see now Adkins 2004; Machinist 2009, 486.

7. Quoting from Sayce 1889c, 4–5.

8. Sayce 1889c, 4–5; 1923, 251–52, and see also 161–73; also previously Sayce 1917, 89–90.

9. Sayce 1923, 251–52; Sayce 1917, 89; for Wilbour's letters, see Capart 1936, 455–57, 461–62; they were written on 15 January and 5 April 1888. On Wilbour's description of Sidrak, see Capart 1936, 455, 461. See also Mynářová 2007, 25; 2015, 45.

10. See again Sayce 1923, 251–52. See also the various comments offered by Mynářová 2007, 25, 33 about this whole episode involving Frénay, Oppert, and the Bulaq Museum in Cairo; numerous others have also recounted the story re Oppert—see, e.g., Artzi 1985, 9; Thompson 2020, 37; and also further discussion below.

11. Petrie 1894, 23–24.

12. Sayce 1917, 89–90.

13. Sayce 1923, 251–52; also previously Sayce 1917, 89–90.

14. Knudtzon 1907 / 1915, 6–7; Mynářová 2007, 16n18. On Ali Abd el-Hajj, see Mynářová 2007, 28; on Tano, see Mynářová 2007, 22; 2015, 39.

15. Thompson 2020, 37, 60, citing Capart 1936, 432–33 (and see also 455–57). On Wilbour, see Thompson 2020, 58–60; Wilkinson 2020, 321–23.

16. On the tablets at the Cairo Museum, however, see Mynářová 2015, 43–45 and further discussion below; see also Mandell 2015, 39. On Daninos, see Thompson 2015, 232 and Ikram and Omar 2021, 37.

17. The other dealers included Todrus Boulos and Panayotis Kyticas; see Mynářová 2007, 36, 38; 2015, 44–45.

18. For a recent example of an archive looted (and then sold) from a site in Iraq, see, e.g., Pearce and Wunsch 2014.

19. Vita 2015, 140 cites Liverani 1998a, 51–52 as suggesting that there may have been as many as three thousand letters exchanged between these Egyptian pharaohs and the other rulers over the time period involved, in which case we now "have barely 10% of the original correspondence." See also the discussion in Bryce 2003, 223–26.

20. For full discussions of the various museums, the dealers, and the various collections of Amarna tablets, see, e.g., Artzi 1985, 4, 9–14; Mynářová 2007, 21–23, 36–39; 2014; 2015, 44–46; also Rainey 2015, 1–2; Mandell 2015, 39–41; Vita 2015, 107–8.

2. Budge

1. Budge 1920, 128–29. For those not acquainted with the geography of Egypt, the northern part of the country, including from Cairo to Alexandria, is known as Lower Egypt, while Luxor and the southern regions are in Upper Egypt, because the Nile River flows from south to north, i.e., from Upper to Lower Egypt. The site of Amarna is considered to be in Middle Egypt.

2. Budge 1920, 132–33; Mynářová 2007, 16; also Wilkinson 2020, 296.

3. Budge 1920, 141–42; quoted also in Wilkinson 2020, 296–97.

4. Budge 1920, 133; Mynářová 2007, 16; also Wilkinson 2020, 296.

5. Budge 1920, 140.

6. Budge 1920, 139–40; see also Mynářová 2007, 17; 2015, 39–42 for a complete recitation.

7. Budge 1920, 70; see now also Thompson 2020, 38.

8. Budge 1920, 139–41; see now also Thompson 2020, 38.

9. Budge 1920, 139–41; see now also J. Thompson 2020, 38.

10. See, e.g., Machinist 2009, 496.

11. Budge 1920, 141; further details, with citations of the relevant documents in the British Museum archives, from Mynářová 2007, 22–23; 2015, 41–42. For the various conversions, see https://www.historicalstatistics.org/Currencyconverter.html and https://www.in2013dollars.com/uk/inflation/1887.

12. Budge 1920, 141.

13. Thompson 2020, 37, 60, citing Capart 1936, 432–33.

14. Capart 1936, 438–39.

15. Budge 1920, 112.

16. Capart 1936, 461–62; Mynářová 2015, 45.

17. See Mynářová 2007, 17–18, 21; 2015, 40–42, who says that Budge may have acquired the tablets already by ca. 22 December, citing relevant letters from Budge in the British Museum archives, including one dated 27 December 1887, in which he says that he already has "secured" at least seventy-one of the tablets.

18. Budge 1920, 146–47; see also Artzi 1985, 9; Mynářová 2007, 18.

19. Budge 1920, 151–52.

20. Budge 1920, 182–84. Budge does note that there was a bit of a quarrel at one point, when the customs agents suspected that he was smuggling whisky, rather than tablets, until they were assured otherwise.

21. On the above details in these paragraphs, see Budge 1920, 236–41, 338; see also Mynářová 2007, 18–19; 2015, 42. On his preliminary publication of the tablets, see Budge 1888.

22. Budge 1920, 241, 334; also quoted in Thompson 2020, 170 and in Wilkinson 2020, 298.

3. Sayce

1. Sayce 1923, 253–58.

2. Sayce 1923, 251; also previously Sayce 1917, 89; most recently see Thompson 2020, 36–37.

3. Langdon 1933; also Griffith 1933a; 1933b.

4. Sayce 1888a.

5. Sayce 1888a, 123; see also discussion in Mynářová 2007, 19–21.

6. Sayce 1823, 258.

7. Sayce 1923, 258. See also Sayce 1917, 90.

8. Sayce 1917, 90. Emphasis mine.

9. Sayce 1917, 90. See also similar comments about Grébaut's actions and their repercussions in his later autobiography (Sayce 1923, 258). Roda is an island neighborhood located in Cairo; as we shall see, Alexandros Rostovitch is likely to be the "Greek gentleman living at Roda."

10. Knudtzon 1907 / 1915, 7–9 (the acquisition number is given by Knudtzon as 28179; he also says that other pieces, acquired in February, were given the acquisition number 28185, and discusses various other tablets and small fragments acquired from various dealers and private collectors).

11. See Mynářová 2007, 26–27; 2015, 38–39, 43–45.

12. See Budge 1920, 113–14; Thompson 2015, 279.

13. Weens 2016, 135.

14. Even earlier, in a letter dated 15 January 1888, Wilbour had also referred to Frénay as a consul; see Capart 1936, 455, 461–62.

15. Sayce 1888b; 1888c.

16. Sayce 1888b; 1888c.

17. Budge 1888, 541.

18. Sayce 1888b, 211; gleefully quoted by Budge 1888, 540–41 and then in Budge 1920, 142; see also Mynářová 2007, 20; Mandell 2015, 41–42.

19. Sayce 1888c, 246–47; again gleefully quoted by Budge 1888, 540–41 and then in Budge 1920, 142; see also Mynářová 2007, 20; Mandell 2015, 41–42.

20. Langdon 1933; also Griffith 1933a; 1933b.

21. Lyon 1896, 131.

22. Langdon 1933, 502; Griffith 1933a, 498.

23. Griffith 1933b, 65–66; see also Thompson 2020, 60.

24. Griffith 1933b, 65–66; see also Thompson 2020, 60.

25. Thompson 1935, 69, quoted by Thompson 2020, 167.

26. Glanville 1947, 11, quoted by Thompson 2020, 166, who also quotes Renouf, the keeper of Oriental Antiquities at the British Museum, as denouncing Budge as "a cowardly, mendacious, and dishonourable scoundrel." See also Wilkinson 2020, 300.

27. Sayce and Grébaut 1888; see also Mynářová 2007, 19–20.

4. The Young Berliners

1. Erman and Schrader 1888.

2. Erman and Schrader 1888.

3. See, e.g., Artzi 1985, 9; Rainey 2015, 1–2; Mynářová 2007, 28; 2015, 44–45; Thomson 2020, 38. A concise listing of the various translations and publications of the Amarna Letters over the years, which underlie the following discussions, can be found in Mynářová 2007; 2014; 2015; Rainey 2015, 5–10; see now also Mandell 2015, 42–49. The most recent translations of the letters to and from the vassal rulers are by Lauinger and Yoder (2025); as mentioned, they can also be found online at http://oracc.museum.upenn.edu/aemw/amarna/, where they have been posted as open access.

4. Capart 1936, 469–70.

5. Until a scholarly concensus was finally reached, there was frequently uncertainty regarding which variant reading of a cuneiform sign should be used—e.g., one could say either Tushratta or Dushratta depending on how one read the TU sign, which is also DÚ. I am indebted to Amanda Podany, professor emeritus of History from California State Polytechnic University, Pomona, for identifying so clearly the reason(s) for the initial confusion in the reading of such royal names (personal communication with the author, 15 July 2024). She also notes that even in his own letters the king's scribes weren't always sure how to spell his name, using Tu-iš-e-rat-ta or "Tuisheratta" in Amarna Letter EA 17 (line 3), for instance.

6. Budge 1888, 541. This would be Budge's only publication on the topic until 1892, when he and Bezold formally published these tablets, as we shall see below.

7. Budge 1888, 541; see also discussion in Mynářová 2007, 20.

8. Precise quotation is from a footnote in Budge's autobiography (1920, 142). See also discussion in Mynářová 2007, 20.

9. Sayce 1888d, 397. In his November 1889 Manchester lecture, Sayce said essentially the same thing to his audience, including the new dating; see Sayce 1889c, 5, 23. Note that Mynářová 2007, 21n53 suggests that the mention of Vienna is another error introduced by Sayce, based on the fact that Graf was Austrian, and that the tablets actually went directly to Berlin; Sayce then repeated this possible error in subsequent publications.

10. Sayce 1888d, 397.

11. The reason for the difference in dating is both simple and complex. It hinges on a still-debated date for a textual record of the sighting of the planet Venus, made by one or more Babylonian astronomers during the reign of King Ammisaduqa, most likely back in the seventeenth century BCE. The debate was ongoing at the time that the Amarna Letters were discovered, following the initial publication in 1870 of a seventh-century BCE copy of this astronomical tablet, which had been found in the ruins at Nineveh. Such an astronomical sighting would

have been possible once every 56 (or 64) years, but since it is not clear exactly when this event was being recorded by the tablet scribe, the three most likely possibilities have given rise to what are usually referred to as the High, Middle, and Low Chronologies, in which the regnal dates of the famous Hammurabi of Babylon could be either 1848–1806 BCE, 1792–1750 BCE, or 1728–1686 BCE, depending upon which date is preferred for the Venus sighting. The Middle Chronology is followed here, as it is by most American scholars, with Hammurabi's rule dated to 1792–1750 BCE, and everything (including the dates for Burna-Buriash II, Amenhotep III, and Akhenaten) following from that.

12. Budge 1920, 142. It is possible that Budge was remembering Bouriant as "the gentleman in Cairo," recalling the four tablets that Frénay initially sent to Bouriant and that Sayce reported on in his initial letters to *The Academy*. However, as we shall see, Alexandros Rostovitch ("Rostovitch-bey") was the only person living in Cairo at the time who was known to have purchased and possessed exactly four of the Amarna tablets, though Sayce did not publish the details of these in the newspaper, as Budge said; instead, he discussed these in his 1889 article in *PSBA*. It is, however, possible that Budge was conflating the four tablets that Frénay initially sent to Bouriant with the four purchased by Rostovitch at about the same time, perhaps misremembering the exact details of what had transpired more than three decades earlier.

13. Budge 1920, 142; see also Artzi 1985, 9; Mynářová 2007, 20.

14. Sayce 1923, 258–59.

15. Budge 1888, 551–52 with specifics in footnote; Sayce 1888e, 488–90; Mynářová 2007, 20 and n48, with references. See Erman and Schrader 1888; Lehmann 1888a; 1888b; 1888c; also Lehmann 1889; Winckler 1888.

16. Budge 1888; Sayce 1888e; Erman and Schrader 1888; Lehmann 1888a; 1888b; 1888c; Winckler 1888; also slightly later Lehmann 1889 and Winckler 1889a; 1889b. Subsequent major German publications included Winckler and Abel 1889–1890; Scheil 1892; Winckler 1896a; 1896b; followed by Knudtzon 1907 / 1915; Schroeder 1915.

5. Šarru Rabû

1. Translation following Moran 1992, 8–10. Note that I have used this same quotation in Cline 2021, 53–54.

2. Translation following Moran 1992, 2. See also "EA 001," Cuneiform Digital Library Initiative, https://cdli.mpiwg-berlin.mpg.de/artifacts/270887. On this correspondence, see also Bryce 2003, 104 and recently Miller 2017, 97–99. Based on petrographic analysis, as well as the relative chronology of the tablets, Goren, Finkelstein, and Na'aman 2004, 30 suggest that EA 1 "was apparently sent from the former capital, Thebes, and brought to Amarna when the royal court moved there."

3. We do not have his original letter in this instance, but his words are being quoted back to Kadashman-Enlil by the pharaoh (EA 1). Translation following Moran 1992, 1. See also "EA 001," Cuneiform Digital Library Initiative, https://cdli.mpiwg-berlin.mpg.de/artifacts/270887.

4. Translation following Moran 1992, 1. See also "EA 001," Cuneiform Digital Library Initiative, https://cdli.mpiwg-berlin.mpg.de/artifacts/270887. See also discussion in Bryce 2003, 102–3; Podany 2010, 233–35.

5. Translation following Moran 1992, 7. See also "EA 003," Cuneiform Digital Library Initiative, https://cdli.mpiwg-berlin.mpg.de/artifacts/270975. Note that I have also previously discussed this and the following in Cline 2021, 54–55 and previously in Cline 1995. See also Bryce 2003, 92–94 and Podany 2010, 247–52 for various problems with gold shipments.

6. See detailed discussions of these topics in Podany 2010, as just one example, for the bibliography on these topics is immense. See, e.g., also Liverani 1999; Bryce 2003, 90–91; Mayes 2016. On the Amarna Age as "an international society in the making," see Ragionieri 2000, 42, 45.

7. On the detaining of messengers, and other related problems, see, e.g., Gestoso Singer 2016; Abo-Eleaz 2018; 2021a; 2023. We will discuss the issue of gold, also mentioned by Abo-Eleaz 2021a, in detail later in this chapter. See also Abo-Eleaz 2021b on Egyptian royal grants and gifts mentioned in the Amarna Letters, in addition to the earlier publications by Cline 1995 and Cochavi-Rainey 1999 on royal gift-giving during the Late Bronze Age; now also Bryce 2003 and Podany 2010. On Suppululiuma I's First and Second Syrian Wars as well as with his other interactions and treaties with Mittani, for instance, including eventually setting up a puppet king (Shattiwaza) on that throne, see recently, e.g., Beckman 1996, 37–50; Bryce 2005, 155–59, 161–63; Podany 2010, 271–73, 291–301; Cordani 2011a; 2013; Devecchi 2013; Zangani 2022b, 50.

8. Translations following Moran 1992, 14, 19. See also "EA 007," Cuneiform Digital Library Initiative, https://cdli.mpiwg-berlin.mpg.de/artifacts/271036 and "EA 010," Cuneiform Digital Library Initiative, https://cdli.mpiwg-berlin.mpg.de/artifacts/270889.

9. Amarna Letter EA 7; "EA 007," Cuneiform Digital Library Initiative, https://cdli.mpiwg-berlin.mpg.de/artifacts/271036; translation following Moran 1992, 14. See also Cline 2021, 55.

10. Following Moran 1992, 16–17.

11. See Moran 1992, 27–37; Rainey 2015, 112–27, 1342–46.

6. An Arzawan Alliance?

1. See now the brief discussion by Waal 2022, 235–37; also previously Hoffner 2009, 7–21 on scribal training in the Hittite kingdom and elsewhere.

2. See now Hoffner 2009, 42 and texts nos. 94–95; Hawkins 2009.

3. Translation following Rainey 2015, 327; previously Moran 1992, 101–3. See also discussion in Podany 2010, 246–47.

4. I have pointed this out previously elsewhere; see Cline 1998 and also Moran 1992, 102n2.

5. Translation following Rainey 2015, 327, 329.

6. Translation following Rainey 2015, 331; previously Moran 1992, 103.

7. See Moran 1992, 382.

8. See Waal 2022, 236–37.

9. Translation following Hawkins 2009, 77, combined with Moran 1992, 103 and Rainey 2015, 331.

10. See, e.g., Waal 2022, 235–37, citing Hoffner 2009, 270, with references; see also Hawkins 2009, 76, who notes that earlier scholars had long ago proposed this order.

11. Translation following Hawkins 2009, 76–77; also previously Moran 1992, 103 as well as Hoffer 2009, 270.

12. The results were published in a book entitled *Inscribed in Clay: Provenance Studies of the Amarna Letters and Other Ancient Near Eastern Texts*; see Goren, Finkelstein, and Na'aman 2004.

13. Goren, Finkelstein, and Na'aman 2004, 45–47.

7. All's Fair in Love and War (and Diplomacy)

1. Translation following Rainey 2015, 189.

2. Translation following Rainey 2015, 215.

3. Translation following Rainey 2015, 193, 215. See also recently the discussions by Podany 2010, 217–18 and Miller 2017, 99.

4. Regarding these various marriages, see the translations of Amarna Letters EA 17, 20–21, 23–24, and 29 by Moran 1992, 41–42, 47–50, 61–71, 92–99; also Rainey 2015, 134–37, 148–59, 184–241, 300–323, 1349–50, 1352–54, 1358–59, 1368–73; see also the discussions in Bryce 2003, 105 and Podany 2010, 196, 217–31. On the unnamed sister and her marriage to Thutmose IV, see most recently Miller 2017, 99.

5. Translation following Rainey 2015, 221, 223.

6. Translation following Rainey 2015, 143, 145.

7. Translation following Rainey 2015, 205, 225.

8. Translation following Rainey 2015, 205, 225.

9. Translation following Rainey 2015, 135.

10. Translation following Rainey 2015, 137. See also Rainey and Notley 2006, 78–79, Podany 2010, 199, 266–67.

11. See, e.g., Cline 2021, 58; also Podany 2010, 267–70; now Frahm 2023, 61–68.

12. See Rainey 2015, 277, 279; also discussion in Rainey and Notley 2006, 79; Podany 2010, 240–41.

13. See Rainey 2015, 282–95; previously Moran 1992, 90. See also the discussion in Goren, Finkelstein, and Na'aman 2004, 42; Rainey and Notley 2006, 79.

14. See Rainey 2015, 297, 299.

15. See Rainey 2015, 303–23.

16. As noted previously, on Suppiluliuma I's First and Second Syrian Wars as well as with his other interactions and treaties with Mittani, including with Shattiwaza, see recently, e.g., Beckman 1996, 37–50; Bryce 2005, 155–59, 161–63; Podany 2010, 271–73, 291–301; Cordani 2011a; 2013; Devecchi 2013.

8. The Hand of Nergal

1. See especially the recent discussions in Miller 2017, 96–97 and Frahm 2023, 61–68; also previously, e.g., Bryce 2003, 75–76.

2. See "EA 015," Cuneiform Digital Library Initiative, https://cdli.mpiwg-berlin.mpg.de /artifacts/271024; translation following Rainey 2015, 128–29, 1347; see also Moran 1992, 37–38. See also Miller 2017, 96. This letter is now in the Metropolitan Museum of Art (24.2.11).

3. See "EA 016," Cuneiform Digital Library Initiative, https://cdli.mpiwg-berlin.mpg.de /artifacts/270976; translation following Rainey 2015, 130–33, 1348; see also Moran 1992, 38–41, Podany 2010, 248–49, and Frahm 2023, 63.

4. Grayson 1987, 105–8.

5. See Rainey 2015, 358–61; also Devecchi 2012.

6. See discussion in Rainey 2015, 362–69; also Devecchi 2012, with earlier references.

7. For the full details, see discussions in Bryce 2005, 180–84, 188; Cordani 2011; 2013, with references; Miller 2017, 99–100; also Cline 2021, with references.

8. Translations following Moran 1992, 104. See, e.g., Rainey and Notley 2006, 79–80; also Goren, Finkelstein, and Na'aman 2004, 48–51, 70–75 on all of this related correspondence. On this specific tablet, see most recently Humphrey 2022, 33–34.

9. Translations following Moran 1992, 105–6. For a brief synopsis, see most recently Humphrey 2022, 34–35.

10. See now Moran 1992, 112; Rainey 2015, 355

11. Translations following Moran 1992, 110. On this letter, see most recently Humphrey 2022, 35–38.

12. See discussions in Bryce 2005, 180–84, 188; Cordani 2011a; 2013, with references; also Cline 2021, with full references.

13. Translation following Rainey 2015, 345. See now the brief comments by Humphrey 2022, 34.

14. Translations following Moran 1992, 107–8, 110. On EA 37, as well as 38–40, which are not discussed here, see again Humphrey 2022, 34, 38–39.

9. No No Necho

1. Sayce 1888e.

2. Sayce 1888e, 494–96; see also Sayce 1889c, 9 for a slightly different, yet still erroneous translation by Sayce. For transliterations and translations, see Moran 1992, 333–34; Rainey 2015, 1124–25, 1596–97; also Mynářová 2007, 25 and now Lauinger and Yoder 2025, 459–60.

3. Sayce 1888e, 498–99. For transliterations and translations, see Moran 1992, 232; Rainey 2015, 738–41, 1497–98; Lauinger and Yoder 2025, 278–79.

4. Sayce 1888e, 501–4. For transliterations and translations, see Moran 1992, 243–44; Rainey 2015, 782–85, 1507; Lauinger and Yoder 2025, 80–82.

5. Sayce 1888e, 499–500. For transliterations and translations, see Moran 1992, 282; Rainey 2015, 932–33, 1543; Lauinger and Yoder 2025, 512.

6. Sayce 1888e, 504–6. See now Moran 1992, 104–5; Rainey 2015, 332–35, 1375–78; "EA 033," Cuneiform Digital Library Initiative, https://cdli.mpiwg-berlin.mpg.de/artifacts/271098.

7. I am indebted to Amanda Podany for her comments and astute observations regarding the various points made in the paragraphs about this tablet; personal communication with author, 15 July 2024.

8. See Knudtzon 1907 / 1915, 278–80. See also, e.g., Winckler 1896a; 1896b, 81, 85–87 (same pages in both) for examples of similar opening paragraphs from other letters exchanged between Cyprus and Egypt.

9. Sayce 1888e, 506–10. For transliterations and translations, see now Moran 1992, 180–81; Rainey 2015, 580–83, 1450–51; Lauinger and Yoder 2025, 184–86.

10. Sayce 1888e, 510–13; Knudtzon 1907 / 1915, 526–29. For transliterations and translations, see Moran 1992, 201–2; Rainey 2015, 640–43, 1466–67; Lauinger and Yoder 2025, 219–21.

11. Sayce 1888e, 514–17; Knudtzon 1907 / 1915, 458–61. For transliterations and translations, see Moran 1992, 176; Rainey 2015, 560–63, 1447; Lauinger and Yoder 2025, 173–75.

12. Sayce 1888e, 519–25; translation following Rainey 2015, 112. For transliterations and translations, see Moran 1992, 27–34; Rainey 2015, 112–27, 1342–46. I am again indebted to Amanda Podany for her comments regarding Sayce's translation of this tablet; personal communication with the author, 15 July 2024.

13. Griffith 1933b, 65–66; see also Thompson 2020, 60.

14. The last tablet (i.e., the eighty-second tablet at the British Museum) was purchased during Budge's fourth mission in 1890–1891; it was registered in the British Museum collection only on 9 May 1891 (BM E 29829). See Mynářová 2007, 23.

15. Budge 1888, 546, 565–68, Plate VIII–IX. See now Moran 1992, 107–8; Rainey 2015, 340–43, 1379–81.

16. Budge 1888, 546, 554–55; see Moran 1992, 84–86; Rainey 2015, 276–81, 1362–64; also "EA 035," Cuneiform Digital Library Initiative, https://cdli.mpiwg-berlin.mpg.de/artifacts/270891.

17. Budge 1888, 550–51, 557–62, Plates I–IV. These include Amarna Letters EA 17, 19, 23, 26, and 28; see Moran 1992, 41–46, 61–62, 84–86, 90–92; Rainey 2015, 134–37, 140–47, 184–87, 276–81, 295–99, 1349–51, 1358, 1362–64, 1367–68.

18. Budge 1888, 551, 562–64, Plates V–VI; see Moran 1992, 18–19; Rainey 2015, 92–95, 1336; also "EA 009," Cuneiform Digital Library Initiative, https://cdli.mpiwg-berlin.mpg.de/artifacts /270888. But see Miller 2017, 96 and 99n9, who sees the letter as having been sent to Akhenaten, not to Tutankhamun.

19. Oppert 1888, 253 (translated from the original French by E. H. Cline).

20. Oppert 1888, 252–53 (translated from the original French by E. H. Cline).

21. Despite now being lost, the tablet is usually referred to as Amarna Letter EA 260; see Artzi 1985, 9; Mynářová 2007, 25 and n72.

10. Lost in Translation

1. Lehmann 1888a; 1888b; 1888c.

2. Lehmann 1888c, 372; see Winckler 1891, 141n2. As we shall see, this may have been the reason, and the context, for a rather barbed and testy comment made by Winckler in an article that he published in 1891.

3. Lehmann 1888c, 373 (translated from the original German by E. H. Cline).

4. Lehmann 1888c, 374. This is now identified as Amarna Letter EA 7; see Moran 1992, 12–16; Rainey 2015, 82–87, 1331–33; also "EA 007," Cuneiform Digital Library Initiative, https://cdli .mpiwg-berlin.mpg.de/artifacts/271036.

5. Lehmann 1888c, 374–75, citing Winckler 1887, 307 in his footnotes regarding Kurigalzu.

6. Lehmann 1888c, 376–77. On Amarna Letter EA 27, see Moran 1992, 86–90; Rainey 2015, 282–95, 1364–67; also "EA 027," Cuneiform Digital Library Initiative, https://cdli.mpiwg-berlin .mpg.de/artifacts/271181.

7. Lehmann 1888c, 394–406. Again, this is now identified as Amarna Letter EA 7; see Moran 1992, 12–16; Rainey 2015, 82–87, 1331–33; also "EA 007," Cuneiform Digital Library Initiative, https://cdli.mpiwg-berlin.mpg.de/artifacts/271036.

8. On "Amarna Akkadian," see, e.g., Mynářová 2007; 2015, with references.

9. See now, e.g., Naunton 2020; Sheppard 2024.

10. Winckler 1888. On the article itself, it says that it was submitted on 1 November, but a subsequent article by Sayce (1889b, 327) says that it was communicated to the Royal Academy of Berlin on 13 December 1888.

11. See Winckler 1888, 1342 (translated from the original German by E. H. Cline); compare, e.g., Moran 1992, 12; Rainey 2015, 80–81, 1330–31; also "EA 006," Cuneiform Digital Library Initiative, https://cdli.mpiwg-berlin.mpg.de/artifacts/271035.

12. See Winckler 1888, 1343 (translated from the original German by E. H. Cline); compare, e.g., Moran 1992, 22; Rainey 2015, 104–5, 1338–40; also "EA 011," Cuneiform Digital Archive Initiative, https://cdli.mpiwg-berlin.mpg.de/artifacts/271037. This was most likely also briefly discussed by Lehmann in his article.

13. Amarna Letter EA 16; see Winckler 1888, 1344–45 (translated from the original German by E. H. Cline); compare, e.g., Moran 1992, 38–41; Rainey 2015, 130–33, 1348–49; also "EA 016," Cuneiform Digital Library Initiative, https://cdli.mpiwg-berlin.mpg.de/artifacts/270976. On Assur-uballit I, see now Frahm 2023, 61–68.

14. Winckler 1888, 1346–48.

15. Winckler 1888, 1351–56. These include what are now labeled as Amarna Letters EA 20, 21, 22, 24, 25, 27, and 29; see, e.g., Moran 1992, 47–61, 63–84, 86–90, 92–99; Rainey 2015, 148–83, 188–275, 282–95, 300–323, 1352–57, 1359–62, 1364–73. They should be reunited with the other Tushratta letters, which are in the British Museum, including Amarna Letters EA 17, 19, 23, 26, and 28.

16. This is Amarna Letter EA 31; see Winckler 1888, 1348–50; Moran 1992, 101–3; Rainey 2015, 326–29, 1374–75; also Knudtzon 1902a; "EA 031," Cuneiform Digital Library Initiative, https:// cdli.mpiwg-berlin.mpg.de/artifacts/270973. I thank Jana Mynářová for pointing out that Winckler was, in fact, correct about the place name.

17. Sayce 1888f, 424–25.

18. See, e.g., Sayce 1889b, 327, written after Winckler sent him the 1888 article.

19. Sayce 1889a, 47; see also Sayce 1889b, 327.

20. See now "EA 003," Cuneiform Digital Library Initiative, https://cdli.mpiwg-berlin.mpg .de/artifacts/270975/reader/50104 and the translations in Moran 1992, 7–8; Rainey 2015, 68–71, 1326–27.

11. Flights of Fancy

1. Delattre 1889a; 1889b.

2. See, e.g., Conder and Kitchener 1882.

3. See "Conder, Claude Reignier" 1912.

4. Conder 1889a, 98; 1889b, 28–30.

5. Sayce 1889b, 326–27; his earlier article was Sayce 1888e. See now also Mynářová 2007, 26.

6. Sayce 1889b, 326–27.

7. Sayce 1888f, 424–25.

8. Sayce 1888f, 425; 1889b, 334–36, no. VI. This is now Amarna Letter EA 39; see Moran 1992, 112; Rainery 2015, 354–55; also "EA 039," Cuneiform Digital Library Initiative, https://cdli .mpiwg-berlin.mpg.de/artifacts/270978.

9. Sayce 1888f, 425; 1889b, 327, 336–40, no. VII; see again Moran 1992, 101–3; Rainey 2015, 326–29, 1374–75; also "EA 031," Cuneiform Digital Library Initiative, https://cdli.mpiwg-berlin .mpg.de/artifacts/270973.

10. Sayce 1888f, 424–25.

11. Sayce 1889b, 344–45, no. IX; see also discussion in Sayce 1889c, 20–21. This is now identified as Amarna Letter EA 158; see the transliteration and translation in Rainey 2015, 786–89, 1508; previously Moran 1992, 244–45; now also Lauinger and Yoder 2025, 82–83. Tutu is also mentioned in several other letters written by Aziru; see, e.g., Amarna Letters EA 164, 167, and 169. On the terminology of kinship in the Amarna letters, see, among many other discussions, Cline 1995; Liverani 2000, 18–19; Pfoh 2016, 36. Tutu's tomb has been located and excavated at Amarna (no. 8); see, e.g., Murnane 1995, 187–98; for a recent full discussion, see Zangani 2022a, also Zangani 2022c, 178; previously Campbell 1964, 72–74, with references.

12. Sayce 1889b, 326. See now also Mynářová 2007, 25.

13. Sayce 1889b, 354–56, no. XIII; the other two are Sayce 1889b, 402–13, nos. XXXII–XXXIII. The three tablets were eventually published by Izre'el 1995 and are now included in Rainey 2015 as Amarna Letters EA 70, 137, and 160. Note that Rib-Hadda's name was often rendered as Rib-Addi or Rib-Adda until fairly recently (including in Moran's 1992 translations).

14. The relevant Megiddo (or related) tablets include Amarna Letters EA 242–48 and 365; there is also a mention of Megiddo in passing in Amarna Letter EA 234. On "Magdali" rather than "Megiddo" in Amarna Letter EA 70, see Rainey 2015, 442–43, 1412–13; also previously Knudtzon 1907 / 1915, 365.

15. Sayce 1889b, 377–79, no. XXIII. Again, this is now identified as Amarna Letter EA 3; see the translation in Rainey 2015, 68–71, 1326–27; previously Moran 1992, 7–8; also "EA 003," Cuneiform Digital Library Initiative, https://cdli.mpiwg-berlin.mpg.de/artifacts/270975/reader /50104.

16. Sayce 1889b, 383–85, no. XXV; Luckenbill and Allen 1916. On Murch himself, see Mynářová 2007, 17, with further references.

17. See discussion in Rainey 2015, 6–7; also Mynářová 2007, 36, 39. This is now simply identified as Amarna Letter EA 26, because of the full join; for the joined tablet and full translation, see now Moran 1992, 84–86; Rainey 2015, 276–81, 1362–64. See also "EA 026," Cuneiform Digital Library Initiative, https://cdli.mpiwg-berlin.mpg.de/artifacts/270897.

18. Sayce 1889b, 388–402, nos. XXVIII–XXXI. As mentioned above, I suspect that there is a good chance that these were the four tablets to which Budge was referring when he discussed "the gentleman in Cairo" who had four tablets which he showed to Sayce. In addition, as mentioned, Rostovitch is also likely to be "the Greek gentleman living at Roda," to whom Sayce later referred in a 1917 article.

19. See Sayce 1889b, 388–92, no. XXVIII; Moran 1992, 90–92; Rainey 2015, 296–99, 1367–68; also "EA 028," Cuneiform Digital Library Initiative, https://cdli.mpiwg-berlin.mpg.de/artifacts /270967.

20. Sayce 1889b, 413.

21. Sayce 1889d.

22. Sayce 1889b, 326. See also Mynářová 2007, 26.

23. Mynářová 2007, 23n64, with full references and documentation.

12. Winckler and Abel

1. Winckler 1889a; 1889b. On the history of the various publications, both those already mentioned and those which will follow, see the very useful discussions by Mandell 2015, 42–49.

2. Winckler 1889b; Lehmann 1889.

3. Winckler 1889a, 42.

4. Winckler 1889a, 43–46.

5. Winckler 1889a, 46–47.

6. Winckler 1889a, 47.

7. Winckler 1889a, 47–48.

8. Winckler 1889a, 48.

9. Winckler 1889a, 48–52.

10. Winckler 1889a, 52–61.

11. Winckler and Abel 1889–1890, vol. 1, unnumbered page at the front (translated from the original German by E. H. Cline).

12. Note that the other letter from Assur-uballit of Assyria (EA 15), which is now in the Metropolitan Museum of Art in New York, was not included in this volume nor was the fragmentary letter from Tarkhundaradu to Amenhotep III (EA 32), even though the latter was in Berlin; those and numerous others (since we are now up to almost fifty such royal letters) would have to wait for inclusion until Knudtzon's volumes in 1907 / 1915, as would the correction that EA 31 had been sent by Amenhotep III rather than to him (Knudtzon 1907 / 1915, 271).

13. See comment in Winckler 1891, 141n1.

14. Winckler and Abel 1889–1890, vol. 2, unnumbered page at the front (translated from the original German by E. H. Cline).

15. Winckler 1896a; 1896b.

16. Capart 1936, 548. From this letter, it is also clear that Wilbour owned a fragmentary statue or sculpture of one of Akhenaten's daughters.

17. Mynářová 2007, 23n64, with full references and documentation.

18. Zimmern 1890a. In Winckler 1891, 141n2 he says: "I expressly note that Dr. Zimmern has published his adaptation of texts in *Zeitschrift* V with my consent" (translated from the original German by E. H. Cline). Zimmern also published another article in this same volume, which was expressly concerned with the grammar of the tablets (see Zimmern 1890c).

19. Zimmern 1890a, 137 (translated from the original German by E. H. Cline).

20. Zimmern 1890a, 138–45.

21. Rainey 2015, 82–87; see also Moran 1992, 12–16. See also Bryce 2003, 72–74; Rainey and Notley 2006, 78; Podany 2010, 206–7. On distances, and the time involved, for messengers to travel round-trip, see Liverani 2000, 21–22.

22. Rainey 2015, 82–87; see also previously Moran 1992, 12–16. See also Podany 2010, 247–52 for various problems with gold shipments, as we will discuss.

23. See Zimmern 1890a, 150–53; Moran 1992, 16–19; Rainey 2015, 89–95, 1333–36; previously Budge 1888, 560–62, Plates I–IV; also "EA 008," Cuneiform Digital Library Initiative, https://cdli.mpiwg berlin.mpg.de/artifacts/271038, and "EA 009," Cuneiform Digital Library Initiative, https://cdli.mpiwg-berlin.mpg.de/artifacts/270888.

24. See Zimmern 1890a, 154–65; Moran 1992, 43–46; Rainey 2015, 140–47, 1350–51.

13. The Lab'ayu Affair

1. See, among many numerous publications, e.g., Bryce 2003, 124–34, as well as the article by Pfoh 2019, who points out that the term for these rulers, *hazannu(tu)*, is frequently translated as "mayor" rather than "king" (p. 252). See now also De Magistris 2024, who notes in addition

that we might consider the territory over which they rule to be more like tribal chiefdoms than city-states or small kingdoms (pp. 255–56); Pfoh 2016, 99–106 touches on the same topic (city-states) as well. For good maps with the locations of these small polities indicated, see, e.g., those in Goren, Finkelstein, and Naʾaman 2004; also the very useful Map II ("Syria in the Amarna Age") shown in Singer 1990, 139; also Map 1 in Vita 2015.

2. David 2000, 59.

3. David 2000, 59–60, also 62, 67.

4. Mynářová 2007; 2015; Morris 2006.

5. Regarding the possible identification of Qilti / Keilah with Hebron, see Morris 2006, 189, citing Several 1972, 126.

6. In this chapter and those following, which are concerned with the vassal letters, please note again that all translations unless otherwise stated are by Lauinger and Yoder (2025). A few of the translations follow Rainey 2015 or Moran 1992, but appropriate reference is made in such instances.

7. See Moran 1992, xxxvi–xxxvii on the dating; also previously Campbell 1964, who is concerned with the chronology of the individual Amarna Letters, including this series. As with many of the topics discussed in both this and the next few chapters, the bibliography on Lab'ayu and Shechem is rather large; see, for example, Campbell 1965; Adamthwaite 1992; Finkelstein and Naʾaman 2005; Rainey and Notley 2006, 83–85; Arie 2016.

8. Lauinger and Yoder 2025, 371. See Rainey 2015, 997; also Moran 1992, 297.

9. Lauinger and Yoder 2025, 373–74. See also Rainey 2015, 1001, 1003, 1561; previously Moran 1992, 298.

10. Lauinger and Yoder 2025, 372. See also Rainey 2015, 999; previously Moran 1992, 297. On the 'apiru much has been written: see, e.g., Rainey and Notley 2006, 88–89, with earlier references; also Rainey 2015, 31–35; Grabbe 2016, 25–26; Lemche 2016, 136–37, 144–45. I am following Rainey and Naʾaman in spelling it as 'apiru rather than *habiru* or *hapiru*, as is sometimes done, including by Lauinger and Yoder.

11. Lauinger and Yoder 2025, 389–91. See also Rainey 2015, 1023, 1025, 1568; previously Moran 1992, 305–6.

12. Lauinger and Yoder 2025, 391–92. On all of this, see also Rainey 2015, 23–25, 1027, 1029, 1569; previously Moran 1992, 306.

13. Lauinger and Yoder 2025, 392–94. See also Rainey 2015, 1031, 1033, 1570; previously Moran 1992, 307; also Lemche 2016, 137–39. On the Egyptian commissioners, see most recently Abo-Eleaz 2021c, with earlier references, and now De Magistris 2024.

14. Lauinger and Yoder 2025, 374–76. See also Rainey 2015, 25–26, 1005, 1007, 1562; previously Moran 1992, 299. Regarding Ba'lu-meher as probably the ruler of Yoqneam, see now Finkelstein and Naʾaman 2005, 174–75; Goren, Finkelstein, and Naʾaman 2002, 227–31; 2004, 250–55.

15. Lauinger and Yoder 2025, 360–62. See also Rainey 2015, 975, 977, 1555–56; previously Moran 1992, 291–92. (Note that Moran thought that the second letter was sent by Satatna, Surata's son and successor as ruler of Acco. Rainey corrected this to say that it is, in fact, a second letter from Surata, but now Lauinger and Yoder have returned to Moran's original assignation to Satatna.)

16. Regarding Yashdata's plight, we are told about this in Amarna Letter EA 248, where it says: "Speak to the king, my lord and Sun god and my god, a message from Yashdata, a loyal servant of the king and the dust of the feet of the king, my lord and Sun god and my god. I fall seven times and seven times. The king, my lord, should know that the entirety of everything that the king, my [lord], gave to h[is] servant, has been taken away. Men of Taanach slaughtered my cattle and drove me away. Now, I am with Biridiya. The king, my lord, should care for his servant." Lauinger and Yoder 2025, 381–82. See also Rainey 2015, 1013, 1564; previously Moran 1992, 301. It is not clear whether Lab'ayu had anything to do with this.

14. The Sons of Lab'ayu

1. Lauinger and Yoder 2025, 377. See also Rainey 2015, 1009; previously Moran 1992, 300.

2. Lauinger and Yoder 2025, 384–87. See also Rainey 2015, 1017, 1019, 1566; previously Moran 1992, 303–4. On the discussion of where this man ruled, see most recently Goren, Finkelstein, and Na'aman 2004, 249–50.

3. See Cline and Cline 2015, 30, 32, 38–39, and figs. 4–8. Previously, e.g., Na'aman 1988.

4. Translation following Moran 1992, 14; see also Rainey 2015, 87; Cline and Cline 2015, 38–39.

5. See Rainey 2015, 89, 91; previously Moran 1992, 16–17.

6. Lauinger and Yoder 2025, 362–63. The letter is concerned with another man, Zirdam-yashda, who had deserted from the service of Biryawaza and came to serve with Satatna instead. Somehow Megiddo was involved in this escapade, since Zirdam-yashdata was apparently with the Egyptian army in that city just before he deserted to Biryawaza, according to Satatna's letter. See Rainey 2015, 979, 981; previously Moran 1992, 292–93.

7. Lauinger and Yoder 2025, 407. See also Rainey 2015, 1249, 1630–31; previously Moran 1992, 365.

8. Lauinger and Yoder 2025, 291–94. See also Rainey 2015, 763, 765, 767, 1502; previously Moran 1992, 238–39.

9. Lauinger and Yoder 2025, 335–36. See also Rainey 2015, 883, 885, 1529; previously Moran 1992, 269–70. See also Amarna Letter EA 52, from Akizzi of Qatna, who also mentions Biryawaza; cf. Rainey 2015, 398.

10. Lauinger and Yoder 2025, 321–22. See also Rainey 2015, 897, 1532–33; previously Moran 1992, 273.

11. Lauinger and Yoder 2025, 322–24. See also Rainey 2015, 899, 901, 1533–34; previously Moran 1992, 273–74.

12. Lauinger and Yoder 2025, 324–26. See also Rainey 2015, 903, 905, 1534–36; previously Moran 1992, 274–75.

15. Jerusalem, O Jerusalem

1. Jensen 1890; Brünnow 1890; Sayce 1890d.

2. Sayce 1890c, 56.

3. Sayce 1890c, 61–90.

4. Sayce 1890c, 57, 59–60. See Winckler 1889a, 53–54, who also sees Dûdu as Aziru's father, without further commenting on the relationship. In contrast, Pfoh 2016, 36, citing previous scholarship, especially by Mario Liverani.

5. Conder 1890. In fact, the whole idea of a supposed "Altaic language family" in and of itself is now generally rejected by modern linguists.

6. See Barton 1925, 14; also the material in *Mitteilungen der Vorderasiatischen Gesellschaft* 1915 (1916) and at https://paleocentrum.ru/popular/gugo-vinkler-1863-1913.html. I am grateful to Klaus Wagensonner, Samantha Clark, and others on social media for their assistance in locating these obituaries for Winckler.

7. Halévy 1890a; quotation from pp. 199–200 (translation from the original French by E. H. Cline).

8. Halévy 1890b.

9. Sayce 1890a, 273.

10. Sayce 1889c, 11.

11. Anonymous 1890, 340.

12. Zimmern 1890b; 1891b; 1891c, 137–40, with notes.

13. Sayce 1890b, 366.

14. Boscawen 1891, 116–18. On Boscawen's career, see Horry 2015.

15. Zimmern 1890c, 142n4; translation following Moran 1992, 334.

16. Sayce 1889c, 1.

17. Sayce 1889c, 7.

18. Cline 2007, 44–45; see previously Matthiae 1977; Shanks 1979; Pettinato 1981; Millard 1992.

16. Publish or Perish

1. Winckler 1891, 141–42 (translated from the original German by E. H. Cline).

2. Winckler 1891, 142 (translated from the original German by E. H. Cline).

3. Winckler 1891, 143–43 (translated from the original German by E. H. Cline).

4. Zimmern 1891a; 1891b; 1891c, 137–40, with notes.

5. Halévy 1891a; 1891b; Conder 1891a; 1891b; Sayce 1891.

6. Delattre 1890; 1891a; 1891b; 1891c.

7. For Delattre on Aziru's real father, see 1891a, 215; 1891b, 320. See previously Delattre 1889b, 84–85 on the use of such terms in the letters between the great kings; there he cites Winckler 1889a, 11n33, but since Winckler's article is on pages 42–64 and there is no note 33, it is unclear to which publication Delattre actually meant to refer.

8. Sayce 1891, 54.

9. Sayce 1891, 54–55.

10. Sayce 1891, 55.

11. Sayce 1891, 60–63; on the meaning of the name, which is now often mistranslated as "city of peace," see, e.g., Cline 2000, 1–2, 16–19, with references. Sayce also noted (p. 65) that Zimmern had sent him an advance copy of a paper entitled "Die Keilschrift-briefe aus Jerusalem," which was to be published in the *Zeitschrift für Assyriologie* (see now Zimmern 1891b).

12. Sayce 1891, 69; see also Zimmern 1891b, 259. This is now identified as Amarna Letter 288.

13. EA 288; Lauinger and Yoder 2025, 453–56. See also Rainey 2015, 1117–19; previously Moran 1992, 331. See also brief discussion of this tablet in Cline 2000, 18.

14. Petrie, private journal, entries from 21–27 December 1891, page 66, Griffith Institute, University of Oxford, available online at https://archive.griffith.ox.ac.uk/index.php/petrie-1-11.

15. Petrie, private journal, entries from 3–9 January 1892, page 75; see now also Mynářová 2007, 33–35; Thomson 2015, 39.

16. Petrie, private journal, entries from 24–30 January 1892, pages 94–95; see now also Mynářová 2007, 33–35.

17. Petrie, private journal, entries from 24–30 January 1892, page 95.

18. Sayce 1894. See the comments by Rainey 2015, 5, who states: "It has been convincingly argued that the texts were not only stored there [at Amarna] but that scribes were trained there as well (Izre'el 1997, 9–13)." See now Devecchi 2012, discussing who wrote the letters sent from the Hittites that were found in the Amarna archive, with earlier references. See also Vita 2012; 2015; and Cohen 2023 on scribes and scribal hands in the Amarna Letters.

17. Bezold and Budge, Finally

1. Bezold and Budge 1892.

2. Bezold and Budge 1892, xiv–xv.

3. Bezold and Budge 1892, xv.

4. Bezold 1893.

5. Bezold 1893, v–vi.

6. Abel 1892; cf. Sayce 1889b, 383–85, no. XXV. The tablet in question, as noted above, is now identified as Amarna Letter EA 26.

7. Boissier 1892.

8. Jastrow 1892; previously Zimmern 1891c.

9. Jastrow 1892, 98–99n11.

10. Jastrow 1892, 103–14, 116–18 and n19, n22.

11. Jastrow 1892, 106n25.

12. Jastrow 1892, 114n37.

13. Jastrow 1892, 118, also 119–22. On the *'apiru* vs. Hebrews, the literature is plentiful, as mentioned, but see again, e.g., Rainey 2015, 31–35; Grabbe 2016, 25–26; Lemche 2016, 136–37, 144–45.

14. Delattre 1892–1893a; 1892–1893b; 1892–1893c; 1892–1893d. See Jastrow 1892, 105n22 re the praise for Delattre.

15. Delattre 1892–1893a, 22–30. See now Moran 1992, 1–5; Rainey 2015, 58–65, 1323–26.

16. Jastrow 1892–1893; 1893.

17. Conder 1892, 711–12. The former is Amarna Letter EA 31 (see Moran 1992, 101–3), which is indeed written in Hittite. The latter tablet is Amarna Letter EA 24 (see Moran 1992, 63–71 and, previously, Winckler and Abel 1889: see the comment on the second page of the unnumbered Table of Contents, where it is no. 27).

18. Conder 1892, 713–14.

18. Facts and Alternative Facts

1. Conder 1893, ix.

2. Conder 1893, ix.

3. Horry 2015, 108–9; Horry states specifically that Boscawen took such classes, while it is my suggestion that Conder may well have done so too, though I have no firm evidence for that at the moment.

4. Conder 1893, x.

5. Conder 1893, 1, 3.

6. Conder 1893, 111–13 and n1, 139n1. On the translation of the Hazor king's name in what is now identified as Amarna Letter EA 228, see now, e.g., Moran 1992, 289–90 and Rainey 2015, 967; I thank Amanda Podany for her insights on this matter.

7. Tiele 1894, 6–7.

8. Tiele 1894, 7–8.

9. Tiele 1894, 18; Budge 1888, 551.

10. Tiele 1894, 13; Sayce 1889b, 377–79.

11. Tiele 1894, 21; Sayce 1888f, 425; 1889b, 344–45.

12. Molendijk 2000, 89.

13. Winckler 1896a; 1896b.

14. Winckler 1896b, v.

15. Winckler 1896a; 1896b.

16. Petrie 1898; Niebuhr 1901, 10. On Krug / Niebuhr, see Merrillees 1987, 19. I am indebted to a number of people, including Suzanne Wilhelm, Eckart Frahm, Laurel Poolman, and Timothy Sailors for their aid in locating and identifying Krug.

17. Knudtzon 1907 / 1915; see brief discussion by Mandell 2015, 44–45. Knudtzon had previously published on various Amarna Letters; see, e.g., Knudtzon 1902a; 1902b.

18. Knudtzon 1907 / 1915; see Campbell 1964, 31; Artzi 1985, 4–6.

19. Schroeder 1915. In addition to the new Berlin tablets, the others include seven tablets acquired in 1918 that are now in the Louvre in Paris, two tablets purchased in Cairo in 1924 that are

now at the Met in New York, a tablet sold to the British Museum in 1925, and a tablet purchased in 1933, which is now in Brussels; see Artzi 1985, 4–6; Mynářová 2015, 45–46; Rainey 2015, 1–2, 9.

20. Mercer 1939; Moran 1987; 1992. Moran's earlier articles have been compiled and republished as Moran 2003, edited by Huehnergard and Izre'el. See full discussion, with additional references, in Mandell 2015, 42–49; also the compilations and discussions by Mynářová 2007; 2014; 2015.

21. Rainey 2015; and see now Lauinger and Yoder's translations 2025 and http://oracc .museum.upenn.edu/aemw/amarna/.

22. Regarding "Canaano-Akkadian," I am grateful to Alice Mandell for her comments in a personal communication, 18 June 2024. See also von Dassow 2004; Izre'el 2005; Tropper and Vita 2010; Rainey 2015, 11–13; Mandell 2015; 2022; 2024; forthcoming-a; Lauinger and Yoder 2025, 12–17.

23. Alice Mandell, personal communication to the author, 18 June 2024; see also Mandell 2022.

24. Amanda Podany, personal communication to the author, 15 July 2024.

25. See, e.g., Podany 2010; Bryce 2003; Cohen and Westbrook 2000. See also Mandell forthcoming-b, which I am grateful to have seen before its publication.

19. The Dog of His House

1. The bibliography on Amurru in the Amarna Letters, including specifically on Abdi-Ashirta, is rather large; see, for example, the discussions in Moran 1969; Altman 1977; Izre'el and Singer 1990; Singer 1990, 124–28; 1991, 141–48; Liverani 1998a; 1998b; Bryce 2003, 137–44; Goren, Finkelstein, and Na'aman 2003; 2004, 101–25; Bryce 2005, 167–70; Rainey and Notley 2006, 80–81; Miller 2008; Devecchi 2010; Morris 2010; Cordani 2011b; Vita 2012; 2015, 15–20; Rainey 2015, 18–19; Kilani 2020, 167–71.

2. Lauinger and Yoder 2025, 74–75. See also Rainey 2015, 419, 1403–4; previously Moran 1992, 131–33. On the many publications concerned with Tell Kazel, see Cline 2021, 109–10 with references; on Kazel and Sumur, see most recently De Magistris 2023.

3. Lauinger and Yoder 2025, 75–76. See also Rainey 2015, 421, 1405; previously Moran 1992, 133.

4. Lauinger and Yoder 2025, 76–78. See also Rainey 2015, 423, 425, 1405–7; previously Moran 1992, 133.

5. See, e.g., Campbell 1964, 77–80; most recently Kilani 2020.

6. Lauinger and Yoder 2025, 112–14. See also Rainey 2015, 445, 447, 1413–14; previously Moran 1992, 140–41.

7. Lauinger and Yoder 2025, 115–17. See also Rainey 2015, 451, 453, 1415–16; previously Moran 1992, 141–42.

8. Lauinger and Yoder 2025, 118–21. See also Rainey 2015, 455, 457, 1416–17; previously Moran 1992, 142–45.

9. Lauinger and Yoder 2025, 122–24. See also Rainey 2015, 459, 461, 1417–18; previously Moran 1992, 145–46.

10. Lauinger and Yoder 2025, 124–26. See also Rainey 2015, 463, 465, 1418–20; previously Moran 1992, 146–47.

11. See also similarly the broken tablet Amarna Letter EA 78; Rainey 2015, 471, 473, 1422–23; previously Moran 1992, 148–49.

12. Lauinger and Yoder 2025, 130–31. See also Rainey 2015, 475, 477, 1423; previously Moran 1992, 149–50.

13. Lauinger and Yoder 2025, 133–35. See also Rainey 2015, 483, 485, 1424; previously Moran 1992, 150–51.

14. Lauinger and Yoder 2025, 135–38. See also Rainey 2015, 487, 489, 1425; previously Moran 1992, 152–53.

15. Lauinger and Yoder 2025, 138–41. See also Rainey 2015, 491, 493, 1426–27; previously Moran 1992, 153–54.

16. Lauinger and Yoder 2025, 141–43. See also Rainey 2015, 495, 497, 1427–28; previously Moran 1992, 154–56.

17. Lauinger and Yoder 2025, 143–47. See also Rainey 2015, 499, 501, 503, 1428–30; previously Moran 1992, 156–58.

18. Lauinger and Yoder 2025, 151–54. See also Rainey 2015, 509, 1431–32; previously Moran 1992, 159–60.

19. Lauinger and Yoder 2025, 149–51. See also Rainey 2015, 511, 513, 1433–34; previously Moran 1992, 160–62.

20. Lauinger and Yoder 2025, 157–60. See also Rainey 2015, 519, 521, 1435–36; previously Moran 1992, 163–64,

21. Lauinger and Yoder 2025, 162–64. See also Rainey 2015, 527, 529, 1437–38; previously Moran 1992, 166–67.

22. Amarna Letter EA 93: Lauinger and Yoder 2025, 164–65. See also Rainey 2015, 531, 1439; previously Moran 1992, 167. Amarna Letter EA 94: Lauinger and Yoder 2025, 166–67. See also Rainey 2015, 533, 1439–40; previously Moran 1992, 168. Amarna Letter EA 95: Lauinger and Yoder 2025, 168–69. See also Rainey 2015, 535, 537, 539, 1440–41; previously Moran 1992, 169. Amarna Letter EA 121: Lauinger and Yoder 2025, 217–19. See also Rainey 2015, 637, 639, 1465–66; previously Moran 1992, 200–201. Amarna Letter EA 127: Lauinger and Yoder 2025, 229–32. See also Rainey 2015, 661, 663, 1471–72; previously Moran 1992, 207–8.

23. Lauinger and Yoder 2025, 154–57. See also Rainey 2015, 515, 517, 1434–35; previously Moran 1992, 162–63.

24. Lauinger and Yoder 2025, 501–2. See also Rainey 2015, 543, 1442; previously Moran 1992, 170–71.

25. Lauinger and Yoder 2025, 170–71. See, e.g., Moran 1969; also Moran 1992, 174–75; Liverani 1998b; Rainey 2015, 553, 555, and especially 1445; Kilani 2020, 170. Note that Altman 1977, 10 was of the opinion that Abdi-Ashirta had actually been captured and taken to Egypt, where he died, though there is absolutely no proof of this.

20. Triple-A Roster

1. The bibliography on Aziru and Amurru, just as with his father Abdi-Ashirta, is rather large; see again, for example, the discussions in Altman 1977; Izre'el and Singer 1990; Singer 1990, 128–44 and the very useful Map II ("Syria in the Amarna Age") on 139; 1991, 148–54; Bryce 2003, 147–56; Goren, Finkelstein, and Na'aman 2003; 2004, 101–25; Bryce 2005, 170–75; Rainey and Notley 2006, 81–82; Miller 2008; Devecchi 2010; Morris 2010; Cordani 2011b; Vita 2012; 2015, 15–20; Rainey 2015, 19–21; Kilani 2020, 169–71.

2. Sayce 1888e, 501–4; 1889b, 344–45, no. IX.

3. Lauinger and Yoder 2025, 80–82. See also Rainey 2015, 783, 785, 1507; previously Moran 1992, 243–44.

4. Lauinger and Yoder 2025, 103–4. See also Rainey 2015, 837, 839, 1519; previously Moran 1992, 258–59.

5. Lauinger and Yoder 2025, 82–83. See also Rainey 2015, 787, 789, 1508; previously Moran 1992, 244–45.

6. Lauinger and Yoder 2025, 88–90. For EA 159–61, see also Rainey 2015, 791, 793, 795, 797, 799, 801, 1508–1511; previously Moran 1992, 245–48.

7. See Bryce 2005, 166–76; 2019, 84.

8. Lauinger and Yoder 2025, 49–50. See also Rainey 2015, 385, 1393–94; previously Moran 1992, 122.

9. Lauinger and Yoder 2025, 51–53. See also Rainey 2015, 387, 389, 1395; previously Moran 1992, 123.

10. On Aitukama's alliance with the Hittites, see Bryce 2005, 163, 175–76, 203; 2019, 85; also, briefly, Zangani 2022b, 50–52.

11. Lauinger and Yoder 2025; 53–57. See also Rainey 2015, 391, 393, 395, 1396–97; previously Moran 1992, 125–26; now also Zangani 2022b, 58–60.

12. Lauinger and Yoder 2025, 57–59. See also Rainey 2015, 397, 399, 1397–98; previously Moran 1992, 126.

13. Lauinger and Yoder 2025, 63–65. See also Rainey 2015, 407, 1400–1401; previously Moran 1992, 128–29. There is also another tablet that is even more fragmentary: Amarna Letter EA 57; see Lauinger and Yoder 2025, 65–66. See also Rainey 2015, 409, 1401; previously Moran 1992, 129.

14. Lauinger and Yoder 2025, 59–62. See also Rainey 2015, 401, 403, 405, 1398–99; previously Moran 1992, 127–28; now also Zangani 2022b, 59–60.

15. See Izre'el 1990, 83, with earlier references; Singer 1990, 158–59, 162–69, 182; 1991, 155; recently Rainey and Notley 2006, 86–87; Rainey 2015, 28–30.

16. Lauinger and Yoder 2025, 268–70. See also Rainey 2015, 719, 721, 1493–94; previously Moran 1992, 227–28.

17. Lauinger and Yoder 2025, 279–83. See also Rainey 2015, 743, 745, 747, 1498–99; previously Moran 1992, 233–35. On the responses, see the comment by Rainey 2015, 1493.

18. Lauinger and Yoder 2025, 278–79. See also Rainey 2015, 739, 741, 1497–98; previously Moran 1992, 232.

19. Lauinger and Yoder 2025, 285–89. See also Rainey 2015, 753, 755, 757, 1500–1501; previously Moran 1992, 236–37.

20. Lauinger and Yoder 2025, 297–99. See also Rainey 2015, 775, 1505; previously Moran 1992, 240–41.

21. Lauinger and Yoder 2025, 283–85. See also Rainey 2015, 749, 751, 1499–1500; previously Moran 1992, 235. For Amarna Letter EA 152, see Lauinger and Yoder 2025, 294–96; also Rainey 2015, 769, 771, 1503–1504; previously Moran 1992, 239–40.

22. Lauinger and Yoder 2025, 291–94. See also Rainey 2015, 763, 765, 767, 1502–1503; previously Moran 1992, 238–39.

23. Lauinger and Yoder 2025, 276–77. See also Rainey 2015, 735, 737, 1496–97; previously Moran 1992, 231–32.

24. Lauinger and Yoder 2025, 274–75. See also Rainey 2015, 731, 733, 1495–96; previously Moran 1992, 230–31.

21. Gaslighting the Pharaoh

1. Lauinger and Yoder 2025, 160–62; previously Rainey 2015, 523, 525, 1436–37; Moran 1992, 164–65. See also Amarna Letter EA 124, in which he repeats many of the details contained in the previous letter; Lauinger and Yoder 2025, 223–25; previously Rainey 2015, 649, 651, 1468–69; previously Moran 1992, 203–4. See also EA 126: Lauinger and Yoder 2025, 227–29; previously Rainey 2015, 657, 659, 1470–71; Moran 1992, 205–7.

2. E.g., Amarna Letters EA 103–4, 109, 117, 131, 362; see Rainey 2015, 561, 563, 565, 567, 619, 621, 623, 679, 681, 1235, 1237, 1447–48, 1460–62, 1477–82, 1627; previously Moran 1992, 176–78, 193–95, 212–14, 359–61.

3. Lauinger and Yoder 2025, 184–86. See also Rainey 2015, 581, 583, 1450–51; previously Moran 1992, 180–81.

4. Lauinger and Yoder 2025, 502–3. See also Rainey 2015, 545, 1442–43; previously Moran 1992, 171.

5. Lauinger and Yoder 2025, 203–6. See also Rainey 2015, 613, 615, 617, 1459–60; previously Moran 1992, 191–93.

6. Lauinger and Yoder 2025, 199–202. See also Rainey 2015, 607, 609, 1457–59; previously Moran 1992, 188–90.

7. Lauinger and Yoder 2025, 236–38. See also Rainey 2015, 675, 677, 1476; previously Moran 1992, 211–12.

8. Lauinger and Yoder 2025, 500–501. See also Rainey 2015, 435; see Moran 1992, 137.

9. Lauinger and Yoder 2025, 247–49. See also Rainey 2015, 695, 697, 1486; previously Moran 1992, 216–17. See now also Kilani 2020, 170–72.

10. Lauinger and Yoder 2025, 250–54. See also Rainey 2015, 699, 701, 703, 1486–87; previously Moran 1992, 218–21. See now also Kilani 2020, 170–72.

11. Lauinger and Yoder 2025, 270–71. See also Rainey 2015, 723, 725, 1494; previously Moran 1992, 228–29.

12. Lauinger and Yoder 2025, 254–60. See also Rainey 2015, 705, 707, 709, 711, 1488–90; previously Moran 1992, 221–25. See now also Kilani 2020, 170–72.

13. Lauinger and Yoder 2025, 264–66. See also Rainey 2015, 713, 715, 1490–91; previously Moran 1992, 225–26. See now also Kilani 2020, 171.

14. Lauinger and Yoder 2025, 266–67. See also Rainey 2015, 717, 1491–92; previously Moran 1992, 226–27. See now also Kilani 2020, 171.

15. Lauinger and Yoder 2025, 28–32. See also Rainey 2015, 803, 805, 807, 1511–12; previously Moran 1992, 248–51; also Lemche 2016, 140–41.

16. Amarna Letter EA 156; Lauinger and Yoder 2025, 79. See also Rainey 2015, 781, 1506–1507; previously Moran 1992, 242.

17. Lauinger and Yoder 2025, 90–92, 96–97. See also Rainey 2015, 811, 813, 823, 825, 1513–16; previously Moran 1992, 251–52, 254–55. Aziru sent a similar message to another Egyptian official, Haya: Amarna Letter EA 166; see Lauinger and Yoder 2025, 94–96; Rainey 2015, 819, 821, 1515; previously Moran 1992, 254.

18. Lauinger and Yoder 2025, 92–94. See also Rainey 2015, 815, 817, 1514; previously Moran 1992, 252–53.

19. Lauinger and Yoder 2025, 272–73. See also Rainey 2015, 727, 729, 1495; previously Moran 1992, 229–30.

20. Lauinger and Yoder 2025, 98–99. See also Rainey 2015, 827, 1516; previously Moran 1992, 255–56; also discussion in Podany 2010, 278–79.

21. Lauinger and Yoder 2025, 101–3. See also Rainey 2015, 833, 835, 1518; previously Moran 1992, 257–58.

22. Lauinger and Yoder 2025, 99–101. See also Rainey 2015, 829, 831, 1517–18; previously Moran 1992, 256–57.

23. Rainey 2015, 1517–18.

24. Beckman 1996, 32–37; see previously, e.g., Campbell 1964, 88–89; Singer 1990, 144–50, 153, 155–59; 1991, 154–58. See now also Kilani 2020, 172–73.

25. Singer 1990 (in Izre'el and Singer 1990) has written extensively about all of this, though he and I differ insofar as I see Amarna Letter EA 162 as a request for his presence in Egypt midway through his reign rather than a final ultimatum, whereas Singer appears to see it as being a final ultimatum from Egypt requesting that he return to the country for a second time (see explicitly Singer 1990, 129–44, 181; also the review by Spalinger 1992). See now also the detailed discussion in Cordani 2011b, 111–12, which I found only after writing up my own suggestions above; we are in lockstep about the chronology of most of these letters, including the fact that EA 162 is not a final ultimatum but is rather the letter that Aziru obeys, journeying to Egypt within a year of receiving it. She says further that "only group EA 159–161 might be dated to after Aziru's return from Egypt, even if with some chronological difficulty." See now also Vita 2015, 122–24, working from the point of view of the scribes who wrote these tablets, citing also Goren, Finkelstein, and Na'aman 2003; 2004, 103–115.

22. If I Forget Thee, O Jerusalem

1. Again, the bibliography on Abdi-Heba and Jerusalem in the Amarna Letters is fairly large; as just a few examples, see Rainey and Notley 2006, 85–86; Na'aman 2011, 31–48; 2022, 218–19; Rainey 2015, 26–28.

2. Lauinger and Yoder 2025, 453–56. See also Rainey 2015, 1117, 1119, 1593–94; Moran 1992, 330–32. For a similar statement, see Amarna Letter EA 285: Lauinger and Yoder 2025, 444–45. See also Rainey 2015, 1105, 1590–91; previously Moran 1992, 325.

3. Lauinger and Yoder 2025, 34–35. See also Rainey 2015, 1251, 1631; previously Moran 1992, 366.

4. Lauinger and Yoder 2025, 407. See also Rainey 2015, 1063, 1579; previously Moran 1992, 315.

5. Lauinger and Yoder 2025, 408–9. See also Rainey 2015, 1065, 1579–80; previously Moran 1992, 315–16.

6. Lauinger and Yoder 2025, 409. See also Rainey 2015, 1067, 1580; previously Moran 1992, 316.

7. Lauinger and Yoder 2025, 410–11. See also Rainey 2015, 1069; previously Moran 1992, 316–17.

8. Lauinger and Yoder 2025, 411–12. See also Rainey 2015, 1071, 1581; previously Moran 1992, 317.

9. Lauinger and Yoder 2025, 431. See also Rainey 2015, 1085, 1585; previously Moran 1992, 320.

10. Lauinger and Yoder 2025, 436–37. See also Rainey 2015, 1095, 1588; previously Moran 1992, 323.

11. Lauinger and Yoder 2025, 435–36. See also Rainey 2015, 1093, 1587; previously Moran 1992, 322.

12. Lauinger and Yoder 2025, 437–38. See also Rainey 2015, 1097, 1099, 1588–89; previously Moran 1992, 323–24. See also Amarna Letter EA 284: Lauinger and Yoder 2025, 439–40. See also Rainey 2015, 1101, 1103, 1589; previously Moran 1992, 324–25.

13. Lauinger and Yoder 2025, 441–43. See also Rainey 2015, 1245, 1247, 1630; previously Moran 1992, 364. Note that Rainey thinks that it is more likely that Surata and Intaruta were fighting against Shuwardata, while Moran (and now Lauinger / Yoder) was of the opinion that they were allied with him.

14. Lauinger and Yoder 2025, 432–33. See also Rainey 2015, 1087, 1586; previously Moran 1992, 321.

15. Lauinger and Yoder 2025, 433–34. See also Rainey 2015, 1089, 1091, 1586–87; previously Moran 1992, 321–22.

16. Lauinger and Yoder 2025, 445–48. See, for this paragraph and the next few dealing with this letter, also Rainey 2015, 1107, 1109, 1591; previously Moran 1992, 326–27, 382; Na'aman 2022, 218–19.

17. Moran 1992, 326, 382.

18. Lauinger and Yoder 2025, 448–52. See also Rainey 2015, 1111, 1113, 1115, 1592–93; previously Moran 1992, 327–30.

19. In Amarna Letters EA 279 and 280.

20. Lauinger and Yoder 2025, 453–56. See also Rainey 2015, 1117, 1119, 1593–94; previously Moran 1992, 330–32. Rainey says that the assassination of Zimri-Haddu reported here (EA 288) "must be related to the sedition" reported elsewhere, i.e., in Amarna Letter EA 333.

21. This letter is unique among all the Amarna Letters, for it is the only one found at its presumed destination—the site of Tell el-Hesi in what is now modern Israel—rather than as a copy found at the originating site of Amarna. See Rainey 2015, 1321, 1623; also Moran 1992, 356. Note also that Zimri-Haddu of Sidon and Zimri-Haddu of Lachish are two very different people and are not to be confused; both names have been previously translated as Zimredda rather than Zimri-Haddu. In addition, Goren, Finkelstein, and Na'aman 2004, 287 believe that there may be yet another ruler of Lachish mentioned in the Amarna Letters: Yabni-Ilu.

22. Lauinger and Yoder 2025, 456–58. See also Rainey 2015, 1121, 1123, 1595–96; previously Moran 1992, 332–33.

23. See again Amarna Letter EA 289; Lauinger and Yoder 2025, 456–58. See again also Rainey 2015, 1121, 1123, 1595–96; previously Moran 1992, 332–33.

24. Amarna Letter EA 290; Lauinger and Yoder 2025, 459–60. See also Rainey 2015, 1125, 1596; previously Moran 1992, 333–34.

23. It's a Small World After All

1. These next two chapters are an abbreviated and updated version of a paper coauthored by myself and my late wife, Diane Harris Cline, which we first presented at a 2014 conference in Prague and that appeared the following year in the conference volume (Cline and Cline 2015); it highlights her experience in applying Social Network Analysis to the ancient world, in which she was a pioneer. I am grateful to Jana Mynářová and the other editors of that volume for permission to include this here, which allows our findings, and her expertise, to now be put into full context.

2. For a brief discussion, see previously Cline 2012, with references to previous studies in various fields.

3. Borgatti, Everett, and Johnson 2009; Brass 2009; 2012, 669; Brughmans 2013.

4. I am grateful to one of the anonymous peer reviewers for bringing up this point and for suggesting that such a network analysis could be eventually done, especially if one uses the data in Vita 2015, for instance, where he has begun the process of identifying individual scribes; see also Mandell 2022; forthcoming-a. A related start was made in 2015 by Diane Harris Cline, in investigating the process involved in creating the individual letters back in the day; see Cline 2015. For a recent account of the writing of the letters and the scribes who produced them, see the series of brief articles published by Alice Mandell on *TheTorah.com*: "The Amarna Letters: An Eight-Part Series," posted 18 March 2025, https://www.thetorah.com/series/the-amarna -letters.

5. De Magistris 2023; 2024; he cites in particular the work of Campbell 1964 in the first of these two articles. However, Campbell, who only listed three main "focal points" (Campbell 1964, 106–30), was investigating all of this for a different reason, for he was trying to figure out the chronology of the various Amarna Letters, in order to put them into chronological order, and was doing so by seeing who was mentioned in each of the letters and thereby documenting the relationships.

6. See previously Cline 1995; also Bryce 2003, and Podany 2010, as cited above.

7. Hansen, Shneiderman, and Smith 2011, 91–102.

8. For examples, see Cline 2012.

9. Smith et al. 2010.

10. See Hansen, Shneiderman, and Smith 2011, 40–41, 71–73; Brass 2012, 669–672; Borgatti, Everett, and Johnson 2013, 164.

11. Wasserman and Faust 1994, 178; Newman 2010, 168; Hansen, Shneiderman, and Smith 2011, 40; Borgatti, Everett, and Johnson 2013, 165.

24. Three Degrees of Separation

1. See Borgatti 1995, 112–15; Hansen, Shneiderman, and Smith 2011, 41; Brass 2012, 672.

2. Newman 2010, 169.

3. Wasserman and Faust 1994, 189; Newman 2010, 185; Borgatti, Everett, and Johnson 2013, 174.

4. Cline 2012, 66.

5. Wasserman and Faust 1994, 347–74, 466–68.

6. Newman 2010, 211–12.

7. See Mynářová 2006; now also Zangani 2022b, 60n54, citing Mynářová.

8. Rainie and Wellman 2012, 122.

Epilogue: After Amarna

1. Mynářová 2014, 16; Rainey 2015, 5, 14; Cline and Cline 2015, 18.

2. See Cline 2021.

3. Beckman 1996, 54–59, 95–102; see now also Miller 2008; Kilani 2020, 173; previously Singer 1990, 150–53; 1991, 159–77.

4. See brief discussion in Cline 2021, 75–78, with earlier references.

5. See brief discussion in Cline 2021, 88, with earlier references. Note that we are unsure where Yanoam is.

6. See Cline 2021; 2024, with earlier references.

7. See Cline 2021, 100–106, with earlier references.

8. See again the brief discussions in Cline 2021, specifically the final chapters, with earlier references.

9. Sherratt 2003, 2017; Zangani 2022c, 28, also 31, 42, 45–47, with further references, especially to the other chapters in Hodos 2017, such as Jennings 2017 and Versluys 2017; also Vandkilde 2016 Moreno García 2021; Cline 2014; 2021, with references to numerous earlier articles.

10. See my numerous earlier publications on this topic, from 1987 onward, including Cline 1987; 1995; 1998, and others listed in the bibliography in Cline 2021; see also now Zangani 2022c, 74–75, 163–64, 168–70, with references.

11. Zangani 2022c, 16.

12. On the question of whether there was or was not an actual Egyptian "empire" in Canaan, particularly in northern Canaan, see now the discussions in Zangani 2022b; 2022c. For a quick rundown regarding the belief by earlier scholars that Akhenaten was uninterested in the southern Levant, which is clearly erroneous, see, e.g., most recently Pfoh 2016, 1–2, with previous references.

13. I am grateful to Mitchell Allen for pointing out some of the various possible parallels presented in the next few paragraphs and for naysaying others.

14. Lemche 2016, 134, 143.

15. Sayce 1923, 251–52; Cohen and Westbrook 2000; De Magistris 2023; 2024; Zangani 2022b; 2022c.

Abel, L. 1892. "Stück einer Tafel aus dem Fund von El—Amarna." *Zeitschrift für Assyriologie* 7: 117–24.

Abo-Eleaz, M.-E. E. 2018. "Neglect and Detention of Messengers in Egypt during the Fourteenth and Thirteenth Centuries BCE." *Journal of the American Research Center in Egypt* 54: 17–34.

———. 2021a. "Fake News and Rumors in the Diplomatic Correspondence between Egypt and the Other Great Powers During the XIVth and XIIIth Centuries BCE." *Revue d'égyptologie* 71: 1–18.

———. 2021b. "The Reward of the Pharaohs: Egyptian Royal Grants and Gifts for the Rulers of Canaan in the Amarna Letters." *Antiguo Oriente* 19: 65–112.

———. 2021c. "Guilty or Not Guilty? An Investigation into the Accusations of Syria-Palestine Vassals against the Egyptian Royal Commissioners in the Amarna Letters." *Zeitschrift des Deutschen Paläistina-Vereins* 137: 1–28.

———. 2023. "The Harsh Life of Diplomatic Messengers in Egypt in the Late Bronze Age." *ANE Today* 11, no, 9: 1–6. https://www.asor.org/anetoday/2023/09/diplomatic-messengers-egypt%7C.

Adamthwaite, M. R. 1992. "Lab'aya's Connection with Shechem Reassessed." *Abr-Nahrain* 30: 1–19.

Adkins, L. 2004. *Empires of the Plain: Henry Rawlinson and the Lost Languages of Babylon*. New York: Thomas Dunne Books.

Altman, A. 1977. "The Fate of Abdi-Ashirta." *Ugarit Forschungen* 9: 1–11.

Anonymous. 1890. "Notes and News." *The Academy* 38, no. 963 (October): 340.

Arie, E. 2016. "The Labayu Affair in the Amarna Letters." In *Pharaoh in Canaan: The Untold Story*, edited by D. Ben Tor et al., 56–57. Jerusalem: The Israel Museum.

Artzi, P. 1985. "The Present State of the Amarna Documents." *Proceedings of the World Congress of Jewish Studies* 1985: 3–16.

Barton, G. A. 1925. "Unlocking the Secrets of the Hittite Language." *Bulletin of the American Schools of Oriental Research* 17: 13–15.

Beckman, G. 1996. *Hittite Diplomatic Texts*. Atlanta: Scholars Press.

Bezold, C. 1893. *Oriental Diplomacy: Being the transliterated text of the Cuneiform Despatches between the Kings of Egypt and Western Asia in the XVth century before Christ, discovered at Tell el-Amarna, and now preserved in the British Museum*. London: Luzac and Co.

Bezold, C., and E.A.W. Budge. 1892. *The Tell el-Amarna Tablets in the British Museum with Autotype Facsimiles*. London: Trustees of the British Museum.

Boissier, A. 1892. "Notes sur les lettres de Tell el-Amarna." *Zeitschrift für Assyriologie* 7: 346–49.

Borgatti, S. P. 1995. "Centrality and AIDS." *Connections* 18, no. 1: 112–15.

Borgatti, S. P., M. G. Everett, and J. C. Johnson. 2013. *Analyzing Social Networks*. London: Sage Publications.

Borgatti, S. P., A. Mehra, D. J. Brass, and G. Labianca. 2009. "Network Analysis in the Social Sciences." *Science* 323, no. 5916: 892–95.

Boscawen, W. St. Ch. 1891. "Southern Palestine and the Tel el-Amarna Tablets." *The Babylonian and Oriental Record* 5 (May): 114–19.

Brass, D. J. 2009. "Connecting to Brokers: Strategies for Acquiring Social Capital." In *Social Capital: Reaching Out, Reaching In*, edited by V. O. Bartkus and J. H. Davis, 260–74. Cheltenham, UK: Edward Elgar Press.

———. 2012. "A Social Network Perspective on Organizational Psychology." In *The Oxford Handbook of Organizational Psychology*, edited by S.W.J. Kozlowski, 667–95. New York: Oxford University Press.

Brughmans, T. 2013. "Thinking through Networks: A Review of Formal Network Methods in Archaeology." *Journal of Archaeological Method and Theory* 20: 623–62.

Brünnow, R. E. 1890. "Die Mitâni-Sprache." *Zeitschrift für Assyriologie* 5: 209–59.

Bryce, T. 2003. *Letters of the Great Kings of the Ancient Near East: The Royal Correspondence of the Late Bronze Age*. London: Routledge.

———. 2005. *The Kingdom of the Hittites*. New Edition. Oxford: Oxford University Press.

———. 2019. *Warriors of Anatolia: A Concise History of the Hittites*. London: I. B. Tauris.

Buchwald, J., and D. Josefowicz. 2020. *The Riddle of the Rosetta: How an English Polymath and a French Polyglot Discovered the Meaning of Egyptian Hieroglyphs*. Princeton, NJ: Princeton University Press.

Budge, E.A.W. 1888. "On Cuneiform Despatches from Tushratta, King of Mitanni, Burraburiyash the son of Kuri-Galzu, and the King of Alashiya, to Amenophis III, King of Egypt, and on the Cuneiform Tablets from Tell el-Amarna." *Proceedings of the Society of Biblical Archaeology* 10: 540–69.

———. 1920. *By Nile and Tigris, a Narrative of Journeys in Egypt and Mesopotamia on Behalf of the British Museum between the Years 1886 and 1913*. 2 vols. London: J. Murray.

Campbell, E. F., Jr. 1964. *The Chronology of the Amarna Letters, with Special Reference to the Hypothetical Coregency of Amenophis III and Akhenaten*. Baltimore: Johns Hopkins University Press.

———. 1965. "Appendix 2: Shechem in the Amarna Archive." In G. E. Wright, *Shechem: The Biography of a Biblical City*, 191–213. New York: McGraw-Hill Book Company.

Capart, J., ed. 1936. *Travels in Egypt (December 1880 to May 1891): Letters of Charles Edwin Wilbour*. New York: Brooklyn Museum.

Cline, D. H. 2012. "Six Degrees of Alexander: Social Network Analysis as a Tool for Ancient History." *Ancient History Bulletin* 26, nos. 1–2: 59–70.

———. 2015. "The Amarna Letters: A Web of Interaction." *Journal of Ancient Egyptian Interconnections* 7, no. 4: 58–60.

Cline, D. H., and E. H. Cline. 2015. "Text Messages, Tablets, and Social Networks in the Late Bronze Age Eastern Mediterranean: The Small World of the Amarna Letters." In *Egypt and the Near East: Crossroads II; Proceedings of an International Conference on the Relations of Egypt and the Near East in the Bronze Age, Prague, September 2014*, edited by J. Mynářová, P. Onderka, and P. Pavúk, 17–44. Prague: Charles University.

Cline, E. H. 1987. "Amenhotep III and the Aegean: A Reassessment of Egypto–Aegean Relations in the 14th Century BC." *Orientalia* 56, no. 1: 1–36.

———. 1995. "'My Brother, My Son': Rulership and Trade between the LBA Aegean, Egypt and the Near East." In *The Role of the Ruler in the Prehistoric Aegean*, edited by P. Rehak, 143–50. Aegaeum 11. Liège: Université de Liège.

———. 1998. "Amenhotep III, the Aegean, and Anatolia." In *Amenhotep III: Perspectives on His Reign*, edited by D. O'Connor and E. H. Cline, 236–50. Ann Arbor: University of Michigan Press.

———. 2007. *From Eden to Exile: Unraveling Mysteries of the Bible*. Washington, DC: National Geographic.

———. 2021. *1177 BC: The Collapse of Civilization*. Revised and updated edition. Princeton, NJ: Princeton University Press.

———. 2024. *After 1177 BC: The Survival of Civilizations*. Princeton, NJ: Princeton University Press.

Cochavi-Rainey, Z. 1999. *Royal Gifts in the Late Bronze Age, Fourteenth to Thirteenth Centuries BCE: Selected Texts Recording Gifts to Royal Personages*. Beersheba: Ben-Gurion University of the Negev Press.

Cohen, R., and R. Westbrook, eds. 2000. *Amarna Diplomacy: The Beginnings of International Relations*. Baltimore: Johns Hopkins University Press.

Cohen, Y. 2023. "Three Amarna Notes: Scribal Training, Scribal Hands and Tablet Provenance." In *"I Passed over Difficult Mountains"—Studies on the Ancient Near East in Honor of Mario Liverani*, edited by F. Di Filippo, L. Milano, and L. Mori, 31–47. Münster: Zaphon.

"Conder, Claude Reignier." 1912. In *Dictionary of National Biography*, 401–3. Supplement. London: Smith, Elder & Co.

Conder, C. R. 1889a. "The King of Arzapi's Letter." *The Academy* 35, no. 875: 98.

———. 1889b. "The Tell Amarna Tablets. *Quarterly Statement of the Palestine Exploration Fund* 1889: 28–30.

———. 1890. "A Hittite Prince's Letter." *Quarterly Statement of the Palestine Exploration Fund* 1890: 115–21.

———. 1891a. "Altaic Letter from Tell Amarna." *Quarterly Statement of the Palestine Exploration Fund* 1891: 245–50.

———. 1891b. "The Tell Amarna Tablets." *The Scottish Review* 17: 292–318.

———. 1892. "Dusratta's Hittite Letter." *The Journal of the Royal Asiatic Society of Great Britain and Ireland* (October): 711–809.

———. 1893. *The Tell Amarna Tablets*. London: The Committee of the Palestine Exploration Fund.

Conder, C. R., and H. H. Kitchener. 1882. *The Survey of Western Palestine: Memoirs of the Topography, Orography, Hydrography, and Archaeology*. Vol. 2, *Sheets VII–XVI: Samaria*. London: Palestine Exploration Fund.

Cordani, V. 2011a. "One-Year or Five-Year War? A Reappraisal of Suppiluliuma's First Syrian Campaign." *Altorientalische Forschungen* 38, no. 2: 240–53.

———. 2011b. "Aziru's Journey to Egypt and Its Chronological Value." In *Egypt and the Near East—the Crossroads*, edited by J. Mynářová, 103–13. Prague: Charles University.

———. 2013. "Suppiluliuma in Syria after the First Syrian War: The (Non-)Evidence of the Amarna Letters." In *New Results and New Questions on the Reign of Suppiluliuma I*, 43–64. Turin: LoGisma editore.

David, S. R. 2000. "Realism, Constructivism, and the Amarna Letters." In *Amarna Diplomacy: The Beginnings of International Relations*, edited by R. Cohen and R. Westbrook, 54–67. Baltimore: Johns Hopkins University Press.

Delattre, A. J. 1889a. "La trouvaille de Tell el-Amarna." *Revue des questions scientifiques* 25: 143–81.

———. 1889b. "Les inscriptions de Tell el-Amarna." *Revue des questions scientifiques* 26: 79–98.

———. 1890. "Trois lettres de Tell el-Amarna." *Proceedings of the Society of Biblical Archaeology* 13: 127–32.

———. 1891a. "Azirou (les lettres de Tell el-Amarna)." *Proceedings of the Society of Biblical Archaeology* 13: 215–34.

———. 1891b. "Quelques lettres de Tell el-Amarna." *Proceedings of the Society of Biblical Archaeology* 13: 317–27.

———. 1891c. "Lettres de Tell el-Amarna." *Proceedings of the Society of Biblical Archaeology* 13: 539–61.

———. 1892–1893a. "Lettres de Tell el-Amarna (5ᵉ Série)." *Proceedings of the Society of Biblical Archaeology* 15: 16–30.

———. 1892–1893b. "Lettres de Tell el-Amarna (6ᵉ Série)." *Proceedings of the Society of Biblical Archaeology* 15: 115–34.

———. 1892–1893c. "Lettres de Tell el-Amarna (7ᵉ Série)." *Proceedings of the Society of Biblical Archaeology* 15: 345–73.

———. 1892–1893d. "Lettres de Tell el-Amarna (8ᵉ Série)." *Proceedings of the Society of Biblical Archaeology* 15: 501–20.

De Magistris, F. I. 2023. "A Tale of Two Cities: Sumur and Kumidi as Egyptian Centres in the Late 18th Dynasty." *Altorientalische Forschungen* 50, no. 2: 150–69.

———. 2024. "The Proximity Principle and the Egyptian Levant in the Late 18th Dynasty." *Bulletin of ASOR* 391: 77–92.

Devecchi, E. 2010. "Amurru between Hatti, Assyria, and Ahhiyawa: Discussing a recent hypothesis." *Zeitschrift für Assyriologie* 100: 242–56.

———. 2012. "The Amarna Letters from Hatti: A Palaeographic Analysis." In *The Ancient Near East, A Life! Festschrift Karel Van Lerberghe*, edited by T. Boiy, J. Bretschneider, A. Goddeeris, H. Hameeuw, G. Jans, and J. Tavernier, 143–53. Leuven: Peeters.

———. 2013. "Suppiluliuma's Syrian Campaigns in Light of the Documents from Ugarit." In *New Results and New Questions on the Reign of Suppiluliuma I*, 81–97. Turin: LoGisma editore.

Erman, A., and E. Schrader. 1888. "Der Thontafelfund von Tell-Amarna." *Sitzungsberichte der K. preussischen Academie der Wissenschaften zu Berlin Philologisch-historische Klasse* 23: 583–89.

Finkelstein, I., and N. Na'aman. 2005. "Shechem of the Amarna Period and the Rise of the Northern Kingdom of Israel." *Israel Exploration Journal* 55: 172–93.

Frahm, E. 2023. *Assyria: The Rise and Fall of the World's First Empire*. New York: Basic Books.

Gestoso Singer, G. 2016. "Fortunes and Misfortunes of Messengers and Merchants in the Amarna Letters." *Fortune and Misfortune in the Ancient Near East: Proceedings of the 60th Rencontre Assyriologique Internationale Warsaw, 21–25 July 2014*, edited by O. Drewnowska and M. Sandowicz, 143–61. University Park, PA: Eisenbrauns.

Glanville, S.R.K. 1947. *The Growth and Nature of Egyptology: An Inaugural Lecture*. Cambridge: Cambridge University Press.

Goren, Y., I. Finkelstein, and N. Na'aman. 2002. "The Seat of Three Disputed Canaanite Rulers According to Petrographic Investigation of the Amarna Tablets." *Tel Aviv* 29: 221–37.

———. 2003. "The Expansion of the Kingdom of Amurru According to the Petrographic Investigation of the Amarna Tablets." *Bulletin of the American Schools of Oriental Research* 329: 2–11.

———. 2004. *Inscribed in Clay: Provenance Study of the Amarna Tablets and Other Ancient Near Eastern Texts*. Tel Aviv: Emery and Claire Yass Publications in Archaeology.

Grabbe, L. L. 2016. "Late Bronze Age Palestine: If We Had Only the Bible . . ." In *The Land of Canaan in the Late Bronze Age*, edited by L. L. Grabbe, 11–56. London: Bloomsbury.

Grayson, A. K. 1987. *Assyrian Rulers of the Third and Second Millennia BC (to 1115 BC)*. Toronto: University of Toronto Press.

Griffith, F. Ll. 1933a. "Professor A. H. Sayce." *The Journal of the Royal Asiatic Society of Great Britain and Ireland* 2: 497–99.

———. 1933b. "Archibald Henry Sayce." *Journal of Egyptian Archaeology* 19, no. 1/2: 65–66.

Halévy, J. 1890a. "La correspondance d'Amenophis IV et la Bible." *Revue des etudes juives* 20, no. 40: 199–219.

———. 1890b. "La correspondance d'Amenophis III et d'Amenophis IV, transcrite et traduite." *Journal asiatique* 8ᵐᵉ serie, 16: 298–354, 402–62.

———. 1891a. "La correspondance d'Amenophis III et d'Amenophis IV, transcrite et traduite." *Journal asiatique* 8ᵐᵉ serie, 17: 87–133, 202–73.

———. 1891b. "La correspondance d'Amenophis III et d'Amenophis IV, transcrite et traduite." *Journal asiatique* 8ᵐᵉ serie, 18: 134–85, 510–36.

Hansen, D., B. Shneiderman, and M. A. Smith. 2011. *Analyzing Social Media Networks with NodeXL: Insights from a Connected World*. Burlington, MA: Morgan Kaufmann.

Hawkins, J. D. 2009. "The Arzawa Letters in Recent Perspective." *British Museum Studies in Ancient Egypt and Sudan* 14: 73–83.

Hodos, T., ed. 2017. *The Routledge Handbook of Archaeology and Globalization*. New York: Routledge.

Hoffner, H. A. 2009. *Letters from the Hittite Kingdom*. Atlanta: Scholars Press.

Horry, R. 2015. "Assyriology at the Margins, the Case of William St. Chad Boscawen 1855–1913." *Iraq* 77: 107–28.

Humphrey, T. 2022. "Power and Diplomacy in the Amarna Letters: Cypro-Egyptian Relations in the Mid-Fourteenth Century BCE." In *Narratives of Power in the Ancient World*, edited by U. Furlan, T. A. Husøy, and H. Bohun, 23–46. Cambridge: Cambridge Scholars Publishing.

Humphries, M. D., and K. Gurney. 2008. "Network 'Small-World-Ness': A Quantitative Method for Determining Canonical Network Equivalence." *PloS ONE* 3, no. 4: e0002051.

Ikram, S., and A. Omar. 2021. "Egypt." In *A History of World Egyptology*, edited by A. Bednarski, A. Dodson, and S. Ikram, 25–67. Cambridge: Cambridge University Press.

Izre'el, S. 1990. "The General's Letter: Philological and Linguistic Aspects." In *The General's Letter from Ugarit: A Linguistic and Historical Reevaluation of RS 20.33 (Ugaritica V, No. 20)*, edited by S. Izre'el and I. Singer, 17–112. Tel Aviv: Tel Aviv University, Chaim Rosenberg School of Jewish Studies.

———. 1995. "Amarna Tablets in the Collection of the Pushkin Museum of Fine Arts." *Journal for Semitics* 7: 125–61.

———. 1997. *The Amarna Scholarly Tablets*. Groningen: Styx.

———. 2005. *Canaano-Akkadian*. 2nd edition. Languages of the World / Materials 82. Munich: LINCOM.

Izre'el, S., and I. Singer. 1990. *The General's Letter from Ugarit. A Linguistic and Historical Reevaluation of RS 20.33 (Ugaritica V, No. 20)*. Tel Aviv: Tel Aviv University.

Jastrow, M., Jr. 1892. "Egypt and Palestine, 1400 B.C." *Journal of Biblical Literature* 11, no. 1: 95–124.

———. 1892–1893. "The Letters of Abdiheba." *Hebraica* 9, nos. 1–2: 24–46.

———. 1893. "'The Men of Judah' in the El-Amarna Tablets." *Journal of Biblical Literature* 12, no. 1: 61–72.

Jennings, J. 2017. "Distinguishing Past Globalizations." In *The Routledge Handbook of Archaeology and Globalization*, edited by T. Hodos, 12–28. New York: Routledge.

Jensen, P. 1890. "Vorstudien zur Entzifferung des Mitanni." *Zeitschrift für Assyriologie* 5: 166–208.

Kilani, M. 2020. *Byblos in the Late Bronze Age: Interactions between the Levantine and Egyptian Worlds*. Leiden: Brill.

Knudtzon, J. A. 1902a. *Die Zwei Arzawa-Briefe. Die Ältesten Urkunden in Indogermanischer Sprache*. Leipzig: J. C. Hinrichs.

———. 1902b. "Weitere Studien zu den El-Amarna-Tafeln." *Beiträge zur assyriologie und semitischen sprachwissenschaft* 4: 279–337.

———. 1907 / 1915. *Die El-Amarna Tafeln*. 2 vols. Leipzig: J. C. Hinrichs.

Langdon, S. 1933. "Archibald Henry Sayce as Assyriologist." *The Journal of the Royal Asiatic Society of Great Britain and Ireland* 2: 499–503.

Lauinger, J., and T. R. Yoder. 2025. *The Amarna Letters: The Syro-Levantine Correspondence*. Columbus, GA: Lockwood Press.

Lehmann, C. F. 1888a. "Aegypten und Vorderasien im zweiten vorchristlichen Jahrtausend: Nach neugefundenen keilinschriftlichen Urkunden im Berliner Museum." *Kölnische Zeiturig*, 4 June.

———. 1888b. "Die in Aegypten neugefundenen keilschriftlichen Dokumente." *Hamburgischer Correspondent*, 20 June.

———. 1888c. "Aus dem Funde von Tell el Amarna." *Zeitschrift für Assyriologie* 3: 372–406.

———. 1889. "Nachträge und Berichtigungen zu dem Augsatze: 'Aus dem Funde von Tell-el-Amarna.'" *Zeitschrift für Assyriologie* 4: 82–86.

Lemche, N. P. 2016. "The Amarna Letters and Palestinian Politics." In *The Land of Canaan in the Late Bronze Age*, edited by L. L. Grabbe, 133–46. London: Bloomsbury.

Liverani, M. 1998a. *Le lettere di el-Amarna*. Vol. 1, *Le lettere dei "piccolo Re."* Brescia: Paideia.

———. 1998b. "How to kill Abdi-Ashirta. EA 101, Once Again." *Israel Oriental Studies* 18: 387–94.

———. 1999. *Le lettere di el-Amarna*. Vol. 2, *Le lettere dei "Grandi Re."* Brescia: Paideia.

———. 2000. "The Great Powers' Club." In *Amarna Diplomacy: The Beginnings of International Relations*, edited by R. Cohen and R. Westbrook, 15–27. Baltimore: Johns Hopkins University Press.

Luckenbill, Daniel D., and T. G. Allen. 1916. "The Murch Fragment of an el-Amarna Letter." *American Journal of Semitic Languages* 33: 1–6.

Lyon, D. G. 1896. "A Half Century of Assyriology." *The Biblical World* 8, no. 2: 124–42.

Machinist, P. 2009. "The Road Not Taken: Wellhausen and Assyriology." In *Homeland and Exile: Biblical and Ancient Near Eastern Studies in Honour of Bustenay Oded*, edited by G. Galil, M. Geller, and A. Millard, 469–531. Supplements to Vetus Testamentum 130. Leiden: Brill.

Mandell, A. H. 2015. "Scribalism and Diplomacy at the Crossroads of Cuneiform Culture: The Sociolinguistics of Canaano-Akkadian." PhD diss., University of California, Los Angeles.

———. 2022. "Speaking Clearly through the Canaanite Amarna Letters: How to Connect with an Audience in Cuneiform." In *One Who Loves Knowledge: Studies in Honor of Richard Jasnow*, edited by B. Bryan, M. Smith, C. Di Cerbo, M. Escolano-Poveda, and J. S. Waller, 263–76. Columbus, GA: Lockwood Press.

———. 2024. "Letters to Pharaoh: The Canaanite Amarna Tablets." *Biblical Archaeology Review* 50, no. 3: 46–53.

———. Forthcoming-a. *Cuneiform Culture and the Ancestors of Hebrew*. The Ancient World Series. London: Routledge.

———. Forthcoming-b. "Remodeling Albright's House in the 21st Century: From a Patrimonial Household to an Open-concept Structure." In *Jehu's Tribute: What Can Biblical Studies Offer Assyriology? Explorations in Ancient Near Eastern Civilizations*, edited by J. L. Cooley and R. I. Lasine Thelle. University Park, PA: Eisenbrauns.

Matthiae, P. 1977. *Ebla: An Empire Rediscovered*. London: Hodder and Stoughton.

Mayes, A.D.H. 2016. "International Diplomacy in the Amarna Age." In *The Land of Canaan in the Late Bronze Age*, edited by L. L. Grabbe, 147–58. London: Bloomsbury.

Mercer, S.A.B. 1939. *The Tell El-Amarna Tablets*. Toronto: Macmillan.

Merrillees, R. S. 1987. *Alashiya Revisted*. Paris: J. Gabalda.

Millard, A. 1992. "Ebla and the Bible: What's Left (if Anything)?" *Bible Review* 8, no. 2: 18–31, 60, 62.

Miller, J. L. 2008. "The Rebellion of Hatti's Syrian Vassals and Egypt's Meddling in Amurru." *Studi micenei ed egeo-anatolici* 50: 533–54.

———. 2017. "Political Interactions between Kassite Babylonia and Assyria, Egypt and Ḫatti during the Amarna Age." In *Karduniaš: Babylonia under the Kassites*, vol. 1, edited by A. Bartelmus and K. Sternitzke, 93–111. Berlin: De Gruyter.

Molendijk, A. L. 2000. "The Heritage of Cornelis Petrus Tiele (1830–1902)." *Dutch Review of Church History* 80, no. 1: 78–114.

Moran, W. L. 1969. "The Death of Abdi-Ashirta." *Eretz Israel* 9: 94–99.

———. 1987. *Les lettres d'El Amarna: Correspondence diplomatique du pharaon*. Paris: Editions du Cerf.

———. 1992. *The Amarna Letters*. Baltimore: Johns Hopkins University Press.

―――. 2003. *Amarna Studies: Collected Writings*. Edited by J. Huehnergard and S. Izre'el. Winona Lake, IN: Eisenbrauns.

Moreno García, J. C. 2021. "Markets, Transactions, and Ancient Egypt: New Venues for Research in a Comparative Perspective." In *Markets and Exchanges in Pre-modern and Traditional Societies*, edited by J. C. Moreno García, 189–229. Multidisciplinary Approaches to Ancient Societies: Interpreting Ancient Egypt 1. Oxford: Oxbow Books.

Morris, E. F. 2006. "Bowing and Scraping in the Ancient Near East: An Investigation into Obsequiousness in the Amarna Letters." *Journal of Near Eastern Studies* 65, no. 3: 179–95.

―――. 2010. "Opportunism in Contested Land, B.C. and A.D.: Or how Abdi-Ashirta, Aziru, and Padsha Khan Zadran Got Away with Murder." In *Millions of Jubilees: Studies in Honor of David Silverman*, vol. 1, edited by Z. Hawass and J. H. Wegner, 413–38. Cairo: Supreme Council of Antiquities Press.

Murnane, W. J. 1995. *Texts from the Amarna Period in Egypt*. Atlanta: Scholars Press.

Mynářová, J. 2006. "Akizzi of Qatna—A Case of Diplomatic Faux Pas?" *Ugarit Forschungen* 37: 445–60.

―――. 2007. *Language of Amarna—Language of Diplomacy: Perspectives on the Amarna Letters*. Prague: Czech Institute of Egyptology.

―――. 2014. "Egyptian State Correspondence of the New Kingdom: The Letters of the Levantine Client Kings in the Amarna Correspondence and Contemporary Evidence." In *State Correspondence in the Ancient World: From New Kingdom Egypt to the Roman Empire*, edited by K. Radner, 10–31. Oxford: Oxford University Press.

―――. 2015. "Discovery, Research, and Excavation of the Amarna Tablets—The Formative Stage." In *The El-Amarna Correspondence: A New Edition of the Cuneiform Letters from the Site of El-Amarna Based on Collations of all Extant Tablets*, vol. 1, edited by A. S. Rainey and W. M. Schniedewind, 37–54. Leiden: Brill.

Na'aman, N. 1988. "Biryawaza of Damascus and the Date of the 1977 'Apiru Letters." *Ugarit Forschungen* 20: 179–93.

―――. 2011. "Jerusalem in the Amarna Period." *Jérusalem antique et médiévale: Mélanges en l'honneur d'Ernest-Marie Laperrousaz*, edited by C. Arnould-Béhar and A. Lemaire, 31–48. Leuven: Peeters.

―――. 2022. "Warm Greetings to the Egyptian Royal Scribe." *N.A.B.U.* 2022/3, no. 3: 218–19.

Naunton, C. 2020. *Egyptologists' Notebooks*. London: Thames and Hudson.

Newman, M. 2000. "Models of a Small World: A Review." *Journal of Statistical Physics* 101: 819–41.

―――. 2010. *Networks: An Introduction*. Oxford: Oxford University Press.

Niebuhr, C. 1901. *The Tell el Amarna Period: The Relations of Egypt and Western Asia in the Fifteenth Century B.C. According to the Tell el Amarna Tablets*. Translated by J. Hutchison. London: David Nutt.

Oppert, J. 1888. "Les tablettes de Tell-Amarn [sic]." *Comptes rendus des séances de l'Académie des Inscriptions et Belles-Lettres* 32–33: 251–54.

Pearce, L. E., and C. Wunsch. 2014. *Documents of Judean Exiles and West Semites in Babylonia in the Collection of David Sofer*. Bethesda, MD: CDL Press.

Petrie, W.M.F. 1894. *Tell el-Amarna*. London: Methuen & Co.

―――. 1898. *Syria and Egypt from the Tell El Amarna Letters*. London: Methuen & Co.

Pettinato, G. 1981. *The Archives of Ebla: An Empire Inscribed in Clay*. Garden City, NY: Doubleday.

Pfoh, E. 2016. *Syria-Palestine in the Late Bronze Age: An Anthropology of Politics and Power*. London: Routledge.

―――. 2019. "Prestige and Authority in the Southern Levant during the Amarna Age." In *The Late Bronze and Early Iron Ages of Southern Canaan*, edited by A. M. Maeir, I. Shai, and C. McKinny, 247–61. Berlin: De Gruyter.

Podany, A. 2010. *Brotherhood of Kings: How International Relations Shaped the Ancient Near East.* Oxford: Oxford University Press.

Ragionieri, R. 2000. "The Amarna Age: An International Society in the Making." In *Amarna Diplomacy: The Beginnings of International Relations*, edited by R. Cohen, and R. Westbrook, 42–53. Baltimore: Johns Hopkins University Press.

Rainey, A. S. 2015. *The El-Amarna Correspondence: A New Edition of the Cuneiform Letters from the Site of El-Amarna Based on Collations of All Extant Tablets.* 2 vols. Edited by W. M. Schniedewind. Leiden: Brill.

Rainey, A. S., and R. S. Notley. 2006. *The Sacred Bridge: Carta's Atlas of the Biblical World.* Jerusalem: Carta.

Rainie, L., and B. Wellman. 2012. *Networked: The New Social Operating System.* Boston: MIT Press.

Rawlinson, H., W. Fox Talbot, E. Hincks, and J. Oppert. 1857. *Inscription of Tiglath-Pileser I., King of Assyria, B.C. 1150.* London: J. W. Parker and Son.

Robinson, A. 2012. *Cracking the Egyptian Code: The Revolutionary Life of Jean-Francois Champollion.* Oxford: Oxford University Press.

Sayce, A. H. 1888a. "Letter from Egypt." *The Academy* 33, no. 824 (February): 123–24.

———. 1888b. "Letter from Egypt." *The Academy* 33, no. 829 (March): 211.

———. 1888c. "Babylonian Tablets from Upper Egypt." *The Academy* 33, no. 831 (April): 246–47.

———. 1888d. "The Name of Moses in the Cuneiform Tablets of Tel el-Amarna." *The Academy* 33, no. 840 (June): 397.

———. 1888e. "Babylonian Tablets from Tell el-Amarna, Upper Egypt." *Proceedings of the Society of Biblical Archaeology* 10: 488–527.

———. 1888f. "Letter from Egypt." *The Academy* 34, no. 869 (December): 424–25.

———. 1889a. "Letter from Egypt." *The Academy* 35, no. 872 (January): 47.

———. 1889b. "The Cuneiform Tablets of Tel el-Amarna, Now Preserved in the Boulaq Museum." *Proceedings of the Society of Biblical Archaeology* 11 (June): 326–413.

———. 1889c. "Letters from Syria and Palestine before the age of Moses." *Transactions of the Lancashire and Cheshire Antiquarian Society* 7: 1–25.

———. 1889d. "Tablets of Tel el-Amarna Relating to Palestine in the Century before the Exodus." *Records of the Past,* n.s., 2: 57–71.

———. 1890a. "Letter from Egypt." *The Academy* 37, no. 937 (April): 273.

———. 1890b. "Jerusalem in the Tablets of Tel el-Amarna." *The Academy* 38, no. 964 (October): 366.

———. 1890c. "Letters to Egypt from Babylonia, Assyria, and Syria, in the Fifteenth Century B.C." *Records of the Past,* n.s., 3: 55–90.

———. 1890d. "The Language of Mitanni." *Zeitschrift für Assyriologie* 5: 260–74.

———. 1891. "Correspondence between Palestine and Egypt in the Fifteenth Century B.C." *Records of the Past,* n.s., 5: 54–101.

———. 1894. "The Cuneiform Tablets." In W.M.F. Petrie, *Tell el-Amarna,* 34–37. London: Methuen & Co.

———. 1917. "The Discovery of the Tel el-Amarna Tablets." *American Journal of Semitic Languages* 33, no. 2: 89–90.

———. 1923. *Reminiscences.* London: Macmillan and Co.

Sayce, A. H., and E. Grébaut. 1888. "The Babylonian Tablets in the Boulaq Museum." *The Academy* 33, no. 835 (May): 315.

Scheil, J.-V. 1892. "Tablettes d'el-Amarna de la collection Rostovicz." In *Mémoires publiées par les membres de la Mission archéologique français au Caire* 6: 297–312.

Schroeder, O. 1915. *Die Tontafeln von El-Amarna.* 2 vols. Leipzig: J. C. Hinrichs.

Several, M. 1972. "Reconsidering the Egyptian Empire in Palestine during the Amarna Period." *Palestine Exploration Quarterly* 104: 123–33.

Shanks, H. 1979. "Ebla Evidence Evaporates." *Biblical Archaeology Review* 5–6: 52–53.

Sheppard, K. 2024. *Women in the Valley of the Kings: The Untold Story of Women Egyptologists in the Gilded Age.* London: St. Martin's Press.

Sherratt, S. 2003. "The Mediterranean Economy: 'Globalization' at the End of the Second Millennium BCE." In *Symbiosis, Symbolism, and the Power of the Past: Canaan, Ancient Israel, and Their Neighbors, from the Late Bronze Age through Roman Palaestina,* edited by W. G. Dever and S. Gitin, 37–62. Winona Lake, IN: Eisenbrauns.

———. 2017. "A Globalizing Bronze and Iron Age Mediterranean." In *The Routledge Handbook of Archaeology and Globalization,* edited by T. Hodos, 602–17. Abingdon, UK: Routledge.

Singer, I. 1990. "Aziru's Apostasy and the Historical Setting of the General's Letter." In *The General's Letter from Ugarit: A Linguistic and Historical Reevaluation of RS 20.33,* edited by S. Izre'el and I. Singer, 113–83. Tel Aviv: Tel Aviv University, Chaim Rosenberg School of Jewish Studies.

———. 1991. "A Concise History of Amurru." In S. Izre'el, *Amurru Akkadian: A Linguistic Study,* 134–95. Atlanta: Scholars Press.

Smith, M., N. Milic-Frayling, B. Shneiderman, E. Mendes Rodrigues, J. Leskovec, and C. Dunne. 2010. *NodeXL: A Free and Open Network Overview, Discovery and Exploration Add-In for Excel 2007/2010.* http://nodexl.codeplex.com/.

Spalinger, A., 1992. Review of *The General's Letter from Ugarit. A Linguistic and Historical Reevaluation of RS 20.33 (Ugaritica V, No. 20),* by S. Izre'el, and I. Singer. *Journal of the American Research Center in Egypt* 29: 220–22.

Thompson, J. 2015. *A History of Egyptology.* Vol. 1, *From Antiquity to 1881.* Cairo: American University in Cairo Press.

———. 2020. *A History of Egyptology.* Vol. 2, *The Golden Age: 1881–1914.* Cairo: American University in Cairo Press.

Thompson, R. C. 1935. "Ernest Alfred Wallis Budge: 1857–1934." *Journal of Egyptian Archaeology* 21, no. 1: 68–70.

Tiele, C. P. 1894. *Western Asia: According to the Most Recent Discoveries: Rectorial Address on the Occasion of the 318th Anniversary of the Leyden University, 8th February 1893.* Translated by Elizabeth J. Taylor. London: Luzac.

Tropper, J., and J.-P. Vita. 2010. *Das Kanaano-Akkadische der Amarnazeit.* Münster: Ugarit-Verlag.

Vandkilde, H. 2016. "Bronzization: The Bronze Age as Pre-Modern Globalization." *Praehistorische Zeitschrift* 91, no. 1: 103–23.

Versluys, M. J. 2017. "The Global Mediterranean: A Material-Cultural Perspective." In *The Routledge Handbook of Archaeology and Globalization,* edited by T. Hodos, 597–601. Abingdon, UK: Routledge.

Vita, J.-P. 2012. "Amurru Scribes in the Amarna Archive." In *Palaeography and Scribal Practices in Syro-Palestine and Anatolia in the Late Bronze Age: Papers Read at a Symposium in Leiden, 17–18 December 2009,* edited by E. Devecchi, 185–200. Leiden: Nederlands Instituut Voor Het Nabije Oosten.

———. 2015. *Canaanite Scribes in the Amarna Letters.* Münster: Ugarit-Verlag.

von Dassow, E. 2004. "Canaanite in Cuneiform." *Journal of the American Oriental Society* 124: 641–74.

Waal, W. 2022. "The Missing Link? Writing in West Anatolia During the Late Bronze Age." In *The Political Geography of Western Anatolia in the Late Bronze Age: Proceedings of the EAA Conference, Bern, 7 September 2019,* edited by I. Hajnal, E. Zangger, and J. Kelder, 229–69. Budapest: Archaeolingua.

Wasserman, S., and K. Faust. 1994. *Social Network Analysis: Methods and Applications.* Cambridge: Cambridge University Press.

Watts, D. 2003. *Six Degrees: The Science of a Connected Age.* New York: W. W. Norton & Company.

Weens, S. 2016. "Mustapha Agha Ayad's House inside Luxor Temple: Providing a Timeline for Its Photographic Records." *Memnonia* 27: 135–47.

Wilkinson, T. 2020. *A World beneath the Sands: The Golden Age of Egyptology.* New York: W. W. Norton and Company.

Winckler, H. 1887. "Studien und beiträge zur babylonisch-assyrischen geschichte." *Zeitschrift für Assyriologie* 2: 299–315.

———. 1888. "Bericht über die Thontafeln von Tell el-Amarna im Königlichen Museum zu Berlin und im Museum von Bulaq." *Sitzungsberichte der K. preussischen Academie der Wissenschaften zu Berlin Philologisch-historische Klasse* 51, no. 2: 1341–57.

———. 1889a. "Verzeichniss der aus dem Funde von el-Amarna herührenden Thontafeln." *Zeitschrift für ägyptische Sprache und Altertumskunde* 27: 42–64.

———. 1889b. "Bemerkung zu den el-Amarna-Briefen." *Zeitschrift für Assyriologie* 4: 404–5.

———. 1891. "Vorarbeiten zu einer gesammtbearbeitung der el-Amarna-texte." *Zeitschrift für Assyriologie* 6: 141–48.

———. 1896a. *Der Thontafelfund von Tell-Amarna.* Berlin: Reuther & Reichard.

———. 1896b. *The Tell-El-Amarna Letters.* New York and Berlin: Lemcke & Buechner / Reuther & Reichard.

Winckler, H., and L. Abel. 1889–1890. *Der Thontafelfund von Tell-Amarna.* 2 vols. Berlin: W. Spemann.

Zangani, F. 2022a. "Textual Evidence for the Diplomatic Role of the Egyptian Official Tutu from Amarna." *Journal of Ancient Egyptian Interconnections* 33: 45–56.

———. 2022b. "Was There Ever an Egyptian Empire in the Northern Levant? Debunking the Egyptological Myth of Dynasty 18." *Journal of Egyptian History* 15, no. 1: 43–82.

———. 2022c. *Globalization and the Limits of Imperialism: Ancient Egypt, Syria, and the Amarna Diplomacy.* Prague: Charles University, Faculty of Arts.

Zimmern, H. 1890a. "Briefe aus dem Funde in El Amarna in Transcription und Uebersetzung." *Zeitschrift für Assyriologie und verwandte Gebiete* V: 137–65.

———. 1890b. "Die ältesten Schriftstücke aus Jerusalem." *Kölnische Zeitung,* 1 October.

———. 1890c. "Das Verhältnis des assyrischen Permansivs zum semitischen Perfect und zum ägyptischen 'Pseudoparticip' untersucht unter Benutzung der El-Amania-Texte." *Zeitschrift für Assyriologie* 5: 1–22.

———. 1891a. "Kanaanäische Glossen." *Zeitschrift für Assyriologie* 6: 154–58.

———. 1891b. "Die Keilschriftbriefe aus Jerusalem." *Zeitschrift für Assyriologie* 6: 245–63.

———. 1891c. "Palästina um das Jahr 1400 v. Ch. nach neuen Quellen." *Zeitschrift des Deutschen Paläistina-Vereins* 13: 133–47.

Note: Page numbers in italic type indicate figures or tables.

A NOTE ON THE TYPE

This book has been composed in Arno, an Old-style serif typeface in the
classic Venetian tradition, designed by Robert Slimbach at Adobe.